W9-COU-658

The Ambiguity of Virtue

Gertrude van Tijn, 1936 *(private collection)*

The Ambiguity of Virtue

Gertrude van Tijn and the Fate of the Dutch Jews

Bernard Wasserstein

Harvard University Press

Cambridge, Massachusetts, and London, England
2014

Copyright © 2014 by Bernard Wasserstein
All rights reserved
Printed in the United States of America

An earlier version of this book was published in Dutch as *Gertrude van Tijn en het lot van de Nederlandse Joden* by Nieuw Amsterdam, © 2013 by Bernard Wasserstein.

Library of Congress Cataloging-in-Publication Data

Wasserstein, Bernard.
[Gertrude van Tijn en het lot van de Nederlandse Joden. English]
The ambiguity of virtue : Gertrude van Tijn and the fate of the Dutch Jews / Bernard Wasserstein.
pages cm
"An earlier version of this book was published in Dutch as Gertrude van Tijn en het lot van de Nederlandse Joden by Nieuw Amsterdam, ©2013"—Title page verso.
Includes bibliographical references and index.
ISBN 978-0-674-28138-7 (hardcover : alkaline paper)
1. Tijn, Gertrude van, 1891–1974. 2. World War, 1939–1945—Jews—Rescue—Netherlands. 3. Holocaust, Jewish (1939–1945)—Netherlands. 4. Jews—Persecutions—Netherlands—History—20th century. 5. World War, 1939–1945—Jews—Netherlands—Amsterdam. 6. Jews, German—Netherlands—Amsterdam—Biography. 7. Jewish women—Netherlands—Amsterdam—Biography. 8. Women social workers—Netherlands—Amsterdam—Biography. 9. Joodsche Raad voor Amsterdam—History. I. Title.
D804.6.W3713 2014
940.53'1809492352092—dc23
[B]

2013036032

Book design by Dean Bornstein

For Tomer

Contents

The Ambiguity of Virtue

The Netherlands, 1940

Prologue

One morning in May 1941 Gertrude van Tijn—a middle-aged Jewish woman bearing a Dutch passport—arrived at Lisbon airport after an adventurous journey from Nazi-occupied Amsterdam.

The Portuguese capital at that time was a place of strange incongruities and topsy-turvy values: an island of peace in a continent at war, the seat of government of an authoritarian police state that boasted of being Britain's "oldest ally," and a magnet for international intrigue. The city was also the main embarkation point for refugees from Nazi-dominated Europe seeking desperately to secure passages to the Western Hemisphere.

Who was Gertrude van Tijn, and why had she come to Lisbon? Hers was a mission of mercy. Though she did not yet fully realize it herself, the trip was an eleventh-hour effort to avert mass murder. Her aim was to extricate thousands of Jews in the Netherlands from the clutches of the Nazis. She undertook her journey with the approval of the Nazi authorities, who, at that stage, were still ready to countenance, indeed keen to encourage, Jewish emigration. In Lisbon she was to meet representatives of the American Jewish Joint Distribution Committee, a wealthy charitable organization concerned with the fate of the Jews of Europe. She was to inquire whether the Joint, as it was known, would finance the exodus of Jews from occupied Europe across the Atlantic. That the Nazis would permit a woman, a Jew, and a person of no apparent standing to carry out such an assignment seemed improbable. Yet Gertrude's flight to Lisbon was the stuff not of fantasy but of bizarre reality.

Gertrude registered at the Palácio Hotel in the nearby seaside resort of Estoril. A luxury establishment opposite the casino, the haunt of exiled monarchs, the Palácio exuded an air of glamour and mystery. Allied and Axis spies rubbed shoulders in the lobby with foreign correspondents and affluent émigrés. The American journalist Eric Sevareid, who had stayed there a few weeks earlier, described the Palácio's bar as "the espionage center for World War II."[1] There, in mid-1941, Ian Fleming, an officer in British naval intelligence, is said to have met Duško Popov, code-named "Tricycle," a double agent working for the German Abwehr (intelligence service) in the British interest. The Estoril Casino reputedly provided the inspiration for *Casino Royale*, the first book in Fleming's James Bond series, for whose hero Popov is alleged to have been a model. Whatever the truth of all that, the plush and rather shady Palácio was an odd destination for a respectable, middle-class housewife from Amsterdam.

How did Gertrude find herself in this surreal environment, burdened with such a terrible responsibility? What was the precise nature of her relationship with her Nazi contacts and with the Jewish community in the Netherlands? Was she merely a pawn of the Nazis, or did her trip offer a genuine opportunity to save large numbers of Jews from death in the gas chambers? How was she received by her interlocutors in Lisbon? And how was the purported German readiness to permit the departure of Jews treated by the United States and other governments? These form one set of questions that I examine in this book.

But Gertrude's mission to Lisbon was merely one episode in a life full of incident that raises broader historical issues. Under conditions of enemy occupation and repression, did the saving of human lives take precedence over all other values? Confronting the absolute evil of Nazism, was there any middle road between outright resistance and abject submission? What compromises might an individual find it necessary to make in order to participate effectively in collective action for humanitarian objectives?

The interplay of Gertrude's personal story with the horrors through which she lived illuminates these larger historical issues of her time. There remains the most fundamental question of all: what kind of moral compass guided her in the face of absolute evil?

CHAPTER ONE

"Ruined Woman"

"Almost all the things I remember of my childhood are acts of rebellion," wrote Gertrude van Tijn in her unpublished memoirs.[1] She called herself an "exasperating child," and the independent-minded outlook with which she approached everything throughout her life was deeply rooted in her character and in the circumstances of her upbringing.

Gertrud Franzisca Cohn, as her name was rendered on her birth certificate, entered the world "during the worst hailstorm in history" on July 4, 1891, in Braunschweig (Brunswick), the historic "Lion City" in Saxony. Her father, Werner Cohn, a merchant, was born in 1854 in the small town of Seehausen and moved to Braunschweig in 1879. Her mother, Thekla, née Levisohn, ten years younger than her husband, married him five years before Gertrude's birth.[2] Gertrude had two brothers, the elder, Ernst, and the youngest of the family, Walter, to whom Gertrude was particularly devoted. The Cohns belonged to the respectable middle class, and Gertrude was imbued from an early age with the social and moral attitudes of the German bourgeoisie: scrupulous manners; tidiness; order; cleanliness; discipline; and respect for authority, education, and conventional morality.

Although the family was of Jewish origin and was officially registered as such, they had all but forgotten their Jewishness. Gertrude's paternal grandfather, Abraham Cohn, had been a merchant in Seehausen. According to Gertrude's later account, he had been "one of the leading men of the emancipation" and had helped establish the famous Israel-Jacobson School.[3] Founded in 1801 in

Gertrude at about age seven *(private collection)*

Seesen on the edge of the Harz mountains, not far from Braunschweig, this was a pioneering school, dedicated to the principles of the German and Jewish enlightenments. From the outset it was interdenominational, with both Jewish and Christian pupils.[4] Gertrude's father and his eight brothers were all educated there and imbibed the influences of acculturated Reform Judaism. But Jewish

Gertrude as a teenager, with her father and brothers *(private collection)*

rituals were not observed at all in Werner Cohn's home, and he and his brothers drifted away from the faith of their fathers.

As a consequence, Gertrude, like many German Jews of her generation, was barely aware in her childhood that she was Jewish. Together with her nanny and her brother Walter, she attended church every Sunday and "firmly believed in God and in Jesus."[5] She may even have been baptized.

During her early years, the family was moderately prosperous, and Gertrude grew used to the presence of household servants. But when Gertrude was eleven years old, an idyllic world suddenly collapsed upon the death of her mother. Soon after, her father suffered a business catastrophe and lost his entire fortune. Unable to cope, he lodged Gertrude and Walter with a succession of foster parents, at the expense of wealthy relatives. These events had a profoundly unsettling effect on the young girl. She became, in her own words, "sullen and obstreperous."[6] Obliged to fend for herself, she started to think for herself—an unusual, even dangerous, venture for someone of her sex, age, and social position.

At the age of about fifteen, Gertrude was shocked to discover that her father had a lover. Formerly he had been a hero to her; now she felt doubly abandoned. The loss of her mother had caused her to jettison her faith in a heavenly God; with the betrayal, as she saw it, by her father, it seemed "as though my God on earth had deserted me."[7] The episode marked a turning point in her life. Looking back, she saw it as the end of her childhood.

Around this time, the family moved to Berlin. The provincial teenager, who had hitherto led a quiet, sheltered existence, was dazzled by the avant-garde culture and social excitements of the imperial capital. She delighted in attending concerts, dances, and the theater.

She also began to experiment sexually. Although she had had crushes on both male and female teachers, she lacked sexual experience. At the age of seventeen, she met a painter, thirty years her senior, who fell in love with her—"violently, as only an older man can fall in love with a very young girl."[8] Gertrude considered herself ugly, but this man gave her confidence for the first time in her own beauty. She repelled his advances but scandal erupted a few months later when he exhibited several paintings and a nude statuette of her, though she protested that she had never sat for him naked.

In Berlin she attended the Lette-Verein, a vocational college "for the promotion of the higher education and employment capacity of the female sex." There she completed a course given by the pioneer German-Jewish social worker and feminist Alice Salomon, of whom Gertrude became a devoted follower. Salomon wanted to escape from what she saw as the pointlessness and lack of opportunities available to young bourgeois women, condemned to do nothing save "feed the canaries and embroider doilies."[9] This was a time when it was not the done thing for *höhere Töchter* (young ladies) to take paid work of any kind. But Salomon sought to train girls to pursue socially meaningful careers. Gertrude became "her star pupil." Salomon "spent much time talking to me about the necessity to fight for equal rights for women."[10] Salomon's influence dictated the subsequent course of Gertrude's life and her eventual choice of career as a social worker.

For a time she was closely chaperoned by her elder brother, Ernst. Eluding his supervision, she met a law student at a fancy-dress ball and enjoyed her "first experience in romance." The two rented a room together and made love. Gertrude's first sexual experience was "so beautiful, so gentle," that she felt serenely happy.[11] When Ernst, a rather stuffy character, found out, he sent seconds to Gertrude's lover and demanded satisfaction in a duel. At her insistent pleading, the young man declined to fight. But she was "irretrievably ruined" in the eyes of her brother.[12] In the hope of avoiding public shame, he sent her to stay with rich relations in London.

By now aged twenty, Gertrude was a spirited, outspoken, and self-confident young woman. Declining her uncle's offer of continued hospitality and a position in his bank, she went to live in a boardinghouse and found a job on her own. She worked first as a secretary for a German who owned a paper business near the docks, later as a factotum for a lawyer-author.

She started taking music lessons from a Viennese singing teacher, a pupil of Schoenberg. "As so often happened in my life with men much older than myself" (she later wrote), he tried to make love to her.[13] At that moment the man's wife entered the room. "I left and never saw him again."[14] Instead, she fell in love with another singing teacher, a Scotswoman who lived in Hampstead. Gertrude moved into her home as a boarder. Later she realized that the teacher was a lesbian and reflected that she herself "might also have become a lesbian if she had in the least encouraged me."[15]

This was a period of great social and political unrest in England. Shocked by the contrast between the opulence of her relatives' homes in the fashionable districts of London and the degradation of working-class existence in the slums of the East End, Gertrude became deeply engaged in social causes. Her landlady encouraged her to join the suffragist movement, then at a high point of its long campaign for women's political rights. Many years later Gertrude wrote to her daughter, encouraging her to read Vera Brittain's *Testament of Youth* (1933): "It's my generation exactly; and I might have written it. You see, I too came out of the 'Women's Movement.'"[16] Gertrude joined Millicent Garrett Fawcett's organization, which, unlike the more militant "suffragettes," employed strictly legal methods in its campaign for women's suffrage. Her relatives seem to have given her some encouragement. "One day my uncle offered me £10 for the movement [a lot of money in pre-First World War currency] if I were to make a soap-box speech at Hyde Park Corner. I did and was promptly chased into the pond. He gave me £20, ten for the speech and ten for the ducking."[17]

The outbreak of war in August 1914 raised a potential conflict of loyalties for Gertrude. As an enemy alien, she was required to report regularly to the police. While continuing her work and political activity, she joined some of her English relations in a relief effort on behalf of the tens of thousands of Belgians who had flooded into England in the wake of the German invasion of their country. This was her first involvement with refugees, a concern that was to become the leitmotif of her life.

In 1915, she was given ten days to leave the country. If she had remained, she would have been interned with other German civilians until the end of the war. As she was "fiercely anti-German," she decided to go to a neutral country rather than return to

Germany.[18] The choice was between Switzerland and Holland. The toss of a coin decided, fatefully, that for the next three decades the Netherlands would be her home base.

Upon arrival in Amsterdam, she took a cheap hotel room. Armed with an introduction from a London relative, she called at the office of Pieter Vuyk, a banker with the Nederlandsche Bank voor Zuid-Afrika. He evidently took a shine to her, and they became fast friends. He introduced her to another banker at the nearby office of Hope and Co. Carel Eliza ter Meulen was one of the most senior and respected financiers in the Netherlands. He too was impressed by Gertrude's self-assurance and vivacity, as well as by her almost perfect English, and hired her on the spot as his private secretary.

Both men remained closely attached to Gertrude for the rest of their lives. Vuyk insisted that she leave her hotel immediately and stay with his family at their home at Zandvoort, a seaside town near Amsterdam. Gertrude admired Vuyk immensely, calling him "one of the finest and wisest" of men. She considered him "extremely handsome, in a distinguished looking way."[19] He was of Calvinist origin, and his wife, Jadwiga, was Polish-Jewish. Vuyk had a reputation as a womanizer. His wife too sought lovers and, for a time, became the mistress of Anton Mussert, later the founder of the Dutch Nazi movement, the NSB.

Were Gertrude and Pieter lovers? Gertrude denied it, insisting that their association "would not have been possible if he had not been such a happily married man and if his wife had been at all jealous. . . . The relationship between P[i]eter and me was also a proof that in rare instances a real friendship, untroubled by sexual complications, can exist between a man and a woman."[20] Only a prurient mind would wish to probe further. But of their intimacy there can be no doubt: for the rest of their lives they lunched together almost every day that they were both in Amsterdam.

Gertrude at Zandvoort, 1917 *(private collection)*

After a few days with the Vuyks, Gertrude moved into a small apartment in a house on the Keizersgracht, one of the most beautiful central canals of the city. She explored Amsterdam and quickly came to love it. She visited the Jewish area (10 percent of the city's population was Jewish), the magnificent old synagogues, and the colorful market on the Waterlooplein.

About this time, Gertrude discovered a new passion: Zionism. At a dinner party, she met "a very attractive young man" (Gertrude does not give his name) who, when she said she was Jewish, began to talk about Zionism. He persuaded her to read some Zionist literature, including Theodor Herzl's *The Jewish State*. "Suddenly my interest was aroused. I read and read. The fact that Jews could be proud of their heritage and actually worked for a renaissance in a country of their own was like a revelation." She felt she had to come to a decision: "stop calling myself Jewish or go over to the Zionists with all my heart."[21]

Gertrude plunged headlong into the Jewish national cause. When her father heard that she had embraced Zionism, he disapproved. "He could not understand it," she later wrote, "seeing how well I had been brought up."[22] This was the typical reaction of an assimilated, middle-class German Jew. But on this, as on so much else in her life, Gertrude, once she had made up her mind, was not to be moved.

Why did she adopt this, at the time, apparently quixotic, even eccentric creed? She certainly had no religious motive, since she had led a thoroughly secular life. She seems rather to have found in Zionism an ideal that she could embrace unconditionally, an outlet for her restless energy, and a circle of young fellow enthusiasts with whom she could engage.

Her earliest recorded formal contact with the Zionist Organization came in a letter in August 1916, addressed to the head office of the Jewish National Fund (JNF) in The Hague. This was the movement's financial arm, concerned with the purchase of land in Palestine for settlement by Jewish immigrant *halutzim* (pioneers). Soon after the outbreak of war, the fund's headquarters had moved from Cologne to shelter under the umbrella of Dutch neutrality. In her letter, Gertrude requested "one guilder worth of stamps of the JNF, preferably with the Herzl portrait." Herzl, the founder of the Zionist Organization, had died in 1904; such stamps bearing his portrait were sold as a fund-raising device. She also asked for "a catalogue of

A Zionist banquet in Holland during the First World War *(Jewish Historical Museum, Amsterdam)*

Jewish literature if something like that exists."[23] Some time later, she visited the JNF office and met its secretary, a Russian-born socialist-Zionist, Shlomo Kaplansky.

Gertrude's knowledge of English, German, and Dutch led to her engagement as a translator of correspondence and publications for the JNF. By February 1917, she was running the JNF's Commissariat in Amsterdam. From her office in the elegant Diamond Exchange building on the Weesperplein, she was soon busy organizing propaganda and fund-raising. Zionist activity in the city was at a low ebb, but Gertrude breathed renewed life into the movement in the Dutch capital. Her Zionist ardor even led her to consider moving to Palestine to work for the JNF bureau there.

Gertrude with Mirjam Gerzon (later de Leeuw), c. 1916 *(private collection)*

But the country was the theater of military operations between its Turkish rulers and an Allied invading army headed by General Edmund Allenby. Settling there was thus impracticable for the time being.[24]

Her work brought Gertrude into the heart of Zionist affairs. She fell in with a group of like-minded enthusiasts—generally young, middle-class intellectuals, several of whom played a part in Gertrude's life long afterwards. Among them was Max Schloessinger, a German-born scholar and businessman in The Hague, who was a director of the Jewish National Fund, and his wife, Miriam Schloessinger-Scheer. Another was Mirjam Gerzon, who became a close friend. Both the Schloessingers and Gerzon emigrated to Palestine in the early 1920s.

Gertrude also met many Zionist leaders, among them Chaim Weizmann. He was at the peak of his prestige as the man who, in November 1917, persuaded the British government to issue the Balfour Declaration, favoring the establishment of a Jewish National Home in Palestine. Like many who encountered him, Gertrude was captivated by the majesty of Weizmann's personality, the pathos of his oratory, and the visionary realism of his politics. She cherished his acquaintance for the rest of her life.

During this period, Gertrude came into contact for the first time with the American Jewish Joint Distribution Committee (commonly known as "the Joint"). She probably owed this connection to Pieter Vuyk, who acted during the war as an intermediary for communications between the Hamburg-based, Jewish banker-philanthropist Max Warburg and the New York headquarters of the Joint, in which his brother Felix Warburg played a central role.[25] With the support of the Joint, Gertrude organized the dispatch of kosher food parcels to Jewish prisoners of war in eastern Europe. Although the Joint offered her a full-time job at an increased salary, she preferred to remain with Ter Meulen, to whom she was by this time unshakably loyal. The link she established with the Joint would nevertheless later became central to her working life.

In February 1920, Gertrude married Jacques van Tijn, a mining engineer two years her junior. They had first met in 1917, when he admired a fiery speech she delivered at a Zionist meeting. Gertrude found him "ugly but with a great deal of charm."[26] His father was a factory owner and an orthodox Jew; his mother came from a family of wealthy Jewish industrialists. Worldly and urbane, with an eye for the ladies, Jacques had spent some time in Russia, an experience from which he retained a penchant for Russian cigarettes. By dint of her marriage, Gertrude acquired Dutch nationality. Her naturalization probably seemed little more than a formality. Only later did it assume great significance.

Gertrude and her future husband, Jacques van Tijn, Enschede, 1918
(private collection)

As an exploration geologist with Royal Dutch Petroleum, Jacques worked mainly overseas, and during the next decade the couple lived a peripatetic life in Switzerland, South Africa, Mexico, Uganda, and Tanganyika. While her husband worked and traveled, Gertrude gave birth to two children: a daughter, to whom they gave the Hebrew name Chedwah Jochewed (familiarly known as "Babs"), born in Amsterdam in 1921; and a son, David, born in Mexico in 1923. For the time being, Gertrude set aside thoughts of a career and looked after the children. They faced many challenges: snakes, locusts, and bushfires in Africa; army ants, banditry, and revolution in Mexico. For several years they lived in a beautiful old Dutch-style house, with magnificent gardens on a thirty-acre estate, at Inanda, outside Johannesburg. The marriage seemed happy, though Gertrude was often upset by Jacques's short temper.

From these experiences, Gertrude acquired a cosmopolitan outlook, an enduring interest in international politics, a stoic resilience in the face of sudden shifts of fortune and changes in living conditions, and a no-nonsense ability to deal effectively with all manner of people, whatever their class, race, or sex. She emerged with a heightened compassion for the wretched of the earth and an as-yet-undirected desire to do what she could to alleviate their lot.

After more than a decade overseas, the family returned to Europe. En route from Africa, they stopped for four weeks in Palestine. This was Gertrude's first visit to the Zionist homeland, now ruled by Britain under a League of Nations mandate. They were able to observe the progress that had been made over the previous decade towards the establishment of the Jewish National Home. Briefly they toyed with the idea of settling there. Gertrude loved the spirituality of Jerusalem and the youthful vigor of the new city of Tel Aviv. They stayed for a few days in the kibbutz of Ein Harod in the Jezreel Valley. But there was no prospect of a job in Palestine for Jacques, and they both felt they "would not have the courage to live in one of the colonies and become peasants."[27] In early 1932 they arrived back in the Netherlands, the country that, for the next twelve years, would become Gertrude's home and where the central historical drama of her life would be enacted.

CHAPTER TWO

Rebuilding Lives

The Holland to which the Van Tijns returned had been radically dislocated by the onset of the Great Depression. No country was immune, but the Netherlands felt the effects with a special intensity. At first it seemed as if, notwithstanding the surrounding turmoil, the family would resume a placid, conventional existence. Jacques found a well-paying job as an engineer with a large company headed by the Jewish industrialist Bernard van Leer. He took a lease on a house belonging to the wealthy Boissevain family in Blaricum, to the east of Amsterdam.

An artists' colony, Blaricum was a delightful small town, really an overgrown village, with old, spacious homes, and well-tended public and private gardens. Its combination of bourgeois comforts, bucolic pleasures, and a slightly bohemian edge fitted Gertrude's tastes perfectly. Het Houten Huis (the Wooden House), with its approaching avenue of trees, tennis court, and adjacent woodland inhabited by brown owls, had room for an entourage, consisting of Gerda, the children's nanny; Hannah, the cook; as well as Glim, the dachshund; Nelly, the cat; and rabbits and chickens.

Gertrude might have settled down to the humdrum preoccupations of a middle-aged, middle-class housewife. Instead, she was suddenly thrust into a maelstrom that transformed her into an actor in a global tragedy.

Soon after their return to the Netherlands, she was offered a job as head of the department of social work of the Dutch Council of Jewish Women. This national body had been established in 1929 as an amalgamation of several local societies. Although a number of Jewish women had been pioneers in the feminist movement in the Netherlands, the council's founders were more concerned with Jewish than gender issues. The organization, whose membership of about two thousand was drawn mainly from affluent segments of the community, engaged in welfare activities and education among the Jewish poor.

Gertrude's work brought her into close contact with the impoverished Jewish working class of Amsterdam, whom she had earlier viewed from a certain distance. When she had first arrived there fifteen years earlier, she had been fascinated by the *Jodenbuurt*, the Jewish district in the center of the city: "The streets there were rabbit-warrens; the houses incredibly old. I learned later how much poverty, inter-marriage [she meant marriage between close relatives] and sickness there was in the ghetto; but it did not hit the eye as it did in London. There seemed to be no slums. I was fascinated by the Jewish markets, which were held in front of the two beautiful old synagogues. Everything was sold there from old rusty nails to silk underwear."[1] Now Gertrude discovered that behind its picturesque façade the quarter had degenerated into a sink of squalor and misery. The peculiar occupational profile of the Jewish working classes had left them even more vulnerable to the depression than their gentile neighbors. Characteristically Jewish trades, in particular the diamond industry, had been especially hard hit. In the *Jodenbuurt*, unemployment was higher and average incomes lower than elsewhere in the city.

Gertrude's routine assumed a steady pattern. Most weekdays she drove twenty miles each way in the family car on the pleasant country road between Blaricum and Amsterdam. She again enjoyed daily lunches with Pieter Vuyk, who had divorced his wife in June 1930 and remarried. Gertrude called him her children's "second Daddy."[2] She also met regularly with her old patron and friend Carel ter Meulen. Given her travels over the previous decade, there was plenty to talk about: both men had banking connections with Africa, and Ter Meulen also with Mexico.

In July 1932, Gertrude attended the second International Conference of Social Workers in Frankfurt. Here she was able to renew her acquaintance with figures who had influenced her in her youth, notably Alice Salomon. The visit gave her an opportunity to witness firsthand the disintegration of the Weimar Republic and the heightened animosity against German Jews. She gained further insight into Nazism on a trip to Berlin in January 1933 for her brother Ernst's wedding anniversary. She thus had a ringside view of Hitler's ascent to power at the end of that month.

Like many German Jews, Ernst was relatively sanguine about the prospects, forecasting that Hitler in government would turn out to be more moderate than his fiery rhetoric might suggest. When Gertrude called at the offices of the main German-Jewish welfare organizations, however, she encountered "a much more realistic assessment of the danger threatening German Jewry," though at this stage the worst that was expected was economic discrimination against the Jews.[3]

One of the first anti-Jewish measures announced by the new regime was a boycott of Jewish retail businesses, set for April 1, 1933. Customers observed it only to a limited degree, and perhaps for that reason the Nazis called it off after one day. But the episode gave a foretaste of worse to come. A significant minority of German Jews resolved to pack their bags. By the end of the year, an estimated forty thousand of the half-million-strong community had fled. Most went to France or other immediate neighbors of Germany; over four thousand arrived in Holland.

Announcement of the boycott had aroused indignation outside Germany and was one of the spurs for Jewish organization in many parts of the world to counter Nazi anti-Semitic propaganda and to aid refugees. In Amsterdam, two interlinked committees were formed: a Committee for Special Jewish Interests and a Committee for Jewish Refugees. Both were organs of the Jewish establishment and included such personalities as Abraham Asscher, a prominent diamond merchant, Liberal politician, and Zionist; and Lodewijk Ernst Visser, a distinguished jurist who was vice-president of the Dutch Supreme Court.

The dominant figure on both committees was David Cohen, a professor of classics at the University of Amsterdam and a longstanding activist in the Zionist movement. Cautious, amiable, and hardworking but also vain and unimaginative, Cohen believed that close cooperation with the authorities was the key to success. He always took pains to demonstrate that he and his colleagues placed Dutch national interests in the forefront of their concerns. The committees held public meetings, disseminated information, and raised funds to assist German Jews who fled to the Netherlands.

Gertrude was invited to serve as secretary of the two committees, though her work was primarily directed towards the refugees committee. She was a logical choice for the position, given her training as a social worker, her administrative experience, her native knowledge of German, and her social entrée to the higher echelons of the Jewish community. Here was an opportunity for Gertrude to combine her social concern with her Jewish commitment. She agreed unhesitatingly to undertake this work, which quickly proved to be more than full-time, without pay.

From the outset, there was a division of labor. Cohen served as the public face of the committees, responsible for relations with the Dutch government and coordination with the Jewish community. His relations with Gertrude were cordial but not intimate. Together with a co-worker Raphaël Henri Eitje, an orthodox Jew, experienced in refugee work, she was in charge of the office and responded to the hundred and one problems faced by German Jews upon arrival in Holland. Because of her command of English and her international connections, she also handled most foreign communications for the committee.

Holland was proud of its historic role as a haven for those persecuted on religious grounds. By contemporary European standards, the country was barely infected with anti-Semitism. The government permitted the initial refugee inflow to continue with little obstruction. Visitors from Germany did not even need a visa until 1938. In a period of severe economic austerity, however, officialdom did not welcome increased burdens. Thus, leaders of the Dutch Jewish community, like the British, gave the government a formal assurance that the costs of providing for Jews arriving from Germany would be met entirely from voluntary funds and would not fall on the public purse. The committee's efforts garnered wide support from both Jews and non-Jews. Gertrude's old friend Mirjam Gerzon—who had married a young Dutch engineer in Palestine, Abraham (Leib) de Leeuw, and returned to Holland in 1926 (followed later by him)—was one of the many who rallied to the cause, advising potential migrants to Palestine on housing and work possibilities there.

Yet Dutch receptivity to immigrants had its limits. The government, like others in western Europe, saw the country as no more than a temporary refuge—a *gare de triage*. The ports of Rotterdam and Amsterdam had long been stages on the migration route from eastern Europe to the Americas. Holland would now again be a way station for "transmigration" to places of permanent residence outside Europe, such as Palestine or the United States. Accordingly, the Jewish Refugees Committee in Amsterdam, like other such bodies in other times and places, saw its primary task not as facilitating settlement on the spot but as organizing onward movement, preferably across the seas.

Early arrivals from Germany included both *Ostjuden* (east European Jews, mainly from Poland, who had settled in Germany) and German Jews. The latter included middle-class businessmen, like Otto Frank, father of Anne, who had been able to export at least some of their capital, and civil servants and professionals who were progressively extruded from their positions by the Nazis. Most of those who remained in Holland settled in Amsterdam, choosing not the historic, central Jewish district but the more modern and salubrious Rivierenbuurt in the south of the city. As with other immigrations, later waves tended to follow their predecessors, so that the area assumed an increasingly German-Jewish character. The nearby Beethovenstraat, with its German pastry shops, cafés, and dressmakers, became jocularly known as "Brede Jodenstraat," a play on the name of the main thoroughfare in the old Jewish quarter, Jodenbreestraat.

Gertrude's work for the committee was far from any Lady Bountiful philanthropic exercise. Refugees required food, shelter, medical aid, and child care; help in dealing with the Dutch bureaucracy; assistance in arranging onward travel; and, in the case of those remaining in the country, guidance towards suitable jobs, language instruction, and much else. Gertrude found herself caught up in a whirlwind of activity. She proved her administrative mettle by securing competent staff and setting up a well-oiled office machinery. The Amsterdam committee was one of several that were set up all over the country, but it developed into the central address for donations and for negotiation with the government, as well as the first port of call for most German Jews reaching the Netherlands.

As locally raised funds were exhausted, the committee turned to Jewish communities elsewhere for support. Gertrude traveled frequently to Paris, London, Berlin, and Geneva to coordinate policy with other organizations. In Paris an office known as HICEM was a joint venture by the Hebrew Immigrant Aid Society of New York and other Jewish philanthropic agencies. Its object was

Fund-raising poster for Jewish refugees from Germany, 1933 *(Beeldbank WO2, NIOD)*

to centralize aid for Jewish refugees heading to the Americas. In Britain, a Jewish Refugees Committee raised large sums; but expenditures in Britain itself were heavy, and little was left over for Holland.

Neither the Dutch Jewish community nor any other in Europe was able to provide resources on the scale required to cope with the large influx. Soon after its establishment, the Amsterdam committee therefore approached the American Jewish Joint Distribution Committee for help. Given her earlier cooperation with the Joint in organizing aid for Jewish prisoners of war, Gertrude was the obvious person to handle these discussions.

She won the confidence of its leaders in her personal integrity and in the efficiency of the committee's operations. But the Joint, in spite of its deep pockets, was operating under enormous pressure, as its support base had been seriously affected by the depression. Simultaneously, the demands on its resources knew hardly any bounds, since it was widely regarded as the fund of last resort, often of first resort, for all Jewish needs around the world. The rise of Nazism, accompanied by a European-wide growth in anti-Semitism, added enormously to calls on the Joint for emergency aid.

Gertrude's was merely one voice in the chorus of supplicants. She knew, however, that she must modulate her demands so as to elicit not merely sympathy but productive results. As early as January 1934, the Amsterdam committee felt so besieged by the flood of refugees and found such difficulty in meeting its financial commitments that it considered closing down completely. That month Gertrude traveled to London to appeal to Jewish leaders there. She asked for £6,000 as a grant towards a special project for the vocational training of young German Jews, who would thereby be enabled to move overseas: she was granted £2,000 on condition that the Americans gave double that sum.[4]

From London she proceeded to Paris to meet the Joint's chief representative there, Bernard Kahn. The relationship that she formed with him, as with later directors of the Joint's operations, proved critical to the success of her committee. Kahn's background was similar to that of Gertrude herself. Born in Sweden, he had been educated in Germany and combined a certain German-Jewish disdain for *Ostjuden* with compassion for their plight that dated back to the period of the Kishinev pogrom in 1903. Like Gertrude, he was a supporter of Zionism; and also like her, he was a person of "complete independence of mind."[5] He had served as European director of the Joint since 1924 and commanded the respect of the organization's head office in New York.

Gertrude evidently made a favorable impression on him. He immediately agreed to advance $15,000 (about £3,000 at the prevailing exchange rate; more than $275,000 in 2014 value) to the Amsterdam committee. Supposedly this was to be the first installment of a long-term commitment to matching sums raised by the committee in Holland.[6] As time went on, the Joint became the main financial guarantor of Jewish refugee expenditures in Holland. Gertrude's role in initiating and sustaining that support over the next decade was crucial.

Reporting to Kahn shortly after her return to Amsterdam, Gertrude noted that local fund-raising was going well, "as people seem to find a sporting pleasure in giving an amount with the knowledge that this will be doubled." But she warned against any expectation that the refugee problem might quickly be "liquidated": "Quite frankly, I do not, personally, see a chance of doing this, unless one or the other country is opened for emigration on a big scale."[7]

Gertrude aimed at more than just temporary relief. Shortly after assuming her position, she helped advance a scheme that, in later years, she saw as her proudest achievement: the establishment of a training farm for young refugees, which would equip them for work overseas in agriculture or handicrafts. This was the special project for which she had raised money in the UK and from the Joint. The inspiration came from the *hachsharah* (training) farms that had been created by Zionists and others to correct what was seen as the socially unhealthy concentration of Jews in urban occupations. One such farm had been set up near Deventer in Holland as early as 1918. As the condition of European Jewry deteriorated in the course of the 1930s, others sprouted all over the continent.

The Werkdorp (work village) Nieuwesluis was built on a *polder* (land reclaimed from the sea) at Wieringen in North Holland. Its purpose was to offer courses in all branches of farming, horticulture, construction, furniture-making, and metalwork, as well as domestic science for girls. Students between the ages of sixteen (later fifteen) and twenty-five were to be prepared for emigration to Palestine or other countries of "permanent settlement." Dutch companies donated some equipment, and the government made available, rent free, an initial area of 60 hectares, later increased to 360 hectares.

Hans Lubinski, the first director of the *werkdorp*, was a progressive educationalist who had previously directed a Jewish reformatory school in Germany. When he moved to Palestine in 1936, his assistant, a young Palestinian Jew, Moshe Katznelson, took over. They engaged as instructors an expert staff of agriculturalists and craftsmen, both Jewish and non-Jewish.

The school was supported by a foundation, the Stichting Joodsche Arbeid, on the board of which Gertrude served as secretary. Her colleagues, all male, were drawn from the Dutch-Jewish elite. The president was George van den Bergh, son of a founder of Unilever, a lawyer and former Social Democrat member of parliament. Van den Bergh had initiated the idea together with George Flatow, a former senior civil servant in Germany.[8] The treasurer, Alfred

Goudsmit, a friend of the Van Tijns, came from a wealthy Jewish family who owned the great Amsterdam department store De Bijenkorf. The ubiquitous Asscher and Cohen also served as members of the board. In its first three years, nearly half the budget for Wieringen was raised in Holland, and most of the remainder from the United States and Britain.[9] German Jews also contributed until prevented from doing so by their enforced pauperization at the hands of the Nazis.

Young men who applied to Wieringen had to commit themselves to remain for up to two years, girls for eighteen months. In March 1934, the first group of eleven boys and four girls moved into wooden barracks plumped in a forlorn landscape, "dark specks on the vast, treeless, still only sparsely inhabited new polder," as Gertrude later described their new habitat. Within a few years the "bleak collection of austere buildings, outlined against an immense horizon," was transformed into "a miniature garden city, surrounded by growing trees, each building the centre of multicolored flowerbeds and shrubs."[10] A spacious central building (which still stands) was erected, surrounded by dormitories, barns, byres, stables, chicken coops, a smithy, workshops, and greenhouses.

The formal opening ceremony of the *werkdorp*, on October 3, 1934, was marked by the presence of James G. McDonald, who bore the cumbersome title of "League of Nations High Commissioner for Refugees (Jewish and Other) Coming from Germany." He was an American citizen, even though the United States was not a member of the League.

A year earlier, the Dutch government had taken the initiative for the establishment of the High Commission, trying to do so in a way that would cause as little irritation as possible to their German neighbors. McDonald's lengthy official handle indicated the reluctance with which the powers authorized his appointment. They attached the stringent condition that no League funds were to be allocated for the purpose. As a result, the high commissioner was compelled to rely on voluntary donations, almost all from Jewish organizations such as the Joint, for the most basic requisites of his office.

McDonald was happy to lend the prestige of his position to reinforce what he saw as an admirable effort in Wieringen. Gertrude liked this tall, handsome midwesterner, and maintained harmonious working relations with him, joining a League advisory committee on refugees. Her close friendship with McDonald endured long after his resignation in December 1935 in despair at the international community's inaction in response to what he called, in an anguished resignation letter, "the terrible human calamity" of German Jewry.[11]

Living conditions at Wieringen were hygienic if spartan. Initially girls were directed to household duties and trained to become "helpful assistants to settlers on the land."[12] Later, under the more egalitarian influence of Katznelson, the policy changed: boys were required to share in domestic tasks and girls to join work in the cowsheds. After some argument, it was agreed by the supervising committee that the kitchen would be strictly kosher even though most of the students were not orthodox. The would-be peasants maintained an interest in culture, literature, and music. The pianist Lili Kraus and the singer Paula Lindberg were among the artists who gave recitals at the *werkdorp* before deeply attentive audiences.

Gertrude took a maternal interest in her charges. "Certain rules were enforced but generally speaking the atmosphere was what to-day would be called 'permissive,'" she later wrote.[13] A certain degree of moral and ideological control was nevertheless exerted over the students. Strict separation was maintained between the living quarters of the sexes, and what was ironically called a "sexual zone" of fifty kilometers was enforced around the farm.

Unsurprisingly, emancipated young people refused to put up with such restrictions. One woman from Berlin relates: "all of us were in our early twenties and found a solution. We exchanged addresses of low-priced Amsterdam hotels where young couples could meet on weekends."[14]

Unlike *hachsharah* farms under the direct control of the Zionists, Wieringen recruited Jews of all political colors. The language of daily intercourse was German, not Hebrew. Political activity was forbidden, the students being required to sign a pledge to abstain from demonstrations. Ideological dissension, even fighting, nonetheless broke out between Zionists and non-Zionists, especially Communists. Gertrude and her committee were anxious that Wieringen should not appear, in the eyes of the Dutch authorities, to be "a centre for the cultivation of Communists."[15] "The presence of an active communist cell in the Werkdorp posed a real threat to its very existence in view of the stringent rules laid down by the host government and the official Dutch anti-communist policies. Yet expulsion of the group was, of course, inconceivable. It would have meant deportation to Germany and almost certain death."[16] This, at any rate, was her retrospective explanation. Actually, the Dutch government rarely deported German Communists back to Germany; such expulsions, when they occurred, were generally over the border with Belgium.

Some of the early students who were Communists asserted that the only place they would go was the Soviet Union. Both Gertrude and Katznelson, who had emigrated from Soviet Russia to Palestine a decade earlier, tried to persuade them to opt for other destinations, such as South America. In the end, only one student went to the USSR. The problem of how to deal with the Communists resolved itself after the outbreak of the Spanish Civil War in 1936, when most of them decided to leave to fight for the endangered republic as volunteers in the International Brigades.

Even though Wieringen was not under direct Zionist control, the original expectation had been that many of the students would migrate to Palestine. But there were difficulties in securing immigration certificates. Out of twenty-seven students in the first Wieringen cohort who sought entry to Palestine in late 1935, just four were initially successful.[17] Eventually, more secured admission. By October 1936, a total of eighty-five had immigrated to Palestine, including a group of twenty-five who settled together in a new kibbutz, Bet Hashita, in the eastern Jezreel Valley, opposite Mount Gilboa. Most of them initially undertook heavy work as stone-breakers and road builders.

In 1936, the British mandatory government of Palestine, in response to the outbreak of a major Arab revolt, introduced for the first time a "political high level" for Jewish immigration. The number of Jews permitted to enter the country was greatly restricted. Precious certificates were preferentially distributed by the Jewish Agency (the Zionist-dominated representative body recognized by the government) to young people in countries where they were judged to be in imminent danger. Those in the freedom of the Netherlands hardly qualified. Although many still managed to get to Palestine, places had to be found for the rest in the Americas, Africa, or elsewhere.[18]

Some, particularly those who settled in kibbutzim in Palestine, remained farmers for the rest of their lives; most drifted back to urban occupations. A survey of former students in the 1960s found a fishmonger in Jerusalem, a travel agent in Tiberias, a foreman at General Motors in Michigan, a probation officer in Melbourne, and so on. The objective of helping to re-create a Jewish peasantry, as in days of yore, out of a nation of shopkeepers thus had only limited success.

Gertrude visited Wieringen regularly, mainly to discuss emigration possibilities. On these occasions, it seems the students were expected to bake a cake in her honor. One observer noted that she conducted these inspection tours rather in the manner of a governess.[19] That side of her emerged particularly when students wanted to get married, complicating already difficult arrangements for emigration. "Send your bride over to the committee one of these days," she wrote to one young man who wanted to take his fiancée with him to Argentina. "We can promise nothing, since she is a Dutchwoman."[20] The couple managed, in the end, to get to Argentina.

A certain haughtiness of manner towards the refugees in general has been detected in Gertrude by the Israeli historian Dan Michman, who quotes a letter she wrote to her office colleague Henri Eitje in 1934: "None of our refugees is so noble, so good, or so needy that one of us should sacrifice his health on that account."[21] Possibly this was an expression of concern for the welfare of her fellow worker; or perhaps she was alluding to the fact that she herself had suffered a heart attack a few weeks earlier (she recovered quickly). Still, the chosen form of words may be revealing of an underlying attitude.

The fundamental benevolence of her disposition and of her intentions nevertheless shone through, and most students left with fond memories of Gertrude and the *werkdorp*. In future years, Gertrude would receive letters from Wieringers in every part of the world, testifying to the influence that Wieringen had had on them and expressing gratitude for the passport to safety that it had provided. "My stay in Wieringen was one of the very few happy times of my youth, which will always stay in my memory," wrote one former student from Australia. "I think it was the spirit and comradeship of the Werkdorp, combined with the friendliness and hospitality of the Dutch people, which helped to re-establish our faith in mankind."[22]

Altogether, at least 684 young people (536 men and 148 women) received training in Wieringen.[23] The experiment elicited much favorable comment in the press in the Netherlands and around the world, and enhanced the already high regard in which officers of the Joint in Paris and New York held Gertrude.

Among the many visitors to the *werkdorp* was a legendary figure, Henrietta Szold, the founder of Hadassah, the American women's Zionist organization (she was a cousin of Gertrude's old friend Miriam Schloessinger). Szold was deeply impressed by what she saw at Wieringen in 1935 and admired Gertrude's combination of humanity and businesslike method. She left full of enthusiasm, but after continuing her journey to Berlin, she wrote to Gertrude expressing a shuddering premonition that given what was happening to Jews in central Europe, "all Jews will sooner or later have to have their names entered on one of your cards and dealt with accordingly."[24]

Together with a German Zionist, Recha Freier, Szold founded Youth Aliyah (*aliya*, literally "ascent," is the Hebrew word for immigration to the Land of Israel) in 1932–1933 with the aim of organizing the large-scale transfer of Jewish youngsters, particularly from Germany, to Palestine. In spite of Wieringen's officially non-Zionist orientation, Youth Aliyah placed a group of about twenty students at the *werkdorp* in 1936.

The pressure on all three of Gertrude's committees, as on Jewish organizations everywhere, increased as Nazi repression of the Jews in Germany intensified. In its first two years of activity, the Jewish Refugees Committee looked after 5,400 refugees, of whom 2,200 were found new homes in other countries.

Over the next few years, Gertrude's correspondence with the Joint and other funding agencies involved constant demands for more money. She secured higher allocations by a deft mixture of negotiating styles. She earned the confidence of overseas supporters by submitting detailed monthly reports showing the spare efficiency with which the Amsterdam operation was conducted in the face of ever-mounting numbers of refugees. Yet she repeatedly threatened that in the absence of further support, her organization would be obliged to "liquidate" its activity. "Our whole position is absolutely deplorable," she wrote to the Joint in a typical letter in July 1934.[25] She also had to find a way to balance the efforts of donor organizations in London and Paris to throw the entire burden on the Americans.

Although the committee sought to focus on "transmigration" and to encourage refugees to move on elsewhere, many remained in the Netherlands, feeding a growing undercurrent of xenophobic hostility. "Life is at present extremely unpleasant and complicated," Gertrude wrote to Bernard Kahn that month. She was being subjected to "violent attacks . . . partly from the non-Jewish side." With uncharacteristic bitterness, she noted that the criticism was "of an entirely destructive nature. From none of the people who are so busy blaming us have I had any suggestion what else we could profitably do with refugees."[26]

As it became ever harder to find homes overseas, refugee organizations in west European cities tried strenuously to bounce unwanted arrivals elsewhere. In January 1935, for example, the London committee wrote to Gertrude asking whether room might be found in Holland for "a very respectable man, the proud possessor of two trades"—chazan (synagogue cantor) and Turkish tobacco factory manager. Since there was no job for him in England, and since, "to be perfectly blunt," the London committee could not afford to maintain him there, they were prepared to give him "his fare and £25 in his pocket" if the Amsterdam committee would take responsibility for him.[27] Gertrude replied immediately that this man could not be accepted. Indeed, the passage of a new law meant that many refugees already in the Netherlands, who had found work there, were being forced out of their jobs. She urged the London committee "to warn the refugees not to go to Holland."[28]

Her British counterparts were equally resistant to Dutch attempts to deposit German Jews in England. In one such case, the London committee wrote to complain about a trainee florist who had been sent to them from Amsterdam. "It is to be regretted that he did not have some lessons before he came here as it is expecting rather a lot for a German Jew (not physically at all attractive and completely ignorant of the horticultural trade) to act as a Vermittler [broker] in Covent Garden when he does not know a word of English!! It is not to be wondered at that he made an initial error, due, I understand, to assuming that 1 bunch of roses = 12 blooms whereas, in fact, 1 bunch of roses = 20 blooms." (Actually, the writer, Wilfred Samuel, got it the wrong way round: the standard in England was a dozen, in Germany a score.)

Samuel, who addressed his letter simply to the Jewish Refugees Committee in Amsterdam, added a further reflection: "As an Englishman writing, I presume, to a Dutchman, may I add that I have always found Germans excessively suspicious of one another. In fact, I often marvel that they are able to trade at all, mutual confidence being the basis of all business."[29] Samuel might have marveled even more had he realized that his addressee was not "a Dutchman" but German-born and female. Gertrude's response, however, demonstrates the extent to which she felt herself fully naturalized as a Dutch citizen and distanced from her German roots. It also hints at what was later to develop into a malignant antipathy between German and Dutch Jews in the Netherlands. She replied that her committee had paid for the would-be florist to have English lessons, and she added, "We quite share your view about the suspiciousness with which the Germans treat each other. It seems to us that they spend half their time quarrelling with each other."[30] London and Amsterdam evidently shared frustrations, but such episodes did little to enhance mutual confidence.

For all concerned, the best solution was, of course, to cooperate in seeking openings for emigrants in some other part of the world altogether—as when Gertrude forwarded to London notice of an opportunity in Baghdad for a "qualified masseuse with knowledge of English and French." Would this perhaps be suitable for a refugee that London was having trouble placing?[31] The fate of this unfortunate woman is not recorded.

A new mass flight from the Reich followed the promulgation in September 1935 of the Nuremberg Laws, which barred Jews from German citizenship, prohibited marriage or sexual relations between "Aryans" and "non-Aryans," and further restricted occupations in which Jews could work. Accompanying the announcement of the laws was a reinforced barrage of anti-Semitic propaganda and sporadic outbreaks of violence.

The effects were felt immediately in Amsterdam, where Gertrude reported a surge of newcomers. Among them were several "mixed-race" couples and men "accused of relationship with non-Jewish women." The refugees committee hoped to be able to send some of these people back to Germany. If they could not return to their original homes, often in small towns, they were directed to large cities, where it was hoped they might blend inconspicuously into the population. Mere economic migrants, who arrived in Holland and claimed to be starving, were, "heartless as it may seem," being sent back. "If we did not, we might soon have thousands and thousands of Jews to care for." "They come to us like hunted animals," Gertrude wrote. But only those threatened with imprisonment or consignment to concentration camps were guaranteed help. Abandoning talk of halting operations, Gertrude issued a renewed, desperate appeal to the Joint and other foreign backers to redouble their financial assistance.[32]

By early 1936, Gertrude wrote that it was "realized clearly by all those who are acquainted with the situation that it will be necessary to liquidate German Jewry systematically by creating chances for large numbers of German Jews to emigrate directly from Germany." In the committee's annual report, she and David Cohen bemoaned its chronic financial predicament: "We are . . . reduced to the state of a 'schnorrer' [beggar] eternally soliciting help." The apparent endlessness of the German-Jewish trauma was rendering fund-raising more, not less, difficult: "Although the pauperization and extermination of German Jewry continues rapidly, to some extent the public has got used to the idea; indignation which is the biggest stimulance for generosity has in many places made place to resignation."[33]

Between 1933 and 1937, the plight of the refugees in Holland deteriorated. Governmental restrictions prevented many from securing employment. Some were reduced to penury, and the committee had to start a soup kitchen and food distribution service to people who would otherwise have starved. The committee paid the lodging and other expenses of destitute families, placed some children in orphanages, organized vocational retraining, and assisted emigrants in organizing their departures for new homes overseas. It also helped those legally permitted to work to find jobs in the few occupations open to foreigners. The committee's office, which was open six days a week, handled, on average, over a hundred callers a day in early 1936.

In that year a Council for German Jewry, headed by the former high commissioner for Palestine, Sir Herbert Samuel, came into being. Based in London, it was a supposedly international consortium that drew support from the United States and elsewhere. But the council's work was hindered by quarrels between Zionists and non-Zionists and by differences between British and American Jewish leaders.

Gertrude hoped that the new body might provide a central fund for Jewish refugee work everywhere, underwriting the expenditures of her committee. In this she was disappointed. Norman Bentwich, the council's director, wrote to her in March 1936: "You always put your case so impressively that you almost persuade me. But not quite. It is really impossible for a Central Organisation to assume financial responsibility for the Refugee Organisations. . . . The Dutch Jewish community, nobly as it has done in the past, must maintain its effort."[34]

Shortly afterwards, Bentwich visited Holland, and Gertrude showed him round Wieringen. Like others, he was impressed, but he remained convinced that Dutch Jews could raise more money themselves. He was fond of Gertrude, with whom he began exchanging what he jokingly called "daily love letters," but he would not relent on the financial issue.[35] "You rather remind me," Gertrude wrote to him, "of a doctor who thinks that according to his theories his patient ought to live without an operation and who after the death of the man puts this down to sheer cussedness and still has faith in his theories." The Dutch, she insisted, simply could not raise much more. "Still, you are English and very English and I don't suppose you will believe what I say."[36]

Gertrude perforce turned once again to the Joint, pleading that "small Holland cannot collect alone the funds necessary to carry on," and urging the Americans to "consider the Dutch committee as one of their branch offices and help us as such."[37] The Joint would not at this stage take her organization under its wing in this way, though it was ready to tide the Dutch over their immediate difficulties. As Paul Baerwald, the organization's effective head, wrote in an internal memorandum in May 1936: "They have just been in London and have been turned down. It is all very well to say that the Dutch Jews should look after this Committee, but they don't, and the JDC seems to be the only place where they can get money."[38]

The original expectation that the majority of Jews leaving Germany would find homes outside Europe was proving increasingly illusory. Gertrude became ever more frustrated. "It is becoming more and more difficult," she wrote, "to emigrate refugees from here, as nearly all overseas countries have of late made the granting of visa more difficult."[39] Apart from other restrictions, most countries now required financial guarantees that prospective immigrants were usually in no condition to furnish.

Of the 4,055 people "transported" by Gertrude's committee up to the end of 1935, 763 were settled in Holland itself, 1,232 elsewhere in western Europe, 232 in Palestine, and 353 in the Americas (of whom just 32 in the United States).[40] The Soviet Union, which had taken in a few hundred German Jews during the first three years of Nazi rule, closed its frontiers almost entirely to immigrants after 1936, save for Communist political émigrés. Improbable expedients such as sending refugees to Bechuanaland (today Botswana) or Cochin China (south Vietnam) began to be discussed. "We are so desperate about the position here," wrote Gertrude in early 1937, "that we should almost wish to send them to the moon."[41]

The Netherlands was the last country in western Europe to continue to admit Jews from Germany without a visa. Those arriving could stay as long as they liked, provided they did not take jobs or set up a business (in practice, these conditions were often relaxed). But as more arrived than left, the number dependent on charity for day-to-day survival steadily grew.

In October 1937, Gertrude visited Berlin and held several long meetings with leaders of German Jewry. They discussed emigration prospects and the possibility of accelerating the complex bureaucratic processes that had to be completed before Jews could leave the country.[42] By the end of the year, a quarter of German Jewry (an estimated 127,000 out of the 501,000 Jews "by religion" in the country in 1933) had fled. Of these, 22,000 had settled or sojourned for a time in the Netherlands.

Gertrude's visit to Berlin gave rise to some controversy, since it was alleged that she had urged her interlocutors to do everything possible to discourage Jewish immigration to Holland.[43] She denied this, explaining that she had stressed the importance of organized transfer as distinct from disorganized mass flight. The latter, she maintained, would be dangerous for the emigrants themselves and for German Jewry as a whole. She warned that those who left Germany without "solid grounds" ran the risk of being sent back and urged that publicity be given in Germany to this danger.[44] "It was harsh," Cohen later admitted, "but only in that way could we ensure that every person under the protection of our committee could get a residence permit from the Dutch police."[45]

Of the total of 4,885 refugees resettled outside the Netherlands under the committee's direct auspices between 1933 and the end of 1937, the single country that received the largest number, 1,093, was Germany.[46] Among these were fifteen young people from the Wieringen *werkdorp*.[47] More than 20 percent of the refugees whose departure from Holland in the first five years of Nazism was paid for by the committee were thus deposited in the very country from which they were trying to escape. At first, German consuls in western Europe aided such repatriations. Some cases of return had tragic consequences. One young German-Jewish woman, who had worked as a secretary for Gertrude, went back to Berlin to be married. She was immediately arrested.[48] As late as September 1938, Jews were still being sent back to Germany.

How could a committee established for the purpose of helping Jewish refugees from Germany justify such a seemingly illogical, hypocritical, or even inhumane policy? We may note a number of mitigating factors. In the first place, most of the repatriations took place in the early Nazi years, 689 of them in 1933.[49] In February 1934, Gertrude wrote, "Things in Germany are much worse again. . . . To send people back to Germany becomes increasingly difficult."[50] Yet strangely, the thought that sending Jews back might place them in renewed danger seems barely to have restrained the committee at this stage. Although Gertrude, in her reports in the later part of this period, used the word "extermination," it is clear that, like most observers before November 1938, she could not envisage anything approaching the mass murder of German Jewry. At worst, people expected an intensification of persecution, leading to the departure of a majority of the community if the Nazis remained in power.

It should also be kept in mind that refugees for whom the committee bought train tickets back to Germany did not necessarily use them; at least a few scattered in other directions. Some may have taken the opportunity instead to cross the lightly policed borders of France or Belgium. Moreover, several of those who returned to Germany between 1933 and 1938 managed to leave again before the outbreak of war.

Refugees were not sent back if they appeared to be under imminent threat of arrest in Germany. In a public statement in April 1935, David Cohen stressed that they were returned only "where . . . it was possible to do so safely."[51] This condition gradually became harder to meet. The committee was certainly aware, on a timely basis and in great detail, of the deteriorating Jewish condition in Germany. It worked closely with the Jewish Central Information Office, headed by Alfred Wiener, which had been set up in Amsterdam in 1933 (the embryo of the Wiener Library that still exists in London). In March 1936, Wiener's office issued a report warning that returning Jews in Germany faced arrest and "reeducation."[52] Still, the number of Jews in concentration camps, of which there were only a handful at this stage, was small before November 1938.

Against impossible odds, all the refugee organizations were trying to arrange, in an orderly, controlled fashion, the systematic removal of hundreds of thousands of threatened people. Why should some jump the queue? The more destitute Jews forced themselves onto the maintenance rolls of charitable organizations, the less money there would be to finance the migration overseas of others who had patiently waited their turn and who had visas to enter countries of permanent settlement.

Seen in long-term historical perspective, the committee's policy is less surprising than it may appear at first sight. Jewish communities in many places and periods had acted similarly in reaction to large-scale arrival of refugees for whose maintenance they might be expected to take responsibility. As far back as the 1620s, we are told, when large numbers of indigent Ashkenazi Jews arrived in Amsterdam, "the first reaction" of the wealthy, established Portuguese Jews of the city "was to help them re-emigrate—often by sea to Poland—rather than encourage them to found a community and a synagogue of their own in Amsterdam."[53]

A comparison with other countries provides some further perspective. In France, the government, at least until the advent of the Popular Front in mid-1936, resorted on a large scale to *refoulements*, removing illegal immigrants from the country. The Paris homologue of Gertrude's committee, the Comité National Français de Secours aux Réfugiés Allemands, Victimes de l'Antisémitisme, was initially quite unsympathetic to the refugees. One of its leaders, Jacques Helbronner, complained that they included far too many "riff-raff, the rejects of society," and he urged the tightest possible closure of French borders.[54] As for those who had already arrived, he argued, they must leave for countries of permanent settlement overseas. The Comité, like its Amsterdam counterpart, repatriated some refugees—417 to Germany and the Saar in 1934 alone.[55] At one point, the Joint's representative in Paris, Bernard Kahn, warned the Comité that it must not act as the government's "sheriff" in executing expulsion orders.[56] After 1936, as Nazi persecution of Jews worsened, *refoulements* from France ceased almost entirely, and the Comité changed its tune and developed into an outspoken advocate of refugees' rights.

Unlike its French equivalent, the Amsterdam committee found itself more and more trapped in the role of the government's "sheriff." Gertrude's colleague, Henri Eitje, declared privately in March 1938: "As I have always told the Ministry [of Justice] and the police, we have kept more Jews outside Holland than the police and Government put together, by informing our contacts in Germany (as we still do today) that we must resist the flood of refugees into Holland."[57] Although it could not return refugees to Germany against their will, the committee was ready, as Gertrude put it, to adopt "the alternative of stopping relief money," which often had much the same effect.[58] To some extent the committee's attitude, particularly in the case of David Cohen, was motivated by a desire to forestall more forceful official action.

The sacrifice (by way of a return to Germany) of 20 percent of the refugees was, in this light, seen as a condition of the salvation of the other 80 percent. If harsh, the calculus was perhaps realistic. But it was the kind of calculus that, carried to an extreme (as it was to be, by Cohen and his colleagues just a few years later), helped bring about terrible results.

Gertrude shared responsibility for these decisions. But as the refugee crisis deepened, she also undertook, independently of Cohen, more adventurous courses in the hope of finding havens for the persecuted. In one case, involving hundreds of refugees, her efforts, as we shall shortly see, were crowned with success.

CHAPTER THREE

"Death Ships"

The 1930s were for Gertrude a decade of personal as well as political upheaval. In 1930, her beloved younger brother, Walter, committed suicide in New York after losing a fortune in the Wall Street crash. In 1933, her close friend Pieter Vuyk died. Although she made a speedy recovery from her heart attack the following year, she felt under enormous strain. In early 1936, she wrote to Norman Bentwich: "I would gladly give five years of my life if I had the strength of character to dissociate myself from this work, but even then I would probably cheat providence, as it will cost me more than that anyhow."[1]

In May 1937, she received a further shock when she discovered that her husband was having an affair with her twenty-seven-year-old secretary, Beatrix "Trixi" Breslauer. Because Gertrude often worked at home, she had invited Trixi to live in Het Houten Huis, where she had her own room "and really became part of the family."[2] Gertrude had always been an unusually complaisant wife. In 1923, when Jacques had flirted with an attractive cousin of hers in New York, Gertrude helped him write "quasi-love-letters he had sent her . . . quite a delicate task, for she [the cousin] was a happily married woman with four children and the letters had to be both ardent and prudent."[3] In South Africa he had had an affair, but Gertrude had decided to let it pass. On this occasion, however, Jacques announced that he was leaving her. He moved out of the house and set out on a trip to the Middle East.

The collapse of her seventeen-year marriage left Gertrude deeply wounded. "I don't think that in any way whatsoever you left anything about me intact . . . the way you made me feel ugly and without charm and power," she wrote to Jacques. Yet with remarkable forbearance, she allowed Trixi to stay at Het Houten Huis while Jacques was away. "She is a nice kid," she wrote to her husband, "and I hate to see her hurt. . . . And the first days after you left she was so confused and unhappy that I felt more sorry for her than for myself."[4]

By August, Gertrude and Jacques were divorced.[5] Gertrude was given custody of Chedwah, now aged sixteen, and David, aged fourteen. Overwhelmed by these events, Gertrude contemplated suicide.[6] Henrietta Szold wrote her a consolatory letter: "You should not reproach yourself for feeling the tragedy deeply, even devastatingly. How could it be otherwise?"[7] Gertrude took a long time to recover. She maintained civil relations with Jacques, but she was distraught at the change in her home life and the absence of male companionship.

Her loneliness was exacerbated by yet another loss shortly afterwards. One day in November 1937, she lunched with her former employer the banker Carel ter Meulen, who had recently retired and just returned from a long visit to the United States. Concerned about her financial position in the wake of the divorce, he said, "You must let me make some provision for you and your children for the sake of my own peace of mind." The next day his chauffeur crashed his Rolls-Royce into a tree, and Ter Meulen was killed. "It seemed to me," she later recalled, "that all the people who had known and loved me for a long time, and whom I had loved, had gone."[8]

The end of Gertrude's marriage led her to plunge all the more fully into her work, which grew steadily more arduous. As persecution of Jews in Germany mounted, more fled. Receiving countries tried to move them on somewhere, anywhere, just so long as they would go. In December 1937, HICEM in Paris, prompted by the Amsterdam committee, sent a stern letter to its affiliate organization, Ezra (the Hebrew word for "help"), in Luxembourg. The letter upbraided Ezra for dispatching refugees elsewhere without prior arrangement: "We fully understand the difficulties. . . . Nevertheless, peregrinations from country to country can only bring about complete anarchy and entirely disorganize the work of assistance."[9]

Even in the Netherlands, hitherto comparatively receptive to the newcomers, the mood was souring, as was demonstrated by an incident at Wieringen in January 1938. One day a police unit surrounded the *werkdorp* to carry out an "administrative inspection," probably the result of a denunciation by some ill-intentioned informer. Upon checking identity cards, the investigating officers discovered six persons whose documentation was faulty and a further twenty who could not produce any documentation at all. Moreover, a number of identity cards were found that did not match any person present. Some of those people were absent because they were ill, and twenty-nine others had already left the country.

A police report commented that in the light of these discrepancies, closer control was desirable in the future.[10] Although the *werkdorp* suffered no immediate consequences, a local paper published a highly colored account, maintaining that the police had been seeking "undesirable, criminal elements."[11] Gertrude was occupied for several weeks in clearing up with the authorities the cases of unsatisfactory papers. Harmless in itself, the episode can be seen as an ominous forerunner of worse things to come.

The *Anschluss* (annexation) of Austria to Germany in March 1938 immediately led to the extension to Vienna of state-sponsored anti-Semitism. Horrific scenes of maltreatment of Jews shocked the world, while leading several countries to tighten rather than loosen immigration restrictions. A new surge of Jews rushed to leave the expanded Reich. The Dutch government responded on May 7 with a circular from the minister of justice, Carel Goseling, instructing officials and border guards that "a refugee should henceforth be considered as an undesirable element for Dutch society and therefore as an undesirable alien, who must be kept out at the border, or, if found within the country, be put over the border."[12] Refugees nevertheless continued to arrive in Holland as elsewhere. As a result, the issue moved up the diplomatic agenda.

At the initiative of President Roosevelt, an international conference convened in July at Evian on Lake Geneva to discuss the emergency. The British and United States governments, which effectively controlled the meeting, were anxious that nothing untoward (such as criticism of British immigration policy in Palestine or of the U.S. "national origins" quota system for immigration) should disrupt the proceedings. The historian Zara Steiner has tartly pronounced the conference "little more than an international façade which allowed delegates to disguise the unwillingness of their so-called civilized governments to act."[13] The only ostensible result was the establishment of an Intergovernmental Committee on Refugees. An American was appointed its director, but he resigned after only a few months. His British successor, Sir Herbert Emerson, served simultaneously as League of Nations high commissioner for refugees. A former governor of the Punjab, Emerson was an indefatigable producer of lengthy memoranda—"pangs without birth and fruitless industry" (as a literate commentator, echoing Dryden, termed them).[14]

Far from opening doors, the conference had the opposite effect. At the suggestion of the Swiss government, the German authorities started marking passports of German Jews with a distinctive letter "J," whereupon Switzerland, as of October 4, 1938, required that holders of such passports obtain a visa before entering the country. At the same time, the Munich agreement, by which

Czechoslovakia was compelled to yield border territory to Germany, exposed yet more Jews to Nazi brutality.

On October 28, German police rounded up eighteen thousand Jews from all over the country who were Polish citizens (though many of them had been born in Germany) and drove them at bayonet point over the frontier to Poland. The Polish government refused to admit them, and they languished in makeshift camps in no man's land. Angered by these events, a young Polish Jew, the son of expellees, attempted to assassinate a German diplomat in Paris. The Nazis seized on this incident as a pretext for a massive escalation of anti-Semitic violence.

An officially sponsored, nationwide pogrom erupted all over Germany on the night of November 9–10, 1938. Synagogues all over the country were burned down. Jewish homes and businesses were ransacked. Twenty thousand Jews were arrested and sent to concentration camps. As punishment for the damage, the Jews themselves were ordered by the government to pay a *Suehnesteuer* (atonement tax), the huge sum of one billion marks. Discriminatory measures against Jews in economic and social life were reinforced. In the wake of what became known as the Kristallnacht (after the broken windowpanes of Jewish-owned shops), it was plain to all that continued Jewish existence in Germany formed no part of the Nazi conception.

The next morning, when David Cohen arrived at the Jewish Refugees Committee office, he found Gertrude "in a very emotional state." She had received reports by telephone from the Rhineland about the "excesses" against Jews.[15] The committee resolved to appeal to the government for help. On November 13, Cohen and Abraham Asscher were received by Minister of Justice Goseling and two senior officials of his ministry. The results were not encouraging. The government had been concerned about the refugee flood for several months. The visitors were told that, notwithstanding Holland's tradition of refuge for the persecuted, the numbers of immigrants must be restricted. Those who arrived would have to be interned, and the committee was required to arrange for their emigration as soon as possible. In addition, the committee was ordered to furnish, within three days, a financial guarantee of a million guilders (over $550,000 in 1938 value, equivalent to around $10 million in 2014) for the cost of establishing and maintaining internment camps.[16] The guarantee was provided, but official policy was clearly moving in a restrictionist direction.

On November 15, the Ministry of Justice issued a circular requiring all men who had entered the country illegally since November 10 to be interned.[17] The Jewish Refugees Committee busied itself with securing their release, but officials required the committee to take responsibility for the upkeep of anyone leaving the camps. It thus found itself more and more drawn into the role of mediator between internees (later, in some cases, prisoners) and the government.

Demand for entry to the United States was now so great that even where applicants were qualified, they had to wait months or years before they could secure immigration certificates. The American consul-general in Berlin, sympathetic to the plight of the Jews, wrote letters for many confirming that they could expect to receive a visa by a given date. This enabled some to find temporary refuge in countries bordering Germany. But when the Dutch government declared that it regarded such letters as a definite commitment by the United States to admit the holders in the future, the consul general was abruptly ordered by the State Department to cease issuing such documents.[18]

In the six weeks following Kristallnacht, the committee was inundated with over eleven thousand letters from Jews in Germany seeking help in emigrating. The number of refugees reaching the Netherlands shot up to over a thousand per week. More arrived in November and December 1938 than in the whole of the previous ten months. The deluge of newcomers, many of them destitute and therefore dependent on charitable support, brought about a great expansion and reorganization of the committee's apparatus.

An outpouring of public sympathy after Kristallnacht also led to new endeavors, including one in which Gertrude played a significant role: what became known as the Kindertransport. The Movement for the Care of Children from Germany was created in Britain after a government announcement that it would allow children from Germany, unaccompanied by their parents, to be admitted and lodged with foster families. The Kindertransport transferred nearly ten thousand children to Britain before the outbreak of war. Holland, Sweden, and Denmark also admitted smaller numbers.

The central figure in the Dutch arm of the operation was Truus Wijsmuller-Meijer, a gentile Amsterdam social worker. Over the next two years, she and Gertrude cooperated effectively, although relations between these highly opinionated and sometimes stubborn middle-aged women are said to have been "cool to the point of hostility."[19] The Dutch government agreed to admit up to fifteen hundred children, provided they would not become a permanent charge on public funds and would remain only so long as might be necessary to meet requirements for immigration to the United States.

On November 14, Gertrude cabled the Joint appealing for emergency financial support for refugee children.[20] The response was immediate and positive. Three days later, it allocated $50,000 (over $800,000 in 2014 value) to Gertrude's committee to cover the care in Holland of children from Germany.[21] Even this unprecedented commitment, however, did not meet the urgency of the moment. The initial discussions envisaged the admission to Holland of 326 children.[22] But reports reaching New York indicated that as many as five thousand were massing "on the Dutch border."[23] On November 19, the Amsterdam committee sent a telegram, signed by Cohen and Gertrude, to Paul Baerwald of the Joint: "Lots of homeless children separated from parents straying in woods or put on trains by desperate mothers whose husbands arrested. Number tremendous. Numerous orphanages destroyed and even sick children driven into streets foodless and penniless. Plight unbelievable. Holland admitting great number but could admit more if immediately reassured by other countries they are willing to absorb children ultimately. Holland could then admit them temporarily and greatest distress would be avoided."[24] The committee hoped that the Netherlands would eventually admit several thousand children and expressed confidence that given the great wave of public sympathy following Kristallnacht, the cost could be covered by local fund-raising. But public interest waned; as new horrors eclipsed old, contributions fell off.

Initial hopes for the Dutch Kindertransport proved to be exaggerated. The government, though willing to admit children, insisted they must remain only temporarily. As for the American administration, although it eased some bureaucratic procedures, it refused to budge from the existing quota system. It emerged that no more than 240 German and Austrian children would be admissible to the United States in 1939, and the same number in 1940.[25] In an effort to liberalize American immigration law, the Wagner-Rogers Bill was presented in early 1939, calling for the admission of twenty thousand German refugee children over a two-year period, beyond the quota. But the bill died in Congress.

Gertrude was at the station in Berlin when the first train left carrying children to Holland. "The scenes were heartbreaking. With their husbands in concentration camps and their children leaving, the mothers tried hard to appear cheerful, but many of them broke down as the train pulled out. Many of the children cried too."[26] The transport arrived in Amsterdam on November 28, and the children were sent to large wooden barracks that had been equipped as a quarantine station.

By the end of April, 1,584 children were being cared for in Holland. Most were housed in orphanages or other institutions; the rest were allocated to Dutch families after being held in quarantine for two weeks. The refugee committee guaranteed to the government the cost of board and upkeep for all the children.

Reporting to the Joint on November 26, Gertrude estimated that about four thousand legal refugees and at least fifteen hundred illegal ones had entered the Netherlands since Kristallnacht. Of the latter, six hundred had been interned. She feared that future illegal immigrants, even if they claimed to be only in transit, would be sent back. "The control of the people who try to enter Holland en route to another country is very severe, and large numbers of people are daily not admitted into Holland." Notwithstanding the sympathetic turn in public opinion, the government was "rigorously determined not to admit more Jews into Holland at present because they say that there are no chances of emigration."[27]

Dutch officials now took stringent measures to stem the flow of immigrants. In early December, a group of twenty unaccompanied children who arrived in Nijmegen, apparently with German police connivance, was sent home.[28] The government announced that after December 17, no more refugees would be admitted, and any who arrived illegally would be deported unless they could prove that their lives were in danger. Border controls were stiffened so as to reduce the number of illegal entries and prevent the *afschuiving* (dumping) of Jews across the frontier by the Nazis.

On December 21, a circular, marked "confidential," from the Jewish Refugees Committee to all its provincial branches warned that the Amsterdam police were sending any illegal immigrants that they encountered back to the border. The same appeared to be happening throughout the country.

> We must therefore request that, apart from exceptional cases in which the police might perhaps grant temporary admission (we are thinking here, for example, of children), you should advise illegal refugees to make their way back to Germany, for otherwise they will be sent back by the police. Of course, there is no objection to your paying their fares. We are sorry to have to write to you thus, but the government takes the position that if the great stream of illegal refugees who have come to the Netherlands recently were to be permitted to continue, the refugee question would become insoluble for the Netherlands.[29]

Once again, the committee was acting as the government's "sheriff." It is impossible to know how many refugees returned to Germany as a result of this advisory notice, since such cases were not included in the official migration figures reported by the committee. That it should have issued such a notice just a few weeks after Kristallnacht is a further sign of its readiness, faced with an almost impossible dilemma, to bow to governmental restrictionism.

Notwithstanding all this, at least seven thousand people were recorded by the government as having arrived in the seventeen months after the deadline, and very few who managed to reach Dutch territory were expelled. Among those who came from Berlin was Gertrude's brother, Ernst. He had been sent to a concentration camp at the time of Kristallnacht but was soon released and reached Amsterdam with his family in January 1939. They were fortunate in obtaining visas to Australia. Most illegal immigrants were deposited in internment camps, where the regime became steadily stricter. Some now turned into something close to prison camps.

When Sir Herbert Emerson visited the Netherlands in February 1939, he found "governmental treatment of refugees" to be "a curious mixture of humanity and restraint, better facilities and more assistance being granted than in many countries, while at the same time there is the imposition of irksome conditions exceeding those which most countries have found it necessary to impose.[30] This policy found expression in a government decision in March 1939 to prohibit refugees from leaving camps to attend the Passover seder (festive meal) with Dutch-Jewish families.[31]

The restrictive new procedures led to considerable Jewish criticism of the refugees committee, which was attacked for not making effective enough representations to official quarters. David Cohen was obliged to issue a public statement pointing out that policy, after all, was decided by the government, not the committee.

In February 1939, Gertrude reported to the Joint that there were twenty-three thousand German-Jewish refugees in the country. The government estimate was thirty thousand, taking account of what officials feared was a large number of unregistered illegal immigrants. Gertrude contested the official figure, since "we do not think that it is possible for any large number of refugees to remain in Holland for any length of time without being detected by the police authorities in their frequent raids in boarding houses, on stations, at the post offices, etc."[32] Gertrude may have been right, but her reference to police raids pointed to the changed atmosphere in which refugees were increasingly becoming hunted fugitives.

The German occupation of Prague on March 15, 1939, not only shattered any lingering faith in the Munich agreement but also raised the refugee crisis to new heights. "One shudders to think of the fate of new tens of thousands driven into the net of Nazi treatment," wrote Morris Troper of the Joint two days later.[33]

Troper, who had taken over from Kahn as head of the Joint's European operations in October 1938, was to play a key role in the organization's relationship with Gertrude. Unlike Kahn, he was an American citizen. A former accountant, he was an efficient administrator who shared Kahn's high estimation of Gertrude's work in Amsterdam.

Early in 1939, the government initiated the idea of closing all the existing internment camps for illegal immigrants and instead establishing a "central camp." Provided the Jewish community assumed full responsibility for all costs, the government would be prepared to legalize the temporary residence of illegal refugees there, pending their emigration to places of permanent residence. In February, the government approved detailed plans for the camp. The chosen site was in the province of Drenthe, in the north of the country, not far from the German border. Westerbork was on a low-lying heath, seven miles from the nearest town, Assen. The location had originally been designated within the Veluwe National Park. Queen Wilhelmina, however, whose summer palace was nearby, objected (not, it would appear, on anti-Jewish grounds—she was demonstratively friendly to her Jewish subjects). The government thereupon decided to locate the camp at Westerbork instead. Shopkeepers in the area looked forward to an increase in business, but the local tourist industry opposed the plan. Some local residents complained that their district was being used as a dumping ground for aliens and that it was "common knowledge" that among the potential residents were asocial elements whose motives for fleeing to the Netherlands were other than racial or religious.[34]

In later years, Gertrude maintained that when the proposal for the camp first appeared, she had been "violently opposed."[35] She, in common with all the other members of the committee's staff, certainly objected to the idea at the outset.[36] This was the first occasion when a serious division appeared between her and David Cohen. Instead of rejecting the project root and branch, she sought to ensure that it was implemented in the most humane and practicable manner. She was one of nine signatories of a letter to the minister of the interior in May that stressed the "moral dangers" of lodging child refugees in the vicinity of adults and proposed instead a detailed plan for providing for children outside the camp. One element of this involved the creation in Wieringen of a children's village adjacent to the *werkdorp*.[37] This was not put into effect, though the government conceded that young children under the age of fourteen would not be sent to the central camp but would be lodged with families elsewhere. Under further pressure from the refugee bodies, it was agreed that people above the age of fifty would also not be placed there. Gertrude reported that the refugee committee's hope was that the camp would be "for emigrable people only" and that "the difference in treatment meted out to the illegal refugees up to now will practically disappear in the Central Camp."[38]

By late June, parliament had passed a bill authorizing a 1.25 million guilder (about $350,000 at the prevailing exchange rate) credit for the construction and equipment of the camp, to be repaid by the Jewish Refugees Committee in annual installments of 200,000 guilders, starting on January 1, 1941. Construction began at Westerbork a few weeks later. Cohen recalled that the committee had no choice but to agree to the government's proposals, even though "nearly all our employees were opposed."[39]

Reporting to the Joint, Gertrude sounded an optimistic note: "Since it becomes more and more clear that the Government will do all in their power to make this refugee village into a first class training centre and since, moreover, we have the greatest confidence in the people who will be entrusted with the management of the community, we look forward to the opening of this camp with the greatest confidence and something like real enthusiasm." She went on to describe the housing arrangements ("newly built wooden barracks with central heating, excellent sanitation and all reasonable comforts"), the private apartments for families, and the area for children above fourteen years of age, which, "although on the same grounds will form a special entity and really be a separate children's village." There would be ample opportunities for work in agriculture, crafts, and upkeep of the camp. She concluded, without any hint of reservation: "The preliminary discussions which we have had with the Government as well as with the camp manager make us feel confident that everything possible will be done to make this experiment of a refugee training village into a success."[40] Westerbork, thus portrayed, seemed on the face of things rather like Wieringen writ large.

Such measures, however, could be no more than palliatives in the face of the accumulating German-Jewish agony. This was demonstrated on May 27, 1939, when the German passenger liner *St Louis* arrived at Havana with 937 passengers, most of them German-Jewish refugees. Even though they held tourist visas for Cuba, they were refused entry, since they did not hold valid onward visas. The United States government rejected requests for emergency visas on the ground that the German quota was full. As a result, the ship recrossed the Atlantic towards Germany. Amid an international outcry and after desperate negotiations, the governments of Britain, France, Belgium, and the Netherlands agreed to admit the passengers on a temporary basis, provided no expense would fall on public funds. The Joint gave the necessary financial guarantee. The Dutch permitted the entry of 181 people, pending their further emigration. Upon disembarkation, they were immediately removed to a camp at Heijplaat (in Rotterdam), surrounded by barbed wire and guarded by dogs. Those below the age of fifty were subsequently to be deposited at Westerbork, then still under construction, pending their departure from the country.

A Joint report from Paris on July 31, summarizing the condition of European Jewry, painted a picture of extreme distress:

> From everywhere reports arrive of Jews roaming the seas without being able to find a haven. One catastrophe follows another. The SS *Rim* caught fire and only with difficulties could the passengers be rescued. According to the latest reports, pestilence has broken out on four ships laden with so-called illegal immigrants to Palestine who were not permitted to set foot on the promised land. There are ships prowling the Danube and one of them is said to have dumped its passengers on a deserted island in the river. Early in June there came reports from Germany that new groups of Polish Jews were being forced over the German-Polish border.[41]

The British government's decision, announced in a white paper in May, to institute stiff new limits on Jewish immigration to Palestine exacerbated the crisis. The new policy was greeted with indignation by the Zionists, who saw it as a betrayal of British commitments and a deviation from the provisions of the Palestine mandate. Non-Zionist as well as Zionist Jews shared in the general outrage that the doors of the Jewish National Home should be virtually closed precisely at the hour of greatest Jewish need.

Extreme difficulty in securing Palestine certificates placed the Jewish Refugees Committee in an acutely awkward position. It had repeatedly promised the Dutch government that the students at Wieringen would leave the country; now it found that it had almost nowhere to send them.

The emergency led Gertrude, among others, into desperate courses. For some time, Zionist agents and commercial racketeers

Professor David Cohen, chairman of the Amsterdam Committee for Jewish Refugees, 1933–1941, cochairman of the Amsterdam Jewish Council 1941–1943 *(Jewish Historical Museum, Amsterdam)*

had been organizing illegal immigration of Jewish refugees to Palestine as well as other countries. Gertrude and a small group of members and associates of the committee decided to cross the line into illegality. They did not inform David Cohen, who was known to be opposed to any activity outside the law.

Several Zionist agents arrived in Europe as representatives of the Mossad le-Aliyah Bet (Institution for Illegal Immigration)—a branch of the Haganah, the underground militia of the mainstream Zionists. Their task was to coordinate the clandestine departure to Palestine of refugees from Holland. Their leader was the German-born Gideon Rufer. His assistant was Shmarya Tsameret, a young American-born member of Kibbutz Bet Hashita, where many former Wieringen students had settled. Tsameret traveled on a United States passport with his birth name of Grey.

In Copenhagen, the two men chartered a small collier (584 gross tons and just 199 feet long and 30 feet broad) that had been built in 1898 at Port Glasgow.[42] Previously registered as SS *Tjaldur*, she was renamed *Dora* in 1939. Although owned by a Greek, she sailed under the Panamanian flag. Her multinational crew was composed mainly of Greeks and Danes. In spite of her origin as a cargo vessel, the *Dora* held a certificate to carry passengers. She was fitted out in rudimentary fashion, with a kitchen, lavatories, and iron bunk beds. Since funds from the Joint could not be used for illegal enterprises, Gertrude's Dutch associates guaranteed £3,000 to cover expenses (the Jewish Agency ultimately bore part of the costs). *Halutzim* (pioneers) from Wieringen were hidden in villages near the coast to await the order for embarkation. But in the course of outfitting the ship, disputes with the crew and friction between the Dutch and the Palestinians jeopardized the venture. At one point, the Zionist leader, Chaim Weizmann, had to intervene to restore peace among the organizers.[43]

The ship was moved from Copenhagen to Amsterdam. Gertrude and one of her committee colleagues, Siegfried Kramarsky—a German-Jewish banker long resident in Holland—inspected the *Dora* in order to satisfy themselves that she was fit for the coming voyage. When they saw the decrepit hulk, they were shocked and wondered aloud whether she was capable of carrying a large complement of passengers through the Atlantic and the Mediterranean to Palestine. They talked of withdrawing their support. Rufer and Tsameret protested that the ship was seaworthy and that it was necessary to take risks in order to save Jews from the Nazis. Tsameret was impressed by Gertrude, whom he called a woman "of experience and humanity."[44] They established cordial relations, but she was still doubtful about the viability of the enterprise, and Kramarsky remained adamantly opposed to allowing the ship to sail. Meanwhile, the undertaking encountered a further setback when Communist stevedores leaked news that a "slave trade" ship was about to embark from the port. Publicity about this "*Dodenschip*" (ship of the dead) threatened to scuttle the venture.[45]

Officially, the Dutch government knew nothing about the preparations for the *Dora*'s departure. Nor did it wish to know. Having reached the end of its tether so far as refugees were concerned, it was happy to facilitate the removal of at least some of them and had little inclination to cooperate with the British in implementing the White Paper policy. Rufer met the Minister of the Interior, Hendrik van Boeijen, who approved the operation and ensured that officials turned a blind eye to what was being organized.

To Gertrude's relief, Dutch marine inspectors visited the ship and pronounced her seaworthy on condition that some minor repairs be made and that lifeboats be brought aboard when she stopped at Antwerp. Gertrude skillfully fielded telephone calls from the press seeking information about the ship's destination.[46] The Communist *Volksdagblad* nevertheless denounced the apparent collusion of the authorities and the refugee committee in the dispatch of this "second *St Louis*" on a "death journey."[47]

The *halutzim* were brought from their hiding places to the harborside Lloyd Hotel in Amsterdam, which functioned at the time as a refugee camp. Gertrude was there with some of her accomplices. Also present were a number of Dutch civil servants and policemen. Every passenger had to sign a form attesting that he or she was embarking of his own free will. Behind a police cordon, the *haverim* (comrades), in groups of ten or twenty, boarded small launches that took them to the *Dora*, waiting a hundred yards from the quay.[48]

A high degree of complicity between the authorities and the organizers was evident. As Zvi Spector, the Haganah chief of the operation, was about to board, the commanding officer of the Dutch immigration police raised a glass and proposed three toasts—to Queen Wilhelmina, to the success of the voyage, and to an independent Jewish state.[49]

In the early hours of Sunday, July 16, 1939, the *Dora* sailed from Amsterdam with about three hundred passengers.[50] Most were Jewish refugees from Germany, including about fifty students from Wieringen. Some were Dutch Zionists who had undergone agricultural training in other *hachsharot*. All were adults, mainly young men. One of the forty or so *haverot* (female comrades) was in her sixth month of pregnancy. Gertrude bade an emotional farewell to the passengers and to Tsameret, who was to travel by train to meet the ship at Antwerp.

The *Dora*'s supposedly covert departure, bound for "a secret destination," was, in fact, widely reported in the Dutch press.[51] The British minister at The Hague, Sir Nevile Bland, lodged a formal complaint, but by then the bird had already flown. Twelve days after the ship's departure, the new minister of justice, Pieter Gerbrandy, wrote to the minister of foreign affairs, advising him that the ship had been allowed to leave "for an unknown destination, supposedly Siam. As to the real destination, of which nothing at present is known, inquiries will be made." Gerbrandy suggested that "the English diplomat" might be told in general terms that the Dutch government, so far as it was able, would not permit the organized departure of illegal immigrants to Palestine.[52] Questions were asked in the Dutch parliament. After several weeks' delay, Gerbrandy replied that the government had in no way facilitated the ship's departure, which, he claimed, had been effected on the sole responsibility of the Jewish Refugees Committee.[53]

More passengers boarded the *Dora* at Antwerp. Kramarsky, who traveled overland from Amsterdam, was furious to discover that beyond the fifty that had been agreed upon, the Haganah organizers had brought aboard over a hundred *haverim* who had been smuggled out of Germany a few weeks earlier.[54] He again threatened to withdraw financial support. Tsameret warned that as the refugees were present illegally in Belgium, they might be sent back to Germany if they did not leave. An enraged Kramarsky telephoned Gertrude and harangued her for an hour. She came on the line to Tsameret and, in milder tones, explained that the Dutch government had been promised that no more than fifty people would board at Antwerp. If a larger number appeared, she said, the passengers from Amsterdam would have to be brought back there.[55] But Tsameret, to Kramarsky's fury, boarded all 157 new passengers anyway. Kramarsky went aboard the vessel himself and tried to persuade them to disembark on grounds of safety. When he failed, he got into his car and left in a dark mood.

Belgian officials, like the Dutch, were keen to see the backs of refugees. The *Dora* left Antwerp on July 17, giving her destination as Bangkok.[56] In her passage through the English Channel, she passed British naval vessels but was not stopped.

The *Dora* took several weeks to reach the coast of Palestine. As Gertrude later wrote, the ship was "overloaded, ill-equipped, not very well provisioned."[57] Off the coast of Normandy, she rolled alarmingly from side to side in high seas. Half the passengers got seasick. As they traversed the Strait of Gibraltar, all except the crew were ordered to remain below deck, lest they be seen by British lookouts. Shortly afterwards, they penetrated deep fog. Then they were blasted by another severe storm. During the final part of the voyage, the Haganah commanders kept in touch with Palestine by radio. They were ordered to take a circuitous route to evade British naval vessels under orders to interdict illegal immigrants. Off southern Anatolia, the ship was subjected to warning shots from Turkish armed forces. And as she neared the coast of Palestine, a near mutiny by the crew demanding more money was averted only after they were bought off with the proceeds of a collection from the passengers.

On the night of August 11–12, the *Dora* reached Palestinian coastal waters. In order to evade British coastal patrols, the passengers were transferred at sea to small boats that Tsameret had purchased in Greece. They landed near Herzliya, north of Tel Aviv. Among those waiting on the shore to greet them was the Haganah commander and creator of the Mossad, Eliyahu Golomb. The passengers were dispersed to various addresses without encountering the British police. It was not until a year later that the mandatory government of Palestine gained complete knowledge of what had happened. Officials then concluded that there was nothing to be done, save to deduct the number of arrivals from the permitted quota of future legal immigration.[58]

The *Dora* was one of several ships that carried thousands of illegal immigrants to Palestine in 1939, but she was the only one to sail from western Europe. The outbreak of war in September precluded any further such ventures from Dutch ports.

Between January and August 1939, the Amsterdam refugee committee managed to transport a total of 2,264 people overseas by legal means. Of these, the largest number, 530, moved to the United States. Next in order were England (393), Australia (370), and Bolivia (224). The number sent to Palestine during this period was just 83, reflecting the tightened restrictions there (obviously, this officially reported number did not include the passengers on the *Dora*). Other destinations included Chile (112), Trinidad (39), China (37), Mexico (20), and even more exotic destinations, such as Samoa, Senegal, and Santo Domingo.

Refugees who failed to leave Holland and could not support themselves were consigned to camps; by the end of August 1939, 1,278 people (731 legals and 547 illegals) were living under various degrees of compulsion in camps and hostels in various parts of the country.[59] The hope was that those who could still not emigrate would be moved to the new "central camp" at Westerbork as soon as it was ready for operation.

By the summer of 1939, the financial position of the committee had again become "critical." The torrent of contributions after Kristallnacht had dwindled to a trickle. Local collections in May yielded only $17,000 against expenditures of $115,000. Difficulties were heightened by the Council for German Jewry's decision to cease its annual subsidy for Wieringen. The *werkdorp* had been given permission shortly after Kristallnacht to expand. By February 1939, it held 278 students, and there was a long waiting list of applicants still in Germany.

Gertrude again threatened to close down the refugee committee altogether unless more assistance arrived from abroad. She urged the convening of "a general conference to be held at as early a time as possible, at which representatives of all the refugee aid committees in Europe might discuss their common problems and present a program to their respective governments."[60]

Sponsored by the Joint and HICEM, such a conference met in Paris on August 22–23, 1939. Participants arrived from the United States; from many European countries, including Germany; and from as far away as Shanghai. A total of about sixty representatives of twenty-nine organizations attended. Noticeably absent were any delegates from Palestine or representatives of Zionist organizations, perhaps because the Zionist Congress was meeting at the same time in Geneva. Gertrude was the sole delegate from the Netherlands. Saly Mayer, a Swiss businessman who had contributed to financing the voyage of the *Dora*, and who was to play an important role in Gertrude's life over the next few years, attended as a delegate of the Federation of Swiss Jewish Communities, which he chaired from 1936 to 1942.

The gathering assembled, as the executive director of the Joint put it, "in the shadow of unknown events"—that is, under the immediate threat of the outbreak of war. Its proceedings were not open to the public and were not published. Apart from the Evian conference, which had been a meeting of governments, not private organizations, this was the first international meeting to deal exclusively with the Jewish refugee question. It was also the last before it was too late.

Delegates from Nazi-controlled territories presented grim reports on their devastated communities. German Jewry had been reduced to penury, terror, and helplessness. Fifty thousand Jews had left the country since the beginning of the year. The downfall of Austrian Jewry had been even more sudden, overwhelming, and shocking. In Vienna, the Jewish population had shrunk from 180,000 at the time of the Anschluss, eighteen months earlier, to just 70,000. Jews had been turned out of their homes; their businesses had been confiscated; they had been dismissed from their jobs; they were forbidden to enter parks, cafés, or places of entertainment; their synagogues had been burned down; and their children had been expelled from public schools. Most were living in wretched poverty, and more than half were subsisting on charitable doles. In the previous month, 12 percent of all Jewish deaths recorded in Vienna had been suicides. The Jewish community had been instructed that the entire Jewish population of Austria must be "cleared out" within a matter of months. Hardly less alarming statements were heard from Jewish communities in other parts of the continent.

Flight out of Nazi territory in these last moments of peace became a headlong rush. The conference expected that all "non-Aryans," except the very old, would have to leave the Third Reich. Refuge would therefore have to be found for at least another 400,000 people. But where? A delegate from England reported that an estimated ten thousand Jewish refugees, including twenty-five hundred children, had arrived there within the previous six or seven weeks. More than nine thousand had reached Italy since the start of the year, many en route to Palestine, Latin America, or Shanghai.

The conferees did not discuss illegal immigration to Palestine. The issue arose, however, towards the end of the proceedings in the course of a speech by Edouard Oungre, the non-Zionist head of HICEM. His refusal to include illegal arrivals in his calculation of the likely number of immigrants to Palestine elicited some objections from his audience. Oungre responded by quoting the celebrated phrase of Léon Gambetta after the German annexation of Alsace and Lorraine in 1870: *pensons-y toujours, n'en parlons jamais* (Let us always think of it; but never speak of it).[61]

Gertrude was the only woman to address the meeting. There were now between five and six thousand refugees in Holland dependent on relief, she said. Of those, about fourteen hundred were children who had arrived without their parents, and another six hundred were young people in Wieringen and similar establishments. She described plans for the Westerbork camp and efforts towards occupational retraining. The Amsterdam committee had spent twice as much as it had received in the first half of the year, and fund-raising was becoming much harder. Rich Jews, both Dutch and German, were fleeing the country as anti-Semitic propaganda increased. Holland, she said, could not accommodate any more refugees.

Together with Saly Mayer, Norman Bentwich, and others, Gertrude was appointed to a committee charged with summarizing the conclusions of the conference. Perhaps inevitably, given the "baffling" nature and the magnitude of the problem, they could record little by way of practical decisions. They echoed earlier calls for "an orderly and planned evacuation" from the Reich over a period of at least four years. Voluntary organizations could not possibly cope; governmental intervention was required. "Impressed by the value . . . of transit camps where those who are waiting for final emigration and settlement can be harboured and prepared," the conference urged on the Intergovernmental Committee on Refugees and other such bodies "consideration of the extension of such camps of refuge with government help."[62]

As the delegates dispersed, news arrived of the signature of the Nazi-Soviet nonaggression pact. War now appeared certain. In private conversations in Paris (there is no documentary record), leaders of the Joint made quiet arrangements in anticipation of the outbreak of war. Their contingency plans were based, in part, on their experience in the First World War. Countries that were expected to remain neutral would have an important role as conduits for money, information, and aid to Jews in Nazi-held territory and for refugees seeking to escape. Saly Mayer and Gertrude, although neither was employed by the Joint, were henceforth treated by its headquarters as its authorized representatives in Switzerland and Holland respectively. Both were accorded full confidence and considerable latitude in political and financial matters by the organization's officials in New York and Paris—support that greatly strengthened their hands and hearts in the coming ordeal.

Gertrude returned to Holland with one of the German-Jewish leaders, Julius Seligsohn, whose wife and children had taken refuge there the previous November. Both Seligsohn's wife and Gertrude begged him not to go back to Germany, but he felt it was his responsibility to help the left-behind Jews, mainly the old and infirm. He left for Berlin on September 4, one day after Britain declared war on Germany.

CHAPTER FOUR

Gertrude's War

By 1939, Gertrude was recovering from the breakup of her marriage. She had always enjoyed male company. After her divorce and the deaths of her friends Vuyk and Ter Meulen, she formed a close attachment to Professor Curt Bondy. An agronomist and educator, Bondy headed a training farm at Gross-Breesen in Silesia until his departure from Germany in November 1938. He acted as an adviser at the Wieringen *werkdorp* before moving to England, where he took charge of a refugee camp. A bachelor, Bondy was a little younger than Gertrude, who visited him in England several times. In intimate conversations, she confessed to him her loneliness and despair following her divorce. Bondy helped her overcome her "frozen unhappiness."[1] "It was as though I was reborn," she later recalled.[2] His feelings for her are not recorded. Bondy's engagement with his youthful charges at Gross-Breesen had had a certain homoerotic element. One of his "disciples" called him "der schönste hässliche Mann" (the most beautiful ugly man), with "a somewhat grotesque face, a broad mouth like an orangutan, but warm eyes and (sometimes) a wonderful smile."[3] For her part, Gertrude's daughter Chedwah considered him very handsome.

When Bondy returned to Holland in the summer of 1939, Gertrude hoped that he would take responsibility "at least temporarily" for "management of the pedagogic and social department" of Westerbork.[4] But he was already planning to leave for America. The camp opened on October 9, 1939, when 22 refugees arrived from an internment camp at Hook of Holland. By January 1940, only 698 remained in other camps, and remaining internees were being concentrated at Westerbork.[5]

In January 1939, the Jewish Refugees Committee had moved to new premises at 366 Lijnbaansgracht. This five-story structure, purchased by a wealthy benefactor, was a former diamond works that had been converted into an office building with space for a staff that now numbered eighty. The same address housed the foundation responsible for the Wieringen *werkdorp*, and most of the furniture in the building was made in the Wieringen workshops. This would remain Gertrude's place of work until 1943.

The outbreak of the European war on September 1, 1939, and Holland's neutrality until May 1940 thrust the Amsterdam committee into the forefront of activity on behalf of Jewish refugees. Gertrude now found herself in a pivotal position. She redoubled efforts to organize onward travel for Jews from Germany whose prewar bookings had been canceled. Gertrude reported to the Joint:

> On the first two days of the war with our help a few hundred people still actually got into Holland. . . . After it was clear, however, that England would no longer admit Jews from Germany, those who tried to enter Holland in the hope that their permits were still valid had unfortunately to be turned back. . . . Still for some days after the frontier had been closed large numbers of Jews with permits and visas tried to get through Holland into England. This caused the most tragic scenes at our frontiers, which scenes unfortunately have become only too familiar to the refugee committees in the frontier places.[6]

In the end, just 140 Jewish refugees entered Holland in September 1939.

As departure from Germany to overseas destinations via Britain was no longer possible, the cost of tickets by other routes soared. Gertrude demanded and immediately received from the Joint a grant of $30,000 to enable the Amsterdam committee to act as a "clearing office" for emigration from Berlin, Vienna, and Prague.[7] The Joint headquarters in New York authorized Gertrude to coordinate arrangements and to use her own judgment regarding emergency cases.[8]

On September 12 she accepted an invitation from the Kultusgemeinde (Jewish community) in Berlin. She was accompanied to the German capital by Truus Wijsmuller-Meijer. Since no trains were running across the frontier, they drove to Germany, leaving the car at the border town of Bentheim. There they boarded a train that, because of military disruptions, took a zigzag route to Berlin. They were met at the station by Paul Eppstein, one of the leaders of the Reichsvereinigung, the officially recognized body of the Jewish community. He told them that two meetings with Jewish leaders had been planned for them, one about potential adult emigration and the other about children. Gestapo agents would be present at both. Wijsmuller-Meijer later recalled, "It was strange to be talking to the community leaders in the presence of two Gestapo men, seated at the head of the table and deciding on each element of our plans. As they said 'yes,' or 'In Ordnung,' or perhaps just nodded, we could proceed a step further. If they said 'no' or shrugged their shoulders, we right away had to propose something new."[9]

After her return to Amsterdam, Gertrude reported to the Joint that the Jews in Germany were "in great fear as to what might develop." They felt they were "living on a volcano." The German government was "of the opinion that Jews should continue emigrating and at present permits Jews of all ages to leave." She warned: "if emigration should come to a standstill because foreign countries refuse them entrance, it is to be feared that very rigorous action will be taken against the Jews of Germany."

Gertrude urged that "all steps should be taken to create immediate possibilities of emigration to enable some tens of thousands of Jews to leave." She proposed the erection of "camps and barracks . . . in some countries like Venezuela" and inquired "whether it might be possible to charter a steamer for the emigration of Jews from Germany . . . to . . . sail under a Red Cross flag." More realistically, she made a number of smaller-scale, detailed proposals for moving emigrants to South America, Australia, and Palestine.

The declaration of war had brought the British Kindertransport to a complete halt. But through Dutch channels, the German government notified the Intergovernmental Committee on Refugees that pressure for Jewish emigration would be intensified. The Germans urged that the committee's work should carry on in spite of the outbreak of war. Jewish leaders in Berlin therefore hoped to be able to organize the departure of Jews, particularly children, to neutral countries such as Denmark and Sweden, as well as the Americas.

In a "personal and strictly confidential" section of her report, Gertrude added, "I have agreed that I shall return, if urgently necessary. If something very bad should occur (f. i. internment of all men) I shall receive a telegram with agreed code-word. . . . In a conversation which was held in an intimate circle, I was frankly told that the worst is to be feared. . . . The way in which our friends continue with the work is truly wonderful." The coded message never came, though this was not her last visit to wartime Berlin.

Gertrude contemplated traveling to Prague, Vienna, and Warsaw—ideas that came to nothing. She suggested that, in view of the state of war between France and Germany, the Joint should transfer its main European office from Paris to Amsterdam. And she pleaded for holders of Palestine immigration certificates, still in Germany, whose permits had been automatically canceled by the British government upon the outbreak of war. Could they be renewed?[10] In the case of this small number of people, the British government relented and, on October 3, informed the Jewish Agency that this limited category of people might proceed.[11]

In her report to the Joint, she also raised what appeared at the time to be the minor issue of the several thousand Germans, mainly from Württemberg, who had immigrated to Palestine since the late nineteenth century. These "Templers" (not to be confused with the Templar knights of the Crusader period), and their descendants were members of a Protestant sect, the Tempelgesellschaft, who sought to hasten the Second Coming by settling in the Holy Land. In the 1930s, many Templers had joined a Palestine branch of the Nazi Party. When war broke out, young men of the community were interned by the British authorities. The Nazi propaganda machine exploited their predicament, claiming that they had been ill-treated. Gertrude commented on the effects of this on the *ha'avara* (exchange) agreement under which, since 1933, the German government had permitted Jews emigrating to Palestine to export a small part of their capital (the Nazis pocketed the rest): "The fact that in Palestine Germans have been attacked by a Jewish mob is being exploited greatly and the authorities refuse to negotiate about any future transfer until proof is given in some way that official quarters will have nothing to do with this. It is of utmost importance that immediately . . . a declaration should be made by the Jewish Agency stating that they will use all their influence to see to it that the lives and property of all people living in Palestine should be respected."[12] Shortly afterwards, the British Ministry of Information issued two statements, denying that any Germans had been maltreated and claiming that German colonists in Palestine had expressed gratitude to the government for their good treatment.[13] So far as Gertrude was concerned the issue lapsed, though it was to reemerge later in a lifesaving manner.

Another delicate matter on which Gertrude's discussions in Germany turned was illegal migration to Palestine. Although Gertrude knew that the Joint would not countenance direct involvement, she pointed out that *Aliyah Bet* (illegal immigration) was "allowed [by the Nazis] if technically and financially feasible." She urged that Pino Ginsburg, a Zionist emissary from Palestine who had crossed from Germany to Holland on September 4, "must investigate whether Dutch ships are available. Embarkation in Trieste." And she offered two contacts for him in Geneva and Amsterdam.

At the Zionist emigration office in Berlin, she had been told that the recent publication of a letter from Chaim Weizmann to the British prime minister, Neville Chamberlain, promising Zionist support for the British in the war, was "considered very dangerous for the Jews in Germany." Whether this was the genuine opinion of her interlocutors or was uttered with a significant glance in the direction of listening Gestapo officials, or both, is impossible to know. (Weizmann's letter was cited by Ernst Nolte as late as the 1980s, in the course of the so-called *Historikerstreit* ["historians' struggle"—a conflict among German historians over interpretation of the Nazi era], as a supposed precipitant of Nazi genocide of the Jews.)[14]

Above all, Gertrude stressed that "if the emigration which at this moment is allowed and demanded does not take place on a large scale," the result would be "a catastrophe."[15]

The Joint received Gertrude's report with the utmost seriousness and reacted promptly. Morris Troper visited Amsterdam and told Gertrude that the organization was considering advancing as much as $200,000 (over $3 million in 2014 value) immediately for greatly expanded activities along the lines that Gertrude had proposed.[16] During the first six weeks of the war alone, the Joint spent $80,000 through Gertrude's office to organize the emigration from Germany of four hundred Jews.[17]

After he left Amsterdam, Troper sent Gertrude a letter in which he warned that the Joint had "a very strict policy," which had "been reaffirmed on several occasions," that it could "under no circumstances participate in *Alijah Beth* activities." He asked the Amsterdam committee to "be especially cautious in connection with the funds now provided . . . to insure that this principle is rigidly adhered to."[18]

Behind this pronouncement lay a more equivocal policy. In an internal document in June 1939, Bernard Kahn admitted that the Joint could not stop local refugee committees supporting illegal immigration, "but no direct JDC participation could be envisaged."[19] At the Paris conference in August, Troper, in a conversation with Saly Mayer, indicated that the Joint would turn a blind eye to the organization of illegal immigration so long as it could not be shown to be directly involved.[20] Given Gertrude's role in the saga of the *Dora*, it is likely that he gave the same advice to her and that his letter was written for the record rather than as a genuine expression of the Joint's position.

The attitude of the American organization on this and other issues was of paramount importance, because by this time it was providing the bulk of the Amsterdam committee's income. Although Gertrude remained nominally answerable to David Cohen, in his capacity as chairman of the network of committees in Amsterdam, it is clear that, from September 1939 onward, she regarded herself as ultimately responsible to the Joint.

About this time, Gertrude received a telephone call from Chaim Weizmann, who was in Geneva. She had known Weizmann since her work for the Jewish National Fund in the previous war. On a recent visit to France, he had heard disturbing reports about German atrocities against Jews in Poland, as well as rumors that the Germans were planning "a Jewish State (or concentration camp) in the Lublin District," where Polish, Austrian, and German Jews would be concentrated. Whether Gertrude shared with him her anxiety about the likely consequences for German Jews of his declaration in support of the British war effort is not recorded. Nor do we know whether they discussed the issue of illegal immigration to Palestine. Weizmann, like the leaders of the Joint, preferred not to be directly involved in this and would certainly not have referred to the subject over an open international telephone line.

In a memorandum to the British government, Weizmann mentioned that Gertrude had "assured him that the Dutch at least did not expect a German invasion."[21] The confidence that Holland would be able, as in the First World War, to ride out the storm as a neutral helps explain Gertrude's hope that Amsterdam might serve as the headquarters of international relief and rescue for Jews in Nazi-held territory. But the Dutch government's approach to the Jewish refugee issue between September 1939 and May 1940 was characterized by bureaucratic formalism, only occasionally mitigated by touches of humanity.

A case in point arose when Truus Wijsmuller-Meijer called at the Ministry of Justice in The Hague to ask that five young German-Jewish women and two men be allowed to enter the Netherlands to receive training at Wieringen prior to their emigration to Palestine. They had all received Dutch entry permits, but these had expired before they had been able to get out of Germany. Gertrude sent a follow-up letter warning that the young people were in extreme danger if they remained in Germany. The request was bluntly rejected.[22] The applicants could not, after all, furnish any guarantee of eventual admission to Palestine. The fates of four out of the seven are known, three of them were murdered by the Nazis.[23] Of course, they might well have suffered the same fate even if they had been granted temporary shelter in Holland. The Dutch government's decision, however, condemned them almost automatically to their fate.

On the other hand, the Dutch authorities quietly issued transit visas to some refugees who were assured of onward passage. At the end of November, Gertrude informed the Joint that her committee's work had "assumed such proportions that it strained our machinery almost to breaking-point. It is work, however, through which even now a large number of Jews from Greater Germany are helped to escape the horrible fate of deportation to a Jewish 'reserve' in Poland, a fate which hangs like a Damocles' sword over every Jew in Greater Germany." Over the previous three months, the Amsterdam committee had, with Joint funds, enabled about thirteen hundred people to escape from the Third Reich. The Dutch, she reported, were continuing to allow genuine "transmigrants" to enter the country, and many continued to the United States and other destinations.[24]

Gertrude succeeded in organizing a group of 180 refugees, who left Rotterdam in late October 1939 aboard the SS *Batavier III* bound for Cadiz. They were to transfer there to an Italian vessel that would proceed through the Panama Canal to Valparaiso in Chile. Their embarkation at Rotterdam was given wide publicity in the Dutch press, thus easing anti-refugee feeling.[25]

The organization of this transport, however, brought Gertrude into conflict with the Paris office of HICEM, which, working in association with the Joint, was supposed to cover the cost of the passages of such migrants. HICEM insisted that it must approve each individual case in advance. Beleaguered by demands on its resources, HICEM often took its time in reaching decisions. It also laid down that, wherever possible, efforts must first be made to secure payment from refugees' relatives in the United States. All this resulted in long delays, endangering the whole enterprise.

On this occasion, Gertrude decided not to wait. "You will probably be surprised [Gertrude wrote to Paris] that notwithstanding the fact that you refused to give your consent or that this consent was still outstanding . . . we sent the people away after all. We did this because we feel that the position here in Holland is so precarious that everybody who has a valid visum should leave."[26] Predictably

HICEM refused to pay, opening a bitter quarrel that dragged on for several months, until superseded by larger developments in the war.[27] This was one of several episodes in which Gertrude's sense of urgency and independence led to trouble with more cautious or conventional spirits. She was fortified, however, by the knowledge that she enjoyed the full confidence and support of the Joint.

In a private letter to Leib de Leeuw in Palestine (he and his wife, Mirjam, had returned there in 1936) on December 4, 1939, Gertrude wrote that she was in "constant direct contact with Berlin, Vienna, Bratislawa, and Danzig" and that any Jews in possession of a valid visa could still leave those places. But she added ominously that there was no communication "as yet" with Warsaw, where conditions were known to be terrible.[28]

Between September 15 and December 20, 1939, Gertrude's committee helped (in many cases was largely instrumental) in organizing the emigration of 3,180 Jews from the Third Reich to the Americas. Most came from Berlin (1,758) and Vienna (1,673), with smaller groups leaving Prague (308), Bratislava, and Danzig. At least 1,980 of these people sailed from Italian or Scandinavian ports, the remainder from Amsterdam and Rotterdam.[29]

By the end of 1939, there were eight camps and "group centers" in the Netherlands housing fifteen hundred refugees, plus four homes for thirteen hundred children. A further thirty-four hundred refugees, including nine hundred children, were being maintained by cash grants. The Jewish community was still expected to cover all the costs, but the Dutch Jews were close to the limits of their charitable capacity. No money at all could come from Britain, now at war. The Joint had perforce to shoulder most of the burden: in 1939, it supplied Gertrude's committee with $439,000 for refugee aid, more than three times its expenditure in the Netherlands the previous year, which had already been at a record level.[30]

In February 1940, Gertrude sensed "extreme nervousness and apprehension" in the country.[31] She continued to struggle to find places of refuge, but fewer refugees were now able to leave. Immigration to the United States, although still restricted by the quota law and hampered by bureaucratic delays, remained possible. Between January and May 1940, the Jewish Refugees Committee helped 1,283 people move from Holland to the United States. Smaller numbers left for other destinations.[32]

The Joint was at this time devoting considerable efforts and resources to the promotion of Jewish agricultural settlement in the Dominican Republic, whose military dictator, Rafael Trujillo, had announced his country's readiness to receive up to 100,000 Jewish refugees. A Dominican Republic Settlement Association (DORSA), underwritten by the Joint, was incorporated in New York. Curt Bondy was engaged to coordinate the recruitment of suitable settlers. He interviewed candidates from Berlin, Vienna, and Prague, as well as the Low Countries (including a few from Wieringen), and tried to arrange passage for them out of Genoa.[33] But political, financial, and transportation complexities hampered the enterprise; of the 250 potential settlers approved in Amsterdam, only 37 reached the Dominican Republic within the next nine months.[34]

At the end of March 1940, Gertrude received a visitor from Palestine. Enzo Sereni, an Italian-born Zionist intellectual and kibbutznik who was organizing illegal immigration to Palestine, came to Holland to meet Zionist leaders. Moshe Katznelson, director of the Wieringen *werkdorp*, showed him round the farmschool.[35] Later Sereni watched as a group of refugees left Amsterdam Central Station: "Figures symbolizing the end of an era," he wrote, "the surviving remnant are emigrating to Zion in the last ships before the final thunderbolt of grief."[36] The departing Jews, who had fled Poland and Germany, were to travel in bulletproof carriages through France and then, it was hoped, by boat to Palestine.

Afterwards, Sereni called on Gertrude at home in Blaricum and later wrote his impressions of her, her children, and Het Houten Huis:

> A woman graced with energy and intelligence. . . . Through her experience and understanding of the ways of the world—she has been through much and knows three-quarters of the world—a wonderful apparatus was created in the Dutch Committee. . . . A long discussion with the children . . . unfolded, returning again and again to literary matters: Hardy and Galsworthy, Stendhal and Tolstoy, Dostoievsky and Goethe. Exchanges of impressions, explanations and elucidations. . . . The pleasant house in the shadow of . . . the high, hoary trees, lapped in its green grasses, its heavy, submerged atmosphere shaded by its antique furniture, its classical library. . . . Here is the young daughter of seventeen—she came here only for a few days. Soon she will return to Deventer and will there prepare . . . for her immigration to Palestine. Her brother, one year younger, will finish school this coming July and go to Jerusalem and to Givat Brenner. . . . V[an] T[ijn] too, in a few weeks, will leave her pleasant home, too spacious for her once her children have left, and will lodge alone in one of the hotels in Amsterdam. These are the last days for this house, which was built with high hopes, after lengthy journeys, which had seemed to be a "good abode," and now is about to be deserted by its inhabitants without sadness or complaint.[37]

Gertrude never met Sereni again. He returned to Palestine and joined the British army. In 1944, he was one of a small number of Zionist agents who were parachuted into occupied Europe by the British to organize anti-Nazi resistance among the Jews. Dropped, by tragic error, directly on German lines in Italy, he was captured and sent to Dachau, where he was shot.

Sereni's presence in Holland may have been connected with further illegal migration activity in which Gertrude again appears to have been involved. The Germans were still willing to explore clandestine cooperation with Zionist agents from Palestine; around this time, Gideon Rufer met an agent of Adolf Eichmann (at the time head of the German security service's "emigration department" in Vienna) and discussed a plan for moving forty thousand Jews from Germany to Palestine, via Italy and Rhodes.[38] But unlike the *Dora* episode, in which a high degree of official collusion had been manifested, the Dutch authorities were now taking a much less friendly interest. On March 20, a police report on "illegal transit of emigrants through the Netherlands" described a system of human trafficking, allegedly organized by Gertrude from her "villa" in Blaricum. The report led the authorities to monitor the activities of the refugee committee closely. In April, four people were arrested for having transferred "illegal foreigners" to Belgium "in cooperation with the refugee committees in Amsterdam, Utrecht, Enschede and Hengelo." The police investigation indicated that these arrests merely scratched the surface of what was depicted as an extensive organization of which the "brains" remained at large.[39]

Such official scrutiny came at a most inconvenient moment. On May 3, 1940, for the first time since its establishment, the Jewish Refugees Committee was compelled to ask the Dutch government for direct financial assistance.[40] But the plea for help was soon swept aside as the Dutch state succumbed to external onslaught.

On May 10, German forces invaded the Netherlands. Gertrude's private life had been dealt a blow two days earlier, when Curt Bondy left for Belgium. The next evening she dined with Alfred Goudsmit and his family at their summerhouse in Blaricum. Alfred walked her back to her home. On the way, "a clear full moon lit up the beautiful landscape. At three o'clock in the morning the sky was full of German airplanes." Later, Gertrude drove through heavy military traffic to Amsterdam, thinking she might be away for a few days. "I did not realize I never again would see Het Houtenhuis."[41]

At this moment of crisis, the British relented a little on their previously adamantine refusal to allow fugitives from enemy territory to enter Britain or the empire. On May 14, Norman Bentwich wrote to Gertrude from London to report that a group of "41 older persons," parents of refugees already living in Trinidad, would be allowed to go there, provided they did not set foot in Britain en route. They would have to proceed from Germany to the West Indies via a Dutch port. Bentwich asked for Gertrude's help in organizing their movement.[42] Unfortunately, amid the chaos of warfare, Gertrude proved unable to pluck these people out of danger. As of March 1941, none had arrived in the colony, and the landing permits were revoked.[43]

On May 14, the Germans bombed and destroyed the center of Rotterdam, killing eight hundred people. The Holland-America passenger liner *Veendam*, which had carried 340 German-Jewish refugees to the United States the previous December, had been due to embark with more on May 10. Unable to proceed because of the outbreak of hostilities, she was severely damaged in the bombardment, and her passengers were stuck in port.

Within days it was clear that the Dutch army had been routed. A panic-stricken exodus from the country ensued. Cohen encouraged his staff to spread the word that a ship was waiting at the port of IJmuiden, near Amsterdam, for Jews who wished to leave. A frenzied throng of civilians gathered there, hoping to get to England. Amid scenes of desperation and confusion, officials tried to regulate the milling crowds. Since most telephones in Amsterdam had been cut off, Gertrude went round the city trying to inform Jews of this "escape chance."[44]

Truus Wijsmuller-Meijer, who had been in Paris at the time of the invasion, hurried back to Amsterdam, anxious about the fate of German refugee children who were being cared for in the Burger-Weeshuis, an orphanage in the city. On the morning of May 14, she wrung an authorization note from the capital's garrison commander to take the children to IJmuiden. She somehow hired five buses and rushed to find Gertrude, to secure approval for their departure. Gertrude was not at her office, but her friend eventually found her at the restaurant of the American Hotel, where she had arranged to wait "for anybody who wished to speak to me."[45] Gertrude noticed that the transportation permit referred in general terms to vehicles rather than just to the children from the orphanage. She therefore tried to fill all the empty places on the buses with other refugee children and with families who had no private cars.

When Gertrude herself tried to leave the hotel, however, she was held up by a zealous official, suspicious of all the foreign visas in her Dutch passport. "I was frantic because every minute was valuable."[46] Just then a radio announcement was broadcast that Queen Wilhelmina and the government had left Holland. "The large restaurant was crowded. There was no sound and no comment. The 'verslagenheid'—the shock—was indescribable. People realized the war was lost."[47]

The buses were due to leave from Gertrude's office on the Lijnbaansgracht. When she finally made her way there from the hotel, she found a chaotic scramble. "The busses were there and there was practically a free fight to get in."[48] At 4:00 p.m. the convoy set off, carrying seventy-four children and forty other panic-stricken Jews. Gertrude followed by car with a colleague, Erich Rosenberg,

German military vehicles on Raadhuisstraat, Amsterdam, May 1940
(Beeldbank WO2, NIOD)

who was seeing off his sick, elderly mother and her nurse. At an excruciatingly slow speed, they drove to IJmuiden through a dense jam of motor vehicles, bicycles, and handcarts. They witnessed "terrifying scenes" as bullets flew across the road.[49]

When they reached IJmuiden, guards would not let them through to the dock, refusing to recognize the validity of the permission note from the garrison commander in Amsterdam. In the end, a naval officer allowed them to pass. The bus passengers boarded the steamship *Bodegraven*, a 5,600-ton cargo vessel, which weighed anchor at 7:50 that evening. Apart from the children, a few hundred other refugees clambered on board. Among those who got away were Jacques van Tijn and Trixi (now his wife). As Gertrude stood on the quay, Jacques was the last person she saw, leaning on the rail of the ship. Rosenberg's mother refused to leave without him. He took her on board and then jumped back onto the quay as the ship was already under way. The *Bodegraven* was the last vessel to leave before the port was closed in order to permit the destruction of oil storage tanks there. Some people succeeded in crossing the North Sea on small craft, in one case on a canoe. Others fled to Belgium and France.

The rest of the crowd went home, disappointed and apprehensive about what might lie in store for them. After seeing off the boat, Gertrude and Rosenberg had to run hard "because the English warned us that before leaving they would blow up the pier. We heard the detonation immediately behind us. We drove back to Amsterdam, passing the burning oil tanks of the Royal Dutch. The road was deserted. The Dutch military authorities who had stopped us every few hundred yards on our way to IJmuiden had left. The Germans had not yet arrived. Then we neared Amsterdam and saw the town blazing with lights."[50] This was to be the last night the city was illuminated until May 1945. The next day German troops marched into Amsterdam.

CHAPTER FIVE

Mission to Lisbon

The Netherlands endured the next five years as a satrapy of Germany. On May 18, 1940, Hitler appointed Arthur Seyss-Inquart as Reichskommissar, or head of the occupation regime. But for the most part, the Germans preferred, at least at the outset, to rule through the existing Dutch administration. Initially, there were just two hundred German civil servants in the country, and the number never rose beyond about two thousand at any point of the occupation.

One of the architects of the Anschluss and a former deputy head of the occupation authority in Poland, Seyss-Inquart was an unswervingly loyal acolyte of Hitler. Operating under the Reichskommissar's nominal direction but with a direct line to the SS chief, Heinrich Himmler, in Berlin, was Hanns Albin Rauter, who had overall responsibility for security and police matters. Rauter was described as "an old party warhorse . . . though not without intelligence and cunning." He was "tough-looking . . . a stern disciplinarian . . . a fanatic."[1] At the time of the Kristallnacht pogrom in November 1938, he had received a commendation for "special merit . . . during the trouble-free Jewish action."[2]

At first, the Germans obtained a considerable measure of Dutch cooperation. The Dutch government, which had followed the queen to exile in London, instructed the secretaries-general (permanent civil service heads) of the various ministries to stay in post. Among them was Hans Max Hirschfeld, a German-born "non-Aryan" in Nazi parlance (his father was Jewish). His efficiency as an administrator of large sections of the Dutch economy was so highly regarded by the occupiers that, notwithstanding his, in their eyes, tainted antecedents, he retained his position throughout the war. He and other officials tried, with diminishing success, to serve as a buffer between the Germans and their Dutch subjects.

Parliament was suspended, and political parties neutered and eventually dissolved. Anton Mussert's pro-Nazi NSB, however, though not accorded real power, was given free rein to engage in Jew-baiting. The mail, the press, radio, and cinema were subjected to censorship. The Dutch machinery of government, including the police force, was eventually induced to collaborate actively in the implementation of discriminatory laws and roundups of Jews for deportation.

A new movement, the Nederlandse Unie (Netherlands Union), was formed in July 1940, calling for recognition of the "changed conditions," national solidarity, and "respect for traditional religious freedom and tolerance."[3] Although its conservative leaders advocated corporatist and antidemocratic ideas, it was seen as an alternative to the NSB and, mainly for that reason, attracted 800,000 members within two months. Even some Jews joined. In early 1941, however, its leaders sought to exclude Jews from "active" membership. The proposal led to internal ructions.[4] The organization soon fell foul of the Germans, who banned it at the end of the year.

Initially, few could imagine the horrors that awaited the Jews, although an "epidemic" of Jewish suicides was reported in Amsterdam in the early days of the occupation.[5] At first the Germans took only limited anti-Semitic measures: in July 1940, Jews were discharged from the Air Raid Protection Service; in August, Jewish ritual slaughter was banned. But unlike in Germany, Jewish doctors and lawyers were allowed, for the time being, to practice, and Jewish businesses were permitted to operate. Some Jews were lulled into complacency. Nevertheless, "a great fear" that worse was in store was reported to be rampant.[6]

Gertrude was then living alone in Amsterdam. As the Germans had confiscated all private cars, she was unable to travel to and from Blaricum and rented an apartment in the capital. She had hoped to obtain a certificate for her son, David, now aged sixteen, to go to Palestine, but this had proved impossible. Instead, he had left for the United States on a student visa shortly before the German invasion. His sister, Chedwah, was working in a hospital in Amsterdam. Gertrude pleaded with her to leave, but she refused to go.

Although several board members and staff fled, the Jewish Refugees Committee persevered in its work. The "always latent" animosity between Dutch and German Jews flared up anew and led to the withdrawal of some German Jews (including two who were Dutch citizens) from the work of the committee.[7] As time went on, even Gertrude, a Dutch citizen for nearly two decades, encountered ripples of such hostility.

The committee's financial problems worsened. A pre-occupation pledge of support from the Dutch government was not honored by the residual administration. Transfers of money from the United States became difficult and eventually stopped. Fearful that refugees would be sent back to Germany, the leaders of the Jewish community levied a special tax to cover the cost of running the Westerbork camp. Most Jews paid up, no doubt in large measure out of solidarity with their brethren. But their compliance may also be seen as a foretaste of later obedience to more painful edicts.

Some clandestine movement of funds from overseas remained practicable, and Gertrude, in her capacity as representative of the Joint, "handled these 'black' amounts as I thought best, though—in order to share the responsibility—I invariably discussed these questions with Professor [Max] Brahn."[8] A leading figure among the German-Jewish refugees in Amsterdam, Brahn would later become Gertrude's lover.

In July 1940, postal and telegraphic communication with the United States resumed, subject, of course, to censorship. Gertrude wrote to the Joint, reporting that Jewish emigration, possibly via Lisbon, was still permitted.[9] A *conditio sine qua non* was that the trans-Atlantic shipping tickets, costing about $250 per person, be paid for in dollars either in Lisbon or in the United States. If availability of these funds were assured, the Portuguese consul in Amsterdam would "probably grant the visa as soon as we can prove to him that the people can leave from Lissabon."[10]

On July 29, Gertrude wrote to the Reichsvereinigung (Reich Association of Jews in Germany) in Berlin, which was still functioning and trying to expedite emigration. Her letter concerned twelve German Jews, among a group of about two hundred who had been arrested as illegal immigrants by the Dutch authorities in December 1938 and held in a series of internment camps. A short time after the occupation of the country, some of them were moved from a camp at Hook of Holland to Dortmund.[11] Gertrude informed the Reichsvereinigung that she had received permission "in principle" for them to return.[12] She later recorded that "miraculously these German Jews were returned to Holland and were interned in Westerbork."[13] Ultimately, however, this did not guarantee their safety. At least one of them was deported from Westerbork to Theresienstadt concentration camp in February 1944—and from there to Auschwitz, where he was murdered a few weeks later.[14]

Over the next few months, Gertrude strained every sinew to extricate Jews from Germany. Since the Dutch administration was still nominally charged with routine decision making, she continued to meet Dutch officials. She wrote or cabled almost daily to New York and to Lisbon, where the Joint had re-established its

European head office in June 1940, just before the fall of Paris. On August 12, a letter from Otto Hirsch of the Reichsvereinigung in Berlin (he had been one of the German-Jewish leaders who had attended the Paris conference a year earlier) reached the Joint in New York. It stated that Gertrude had been in touch and was still hoping to facilitate emigration of German Jews via Lisbon.[15]

As new obstacles replaced old, the prospects of success rose and sank. Gertrude's spirits fluctuated in unison. In August 1940, Gertrude worked to dispatch a group of 331 people who would travel to the United States, Chile, or some other Latin American state. The problems of visas and exit permits (for which application had to be made to the Germans through the Dutch authorities) were largely solved, but shipping passages were in short supply. These had to be paid for in dollars either by relatives of the emigrants overseas or by the Joint. Fortunately, Gertrude still had substantial funds available in Amsterdam that had been supplied by the Joint before the occupation. The Joint authorized her to borrow money in guilders locally "with the assurance that [the Joint would] reimburse these loans when feasible, without aiding the enemy."[16] But there were many snags: by the time tickets were obtained, visas had often expired. Gertrude's office was involved in a never-ending paper chase to synchronize all the arrangements and documentation. Moreover, when people left, they were generally required to leave behind all their property and departed penniless.

In September, Morris Troper delivered a moving address in New York to the board of directors of the Joint that indicates the confidence that the organization reposed in Gertrude, as one of the chief figures in its effort to give succor to European Jewry: "Where I stand before you this morning, I am here not as Morris Troper alone; I am here as Hirsch of Berlin, Loewenherz of Vienna, as Giterman, Guzik and Neustadt of Poland, as Eppler of Budapest and Friedmann of Prague . . . as Van Tijn of Amsterdam . . . and d'Esaguy of Lisbon. . . . They have nothing to look forward to except starvation, disease and ultimate extinction. . . . Ours is the sacred task of keeping our brethren alive—if not all, then at least some."[17] Gertrude was the only woman among those named by Troper. Most had had opportunities to leave for safety but, like Gertrude, had chosen, out of a sense of duty, to remain at their posts. Several paid for that choice with their lives.

Gertrude strove tirelessly to promote the emigration of children. In November she wrote to the German-Jewish Children's Aid Committee in New York, outlining the various categories of children, generally those with parents or close relatives in the United States, for whom, she wrote, "so far as we can judge at present, we shall be able to get the exit permit." She had ascertained that the United States consul was "still willing to consider the sending of children to America" and that the plan was for them to travel via Lisbon.[18]

A significant evolution in Gertrude's responsibilities had in the meantime occurred. She was no longer concerned solely with refugees from Germany. Many Dutch Jews were now clamoring to leave. As anxiety turned to panic, Gertrude's office broadened the scope of its activity and sought to arrange emigration for as many Jews as might be able to procure tickets and visas.

But hardly was one obstruction surmounted than another loomed. A group of about 150 refugees who had been due to leave Holland for the United States on May 10, 1940, probably on the *Veendam*, found that the German invasion led to the cancellation of their departures. Their U.S. visas had lapsed, and they had to begin again the cumbersome application process. The German bombing of Rotterdam had destroyed the American consulate there, together with its archives, leaving many would-be emigrants without the needed documentation. The American consul in the city adopted an unhelpful, strict-constructionist approach to such problems. Gertrude appealed to the Joint for intervention at the State Department, since the consul's attitude was causing "grave injustice."[19] But there was little readiness in Washington for any flexibility on immigration issues.

At the same time, HICEM—now, like the Joint, displaced from Paris to Lisbon—demanded control of all decisions regarding individual cases of Jewish migration, even those for which it was not footing the bill. Citing stipulations of the International Police in Lisbon, HICEM also required that visas granted by consuls in Holland be confirmed by their governments in the form of a cable to their consuls in Lisbon—a procedure that Gertrude protested would be not only time-consuming but also technically impossible. Her relations with HICEM, never cordial, came close to snapping. HICEM's procedures, she wrote to the Joint, "would be a frightful waste of time and complicate matters unnecessar[il]y." Only the solid backing of the Joint sustained her in the "extraordinarily difficult conditions" under which her committee now operated.[20] By December 1940, she was so exasperated with HICEM's policies that she refused to correspond directly with the organization and instead communicated through the Lisbon office of the Joint.[21] Only HICEM's heavy financial dependence on the Joint brought some relief.

Although the refugee committee had originally been formed to organize Jewish emigration, it had found itself increasingly obliged since November 1938 to furnish welfare aid to refugees within Holland. By the end of December 1940, it was supporting over 6,000 refugees, including 714 children. Among those for whom it cared were the Jewish inhabitants of Westerbork, now numbering 972, of whom 142 were children. (Westerbork also housed more than 200 non-Jewish refugees).

Another project in which Gertrude became deeply involved at this period was Jewish emigration to Dutch colonies—the East Indies (today Indonesia) and Dutch Guiana (Surinam). Schemes for Jewish settlement in the Dutch Empire had been much discussed before the war, especially on the far right, though they never approached implementation. The revolutionized circumstances of the war, however, rendered the colonial empire attractive as a destination for Jews. But the colonies remained under the jurisdiction of the Dutch government-in-exile in London, and the prime minister, Eelco Nicolaas van Kleffens, was at first not keen to help. In November 1940, he told the British minister, Sir Nevile Bland, that Jewish refuges were "mostly unsuitable" for the East Indies.[22]

Nevertheless, shortly afterwards, perhaps as a result of British pressure, Dutch diplomats in Lisbon offered to provide emigration facilities to the Indies for their nationals in Portugal. The plan envisaged sending two hundred families, of whom about half would be Jewish. The government was prepared to pay the cost of transportation; the Joint was asked to help finance the migrants in their new home. The Joint undertook to guarantee loans to the prospective settlers to enable them to "start a new life" in the Dutch colony.[23] In early December, about sixty-six Dutch-Jewish refugees left Lisbon for the Dutch East Indies aboard the SS *Angola*. They arrived in Batavia (today Jakarta) in February 1941. The Japanese occupation of the Dutch East Indies a year later precluded further such migration, but most of the Jews already there survived the war.

In February 1941, Solomon Trone, a representative of DORSA and the Joint, visited Amsterdam. A retired executive from General Electric, known as "the American who electrified Russia," Trone was a dynamic, can-do businessman as well as a sophisticated man of culture.[24] He had been sent to Europe to take control of recruitment for Jewish settlement in the Dominican Republic. His fortnight-long stay in Amsterdam marked the start of a lifelong friendship. Gertrude was delighted, after such a long interval, to be able to talk, without fear of censorship, to a representative of the organization that was now, effectively, her employer. She told Trone about her intense frustration with HICEM. As a result, she was finally relieved of this millstone: the Joint took over from HICEM direct responsibility for Jewish emigration from Holland.[25] "I can hardly tell you," she wrote to Troper at the Joint headquarters in New York, "how glad I am that at last, after a struggle lasting for years, we no longer need the HICEM but that in future we shall only have your organisation to deal with." Evidently buoyed up, she added, "It is possible, but not yet certain, that emigration from Holland will shortly take place on a very large scale."[26] Gertrude promised Trone that she would go to Santo Domingo (capital of the Dominican Republic) if he summoned her—but "to tell you the truth," she wrote a few weeks later, "I want to persevere here."[27]

Meanwhile, an accumulation of decrees and regulations was forcing Jews in Holland out of civil society. All government employees, including judges, university professors, and schoolteachers, were required to sign attestations of racial origin. Nearly all "non-Aryans" were ejected from civil service and public positions. Among those who lost their jobs were David Cohen, who was removed from his chair at Amsterdam University, and Lodewijk Ernst Visser, president of the Supreme Court, whose dismissal, on German orders, was approved by a shameful 12 to 5 majority of his judicial colleagues.

Jews (i.e., any persons with at least one Jewish grandparent) were ordered to register with the authorities: their names were marked with the letter "J" in the population registry. Few failed to heed the order.[28] A total of 140,522 so-called "full" Jews registered, of whom 79,352 lived in Amsterdam. An additional 20,268 so-called *Mischlinge*—persons with one or two Jewish grandparents—brought the total "non-Aryan" population to 160,790. Subsequently, Jews were issued, upon payment of a fee of one guilder, yellow identity cards. They were barred from entering cinemas; from sitting on park benches; from visiting beaches, public baths, race meetings, cafés, and restaurants. They were ordered to hand in radio sets. Jewish students were expelled from universities. Jewish-owned businesses were registered. The stock exchange, the Concertgebouw Orchestra, and—from May 1941—the legal and medical professions were purged of Jews.

During the first months of the occupation, Dutch society, though hostile to the Germans, was generally submissive. Only a small minority supported the pro-Nazi NSB, whose militants delighted in provoking clashes with Jews in the streets. In February 1941, following one such fray that left several NSB men wounded (one died three days later), the Dutch police, under orders from the Germans, temporarily sealed off the predominantly Jewish area near the center of Amsterdam. Signs appeared marking it as a *Joodsche Wijk* (Jewish quarter), though no closed ghetto was ever created.

On February 12, H. Böhmcker—Seyss-Inquart's delegate in Amsterdam (*Beauftragte für die Stadt Amsterdam*)—ordered Jewish leaders to form a Jewish Council, with responsibility for maintaining order in the community. Different models for such a body existed in the Reichsvereinigung in Germany, the Judenräte (Jewish Councils) created in occupied Poland in the autumn of 1939, and Jewish representative organizations that had been established under Nazi auspices in France and Belgium in November 1940. The Germans designated Abraham Asscher and David Cohen co-chairmen of the Amsterdam council, and gave them the authority

The Jewish Council, Amsterdam, 1941; co-chairmen Abraham Asscher and David Cohen are seated at left. *(Jewish Historical Museum, Amsterdam)*

to select other members. Asscher and Cohen consented to serve, as did nearly all their nominees, drawn mainly from the bourgeois elite of the Jewish community.

The Nazi authorities instructed the council to issue an appeal to Jews to surrender weapons. The order was accompanied by a warning that the alternative would be a Nazi assault on the Jewish quarter. At the body's first meeting, members declared that they would not "accept orders that were dishonourable to Jews."[29] The restricted meaning they attached to this qualification soon became apparent. They immediately issued an ultimatum to Jews to hand over all weapons.

A few days later, after further civil unrest, German police raided the Jewish quarter around the Waterlooplein and, with demonstrative brutality, seized 425 young men as "hostages." In this, as in subsequent roundups of Jews, the Dutch police force, which the Germans were in the process of Nazifying, assisted the Germans. Most of those arrested were sent to the Mauthausen concentration camp in Austria. From there, within a few months, official notices of death were sent to their next of kin, together with small cardboard boxes containing their ashes.

These outrages aroused deep indignation among the population of Amsterdam. In an episode unique in Nazi Europe, the underground Communist Party (which had opposed the war effort in 1940 as a "massacre in the interests of capitalism")[30] called a protest strike. While demanding the release of the arrested Jews, the Communists took the opportunity to attack the " 'mediation' of Asscher, Sarlouis [L. H. Sarlouis, chief rabbi of Amsterdam], and Cohen. . . . These great capitalists are afraid of the imposition of a fine and they hold their dough more dear than they do the Jewish working people!"[31] On February 25–26, the port, factories, and public services of the city came to a halt. German forces suppressed rioting, leaving nine dead. Enraged by the strikers' demonstration of defiance and solidarity with the Jews, the German authorities warned the Jewish Council that unless the strike were called off, another five hundred Jews would be arrested. The council leaders begged the strikers to resume work. They did so the next day.

The council's conduct was not universally endorsed by Dutch Jews. Visser, the deposed president of the Supreme Court, advocated a more robust policy of non-cooperation with the occupiers. He warned that the council risked being dragged into the role of accomplice in crimes against international law. In December 1940, Visser had created a Jewish Coordination Committee, incorporating members of all Jewish political and religious trends in the country (including, for a time, David Cohen), with the objective of protecting Jewish interests. But Visser's group was sidelined by the Jewish Council and soon dissolved. Visser died a year later. With few exceptions, most members of the Jewish Council preferred, as more realistic, the course adopted by Cohen and Asscher.

In March 1941, the council was given authority over all other Jewish organizations in the city, several of which were shut down. In order to facilitate the promulgation of German decrees, the council was allowed, from April onwards, to issue a newspaper, *Het Joodsche Weekblad*, henceforth the only Jewish paper in the country. The two heads of the Jewish Council, who were responsible to the Germans for everything in the *Weekblad*, used it as a vehicle for repeated admonitions to Jews to follow German instructions. It issued strictures against rumor-mongering together with a leavening of articles on communal and devotional topics. Since non-Jews rarely saw it, the paper served as a convenient method of limiting general public awareness of the full rigor of German anti-Jewish measures. The gentile population was thus shielded from direct confrontation with Nazi anti-Semitic persecution, and those who wished to avert their gaze could do so more easily.

Among the bodies closed by order of the occupying power was the Committee for Jewish Refugees, the functions of which were taken over by two new departments of the Jewish Council: one for "support and social work," the other for emigration. The heads of the council announced that the staff of the latter department would be identical to that of the former refugee committee.[32] Gertrude therefore continued her work seamlessly. Her department's objectives were defined as "promoting . . . the interests of non-Dutch Jews" and serving as a "general emigration office."[33] As before, Gertrude worked under David Cohen. And as before, she regarded the Joint as her real employer.

Gertrude applied herself to the same tasks, at the same desk, with the same colleagues, and even used the same notepaper, overprinted with the letterhead of the Jewish Council. Yet her position had subtly altered. She was now answerable not to an independent charitable body but to an organization created by and subservient to the Nazis. Whereas she had previously played a major role in the deliberations of the refugee committee, she was now reduced to a functionary of the Jewish Council, of which she was not even a member; unless invited, she could not attend its meetings. By consenting to serve the council, however, she was inevitably tarred with its brush. This was responsibility without power—a stance that she found ever more painful over the next two years.

Gertrude carried on working mainly in the hope of being able to bring about large-scale emigration of Jews from the Netherlands. In the weeks following the creation of the council, she was able to arrange for the legal exit of a small number of Jews, who crossed France and Spain to Portugal, and then obtained passages from Lisbon to the Americas. Among these was Gertrude's daughter, who left with a group that included a branch of the wealthy Warburg banking family and some of their employees.

After Chedwah's departure, Gertrude had a "real collapse."[34] A telegram on March 8 reassured her that Chedwah had arrived safely in Lisbon. Although Gertrude felt enormous relief, at the same time she confessed, in a letter to her children, to extreme loneliness. But then, she philosophized, "everyone is lonely from the cradle to the grave—at least everyone who thinks and feels—yet there are degrees in which one suffers—that's what I'm finding out now you are both gone."[35]

Two days later, David Cohen and Gertrude sent a memorandum to the German Security Police, in which they outlined the work of the Committee for Jewish Refugees over the previous eight years. They estimated that the committee had helped a total of about 18,500 refugees leave the country. They were still working, they added, to prepare for the eventuality that emigration would again become possible. "At the moment, in spite of the fact that hundreds of people hold valid emigration visas, it is at a standstill, since the German authorities do not grant exit visas." If it were to resume, the committee would require substantial funds to pay for passages. "It is to be hoped," they continued, "that within certain limits these funds will be made available by the same Jewish charitable organizations in neutral foreign countries that are financing emigration from Germany."[36]

Gertrude submitted her last report on the activity of the committee to the Joint a month later. Unlike the dozens that had preceded it since 1933, it was written in German, not Dutch or English. Also unlike most of its predecessors, it was unsigned and contained only statistical data, without accompanying narrative in Gertrude's characteristically crisp prose. No doubt it was drafted as much for potential readers in the German occupation regime as for the Joint offices in New York and Lisbon. In 1940, the document stated, 1,661 persons had left the country under the auspices of the committee, as against 9,935 in 1939. But nearly all of these had gone in the first five months of the year; "since May 1940 no emigration worth mentioning from Holland nor any transmigration occurred."[37]

During this period, however, a few Jews made their way out of Holland illegally. Since the summer of 1940, an organization initiated by the former Dutch consul-general in Paris had opened a series of *Offices néerlandais* in unoccupied southern France, in places such as Toulouse and Perpignan. Their specific purpose was to aid Dutch citizens, particularly Jewish and political refugees, to escape across the Pyrenees to the Iberian Peninsula.[38] Several individuals and families paid smugglers or *passeurs* (guides) to lead them over frontiers. Many made their way to Lisbon, hoping somehow to secure passages across the Atlantic.

In Lisbon, however, their journey often came to a full stop. The Dutch legation and consulate seemed unsympathetic. Dutch-Jewish refugees complained bitterly that "the Consul's first question to Dutch subjects is 'Why don't you go back to Holland?' "[39] Canada, the United States, and South Africa generally refused to admit them. As for Britain, Sir Nevile Bland commented that "we had, quite understandably, not taken more than a limited number."[40]

Gertrude still hoped to obtain German permission for a large-scale exodus of Jews. To that end, she determined to visit Lisbon in the hope of loosening the bottleneck there—an idea that had first been mooted by the Joint in August 1940. Gertrude applied forthwith for an exit permit. The Dutch authorities undertook to help, but they needed German approval. At first Gertrude expressed optimism about receiving permission.[41] Months passed, and by the end of 1940, although she was "moving heaven and earth" to obtain the permit, she was "extremely doubtful" that it would be granted.[42]

On December 30, an official of the Department for Alien Affairs of the Dutch administration conferred with a German adviser, Kriminalkommissar Wolff, about Gertrude's application for an exit and return visa. Wolff declared that for the time being there was "nothing doing." The conversation turned to Jewish emigration from Germany, Belgium, and Denmark. Wolff said there was no immediate prospect of that from Holland. He himself, through the Gestapo in Berlin, had issued several *Unbedenklichkeitsbescheinigungen* (certificates of no objection to departure). But although many visas for travel abroad had been granted, these were generally of limited duration, and the results in terms of emigration had been practically zero.[43]

Shortly afterwards, however, the German position shifted. The Nazis at this time were still not opposed on principle to Jewish emigration. Indeed, they permitted and even promoted Jewish departures. In late 1940, sealed trains carrying Jewish refugees traveled from Germany across France towards Lisbon and Spanish ports.[44] In January 1941, Paul Meyerheim and Josef Löwenherz, representatives respectively of the Berlin and Vienna Jewish communities, were allowed to go to Lisbon to discuss Jewish emigration possibilities with officials of the Joint. Both returned to Nazi territory. (Meyerheim died in a concentration camp; Löwenherz survived the war.)[45]

By this time, growing numbers of Dutch citizens, both Jews and non-Jews, were congregating in Lisbon, stuck there for lack of tickets or visas that would enable them to leave. As the Battle of the Atlantic escalated in the course of 1941, passenger shipping space became scarce. Trans-Atlantic liners were booked solid six to nine months ahead. The cost of tickets rose as high as $1,200, ten times the prewar price. Nevertheless, one estimate has it that as many as forty thousand Jewish refugees passed through Lisbon in the course of 1940 and 1941.[46] The Portuguese government, alarmed at the flood of refugees, blocked entry even to many who had valid visas for countries such as Brazil and Argentina.[47]

In April 1941, Gertrude was suddenly summoned to appear before a senior SS officer in Amsterdam. According to her later account, this officer was SS Hauptsturmführer Wilhelm Zoepf. Gertrude may, however, have been mistaken about his identity.[48] A lawyer and a Nazi Party member since 1933, Zoepf was an educated man with literary and musical interests (his office was full of musical instruments confiscated from Jews).[49]

The SS officer, she recalled, questioned her about possibilities for Jewish emigration:

> I told him that I thought quite a number of Jews either were already in possession of valid visa[s] for countries overseas or

> could still procure them but that emigration had, since the occupation, not been possible because of the withholding of exit permits. Zoepf thereupon asked me how I thought the difficulty of passage money could be overcome and I told him that that question too might be able to be settled with the aid of the J[oint] D[istribution] C[ommittee]. I explained to him that such dollar amounts as might possibly be made available for Jewish emigration from Holland would, however, be held in a neutral country to be used exclusively for passages after the Jews had actually left Germany and that on no account would any dollars be available for work in occupied Holland. It was thereupon arranged that I should go to Lisbon and try to get as large a credit as possible for the above-mentioned purpose. If I was successful, Zoepf asserted emigration could commence. He also told me, I believe for the first time officially, that a special office, the "[Z]entralstelle fuer Juedische Auswanderung" would be established for that purpose and would start work shortly. He told me that the necessary emigration forms had already been printed.[50]

Soon after this interview, Gertrude received an exit permit to proceed to Lisbon.

Gertrude's trip was connected with the establishment of an Amsterdam Zentralstelle (central office), designed along similar lines to the bureau established by Eichmann in Vienna in August 1938 and subsequently copied in Prague. That office has been called "a conveyor belt of dispossession—a Jew would enter the building as a man of means and come out with nothing but an emigration permit."[51] In a draft presented to Seyss-Inquart on April 18, 1941, Hanns Rauter explained that this body was to "serve as an example for the solution of the Jewish problem in European states in general." It was to be responsible for "the supervision of Jewish life and the central control of emigration." As in the case of the Zentralstelle in Prague, Jewish resources would finance such emigration "and the forthcoming final solution of the Jewish problem in Europe."[52]

In order to present guidance to Jewish leaders in Holland on relations with this new body, two representatives of the Prague Jewish community, Jacob Edelstein and Richard Friedmann, were sent to Amsterdam. The two young men arrived in the entourage of Hans Günther, Nazi head of the Prague Zentralstelle and right-hand man of Eichmann. The visitors spent two months in the Dutch capital, from March 17 to May 17, 1941.

Edelstein and Friedmann had been among about a thousand Jews from former Czechoslovakia deported to occupied Poland in October 1939. They had witnessed appalling German treatment of the deportees for "planned resettlement" in the so-called Nisko reservation, a projected dumping ground for Jews. After a few weeks, the two were able to return to Prague. Subsequently, Edelstein was authorized to visit Trieste, Berlin, and other places. The Germans apparently hoped he would help coordinate Jewish emigration from Nazi-occupied Europe with Zionists and others. In meetings with Jewish representatives in those cities, he provided a firsthand report about the condition of Jews in the "Nazi inferno."

During their stay in Amsterdam, the two reported regularly to the German Security Police but otherwise were given little to do. Two secretaries from the Jewish Council showed them the sights of the city.[53] Cohen and Asscher behaved in a rather cool fashion towards them, perhaps wary of the Nazis' sponsorship of their visit. By contrast, Gertrude joined them in a Passover seder and had several further meetings with them. Cohen seems to have resented her participation in these discussions.[54] Edelstein recounted to his hosts what he had seen in Poland and declared unambiguously, "The Germans intend to kill us all."[55] He himself was shot dead in Auschwitz on June 20, 1944.

At the end of April 1941, Gertrude left for Portugal, traveling first by train to Berlin. The Jewish position there had deteriorated since her last visit in October 1939. Many of the leaders of the Reichsvereinigung had been sent to concentration camps. Julius Seligsohn, who had insisted on returning to Germany upon the outbreak of war, had been arrested in late 1940 after he called on rabbis to announce a day of fasting in response to the expulsion of Jews from Baden and the Palatinate. Gertrude was nevertheless able to meet remaining Jewish leaders and to discuss arrangements for prospective Jewish emigration (still not proscribed) via Lisbon.

Among those she met for the last time were Cora Berliner, head of the emigration department of the Reichsvereinigung, and Hannah Karminski, one of the organizers of the Kinderstransport. These women were among the most impressively humane and self-sacrificing figures in German Jewry. They could have escaped from Germany much earlier but stayed to help others leave; both were deported and murdered in 1942.

From Berlin, Gertrude proceeded by air via Madrid to Lisbon. Arthur Koestler, who had passed through Portugal on his way to England a few months earlier, called the city "the bottleneck of Europe, the last open gate of a concentration camp extending over the greater part of the Continent's surface." "The procession of despair," he wrote, "went on and on, streaming through this last open port, Europe's gaping mouth, vomiting the contents of her poisoned stomach."[56]

Portuguese entry regulations were tightened repeatedly after 1938 but failed to staunch the flow of arrivals. By the spring of 1941, the Portuguese government was approaching the limit of its endurance. In March, a trainload of Jews from Luxembourg, which had been dispatched towards Lisbon by the Nazis, was stopped at the frontier by Portuguese border police and refused admission. The train returned to Luxembourg, from where most of the Jews were subsequently deported to death camps in the east.

Both the British and the Germans maintained active espionage and subversive warfare teams in Lisbon. Some agents of the Portuguese secret police, the PVDE, were in the pay of the Germans. One, a member of the counterespionage department, copied for the Nazis the passports and documents of refugees, and facilitated the arrest of Jewish and other foreigners who were objects of German interest. One notorious case was that of Berthold Jacob, an anti-Nazi journalist: he was kidnapped by Gestapo agents in Lisbon in October 1941 and bundled back to Berlin, where he was imprisoned and tortured. He did not emerge alive.

The thousands of refugees, including many from the Netherlands, who were stuck in Portugal feared that the country might join the Axis camp at any moment. They scrambled for visas to countries of permanent refuge and for passages on ships to the Americas or, in the case of the wealthy, seats on the Pan Am Clipper flying boat to New York. A lucky few, generally prominent writers and artists, were granted emergency visitor visas to the United States outside the normal quota regulations. Among those in this category was the German-Jewish philosopher Hannah Arendt, later to become famous for her *Eichmann in Jerusalem*, with its savage indictment of the role of the Jewish councils in Nazi-occupied Europe.

On March 15, 1941, the U.S. Maritime Commission refused permission for the SS *Washington*, a large passenger liner, to ply between Lisbon and New York. Some other vessels, however, were still sailing from Lisbon. In April, the Portuguese liner SS *Mouzinho* carried 816 passengers, mainly refugees, to New York. But on April 24, the Portuguese government announced that it would cease issuing transit visas to refugees heading across the Iberian Peninsula to the Americas.

Morris Troper, head of European operations of the American Jewish Joint Distribution Committee, with secretary, in his office in Lisbon, 1941 *(United States Holocaust Memorial Museum)*

The prospects for Gertrude's mission were not improved by the publication in the *Saturday Evening Post*, on March 29, of an article headlined "War by Refugee." It maintained that the Nazis were scheming a "human export drive": "For $485 in United States currency put up in New York, the Nazis proposed to transport any Jew of nonmilitary status to Lisbon, where he or she could board ship for American ports. Schedules were drawn up for from two to five trains a week between Aachen and Lisbon. Each train was to carry 500 persons, the cars sealed to prevent escape en route." The Nazis were said to be willing to guarantee the delivery of 750 persons every fortnight, up to 450,00 people altogether, if trans-Atlantic shipping were provided—and if the requisite ransom were forthcoming.[57]

Gertrude arrived in Lisbon on May 2. The Joint's chief European representative, Morris Troper, met her at the airport and escorted her to the Palácio Hotel. After resting from her journey, she quickly got down to business and exchanged information with Troper on the plight of the Jews in occupied Europe. She reported that conditions for Jews in Holland were "rapidly worsening." Recently, "very disturbing articles" by Dutch Nazis had appeared in the press calling for the deportation of German Jews to the so-called Lublin reservation in Poland. The Westerbork refugee camp had been transformed into "a hermetically closed labour camp," though it remained under the administrative control of a Dutch military commandant.

The main objective of Gertrude's visit was to ask for help from the Joint in securing trans-Atlantic passages for refugees reaching Lisbon from Germany and the Netherlands. She confronted formidable hurdles. To Portuguese obstruction, severe competition for limited shipping space, and American quota restrictions were added growing American anxiety about spies and fifth columnists. Even as Gertrude was in Lisbon, Assistant Secretary of State Breckinridge Long testified to Congress that tighter visa controls were essential "as a sieve or screen . . . excluding persons who might be sent into the United States by interested governments in the guise of refugees."[58]

Without making any specific dollar commitment or limitation, Troper undertook that the Joint would do whatever was feasible to obtain trans-Atlantic passages for refugees reaching Lisbon. Also in Lisbon at this time was Solomon Trone, who was working with the Joint on the Santo Domingo settlement scheme. Trone undertook to arrange for as many Dominican visas as possible to be dispatched to Amsterdam.[59]

Gertrude and Troper coordinated another arrangement to facilitate emigration, at least for some Jews. Before leaving Holland, they would hand cash to Gertrude, who would help arrange their departure to a neutral country such as Switzerland. Once there, the money would be repaid from funds provided by the Joint. Although this would directly benefit only better-off Jews, it would provide a mechanism for illicitly moving Joint funds through the Allied blockade to finance aid to Jews in Holland.

Realizing that she was probably being watched by both the Portuguese and the German secret police, Gertrude made no contact with Allied diplomatic or intelligence representatives in Lisbon. The Dutch legation, loyal to the London government, seems to have had no inkling of her visit.

Troper tried to persuade her to stay in Lisbon while the Joint arranged a passage for her across the Atlantic. She telephoned her children in America, who both pleaded with her not to return to Amsterdam. "It was a hard decision to make," she wrote later, "particularly as I had no illusion about my ultimate fate. But I knew that, were I to choose safety over duty, I would never be able to live at peace with myself again." Moreover, "at that time I sincerely believed the Germans would allow Jews to emigrate and that their ability to do so for many was dependent on my bringing back confirmation of dollar deposits for their passages."[60] It was a brave, potentially suicidal, decision, which must be weighed in any assessment of her actions following her return.

Gertrude left Lisbon on the night of May 6–7. On the return journey, she stopped again in Berlin, where the Jewish position had grown even more sepulchral. She came back to Amsterdam optimistic that some significant Jewish emigration via Lisbon might now be possible. At first the signs were promising. The Portuguese government acceded to pressure and lifted the ban on transit of refugees.[61] In an effort to reduce the cost of passages, the Joint, together with HICEM, chartered the SS *Mouzinho*, which sailed from Lisbon in June and August with several hundred passengers.

Among them were many children from France and some Jews from both Germany and the Netherlands.

But new stumbling blocks emerged. On June 5, the State Department directed consuls to withhold visas from aliens with close relatives in Germany and German-occupied countries. It also warned consuls to beware of applicants who tried to conceal the existence of such relatives.[62] On June 14, President Roosevelt issued an executive order forbidding all transfers of funds from the United States to Axis, Axis-occupied, or neutral states in Europe, save by special Treasury license. From July 1, a new and more stringent policy further limiting the grant of visas by U.S. consuls came into effect. Meanwhile, in a sign of the steadily worsening relations between the United States and Germany, all German consulates in the United States and all American consulates in Germany and German-occupied territories closed.

Given the impossibility of securing a U.S. visa without access to an American consul and the diminution of passenger traffic across the Atlantic, the number of Jewish immigrants entering the United States dropped precipitately—from 36,945 in fiscal year (July to June) 1939–1940 to 23,737 in 1940–1941. Thereafter, the numbers dwindled even further: to 10,868 in 1941–1942 and just 4,705 in 1942–1943. As the last escape routes were sealed, Jews in Holland, as in the rest of Europe, faced extreme peril.

CHAPTER SIX

Crisis of Conscience

Immediately upon Gertrude's return to Amsterdam in the second week of May 1941, she was again summoned to SS headquarters to report on her trip to the same official who had dispatched her. According to Gertrude's account, he addressed her with crude discourtesy and made her stand throughout the interview. He seemed dissatisfied with the Joint's failure to commit a specific sum for shipping passages, although Gertrude assured him that whatever was necessary would become available.

A few days later, Gertrude wrote to Lisbon that "the situation here is extremely trying and the nerves of all our friends, who are waiting for their exits, are very much on edge."[1] But Gertrude remained optimistic that a larger exodus might be feasible. "We still have no organized emigration," she wrote to Saly Mayer in Switzerland on May 28, "but we suppose that it will soon begin."[2]

The Germans still remained interested in the departure of Jews from Europe, though they now prioritized getting rid of those closest to home. Hermann Göring, effectively the number two man in the Reich, issued a decree that month ordering Jewish emigration from Germany and the Protectorate of Bohemia and Moravia to be "stepped up in spite of the war, in so far as this was humanly possible," though, in order to facilitate the removal of Jews from the Reich, departures from France and Belgium were to be prohibited.[3]

In the case of the Netherlands, Nazi policy seemed to be in flux. Over the previous few weeks, policy towards the Jews in Holland had become an object of infighting among competing elements in the Nazi machine. Seyss-Inquart, wishing to retain at least some degree of control over the Jewish issue, had no desire to empower the SS and so delayed approving Rauter's guidelines for the Zentralstelle. The matter was not settled until the end of July, when an order from Göring placed full authority for the solution of the Jewish problem "in the form of emigration or evacuation" squarely in the hands of the SS.[4]

Gertrude now came into contact with another SS officer, at that time junior and little known. Klaus Barbie had arrived in Amsterdam a few weeks after the German occupation. Operating under the head of the Sicherheitsdienst in the city, Willy Lages, Barbie was installed in an office in a fine old merchant house at 485–7 Herengracht at the Gouden Bocht (golden curve) of the city's most majestic canal. Aged twenty-six, Barbie had been put through his paces in minor capacities in Nazi security organs in Germany. The Netherlands was his first foreign posting, and he had recently been promoted to the rank of Untersturmführer. A Dutch interpreter who worked for the Germans recalled, "Klaus was a very small guy so when he was in uniform he looked quite comical. But when it came to his work, he was a towering figure. He was a canny operator was Klaus."[5]

Barbie's encounter with Gertrude arose from her continuing responsibility for the farm school at Wieringen. The school's director, Moshe Katznelson, a Palestinian citizen, had been offered an opportunity by the British consul to go to England at the time of the German invasion. Katznelson decided to remain with his charges and was interned as an enemy alien for the duration of the war. Apart from his absence, life on the *werkdorp* during the first ten months of the occupation passed with little change; hardly a single German soldier appeared. But the occupation made it very difficult to arrange for the emigration of students from Wieringen once they completed their studies. Back in August 1940, the Dutch Ministry of Social Affairs had suggested that such students be sent to Westerbork, where they might usefully occupy themselves without encroaching on the Dutch labor market.[6] But the matter was left in abeyance for the time being.

Because there had been some talk of sending students back to Germany, Gertrude had made a special effort to find overseas havens for them. In October, the Joint informed her that forty to fifty places might be found for them in the Dominican Republic, at the agricultural colony in Sosúa that Trone was organizing.[7] Gertrude reported in December that twenty-six candidates from Wieringen and another fifteen from a similar group at Deventer had been selected, and were awaiting visas and exit permits. In the meantime, they were "all learning Spanish."[8] But in March they were still awaiting permits.

Katznelson's stand-in as director, the lawyer and journalist Abel Herzberg, sounded a pessimistic note in a speech to the students on the normally joyous festival of Purim on March 13, 1941. He said he just hoped they would all be able to stay at Wieringen for a long time. That hope was speedily shattered.

On the morning of March 20, seven blue Amsterdam buses drew up and parked near the entrance to the farm. A siren summoned all the students to the dining hall. Waiting for them were the drivers of the buses accompanied by several German officials, among them Barbie. Shortly afterwards, the chief of the Amsterdam SD, Willy Lages, arrived and barked out orders. Sixty students were to remain on the farm for another six months to finish harvesting and carry out essential maintenance duties. The remaining 210 were given ten minutes to pack their belongings and were transported to Amsterdam. Gertrude had meanwhile received an order by telephone from the German authorities to find

Roundup of students at the Wieringen *werkdorp*, March 20, 1941 *(Beeldbank WO2, NIOD)*

accommodation for them in the city that same day. She met them at the Asscher diamond factory, from where they were dispersed to the homes of Jewish families.

Four days later, Gertrude and David Cohen sent a memorandum to the SS outlining the history and objectives of the *werkdorp*.[9] Although the document did not specifically ask for the return of the students to Wieringen, it was evidently designed to reassure the Germans as to the harmlessness of the enterprise. It emphasized that students were being prepared for emigration overseas. On March 28, Cohen wrote again to the SS, requesting that at least two girls be allowed to go back to the farm.[10] No reply is on file.

While she was in Lisbon, Gertrude reported to Morris Troper on these developments. She had little hope that the *werkdorp* could reopen, and she feared that since the students were "all young and healthy boys and girls, there is a certain danger that they will be drafted into some kind of labour service."[11]

In early June, the outlook for the school seemed to brighten. Barbie summoned Cohen, Gertrude, and the treasurer of the *werkdorp* to his office and asked for the addresses in Amsterdam of the students who had been ejected.[12] He needed this information, he said, in order to arrange for their transportation back to Wieringen. "When I pointed out to him [Gertrude later recalled] that all the names and addresses were known to the Germans [presumably from the Population Registry, which recorded changes in address], he said that was so but it would be simpler for them if we submit this list." Gertrude and her colleagues discussed what should be done and agreed that "it would be in the interest of the boys" to comply.[13]

The same day Gertrude sent to the Sicherheitspolizei, "as requested," a list of the students' addresses in Amsterdam. In an accompanying letter she wrote, "As we have already stated orally, we should very much welcome it if, in view of the large scarcity of work and the encouraging prospects for emigration of the students, they could return to Wieringen as quickly as possible."[14] Gertrude told some of the Wieringers in Amsterdam "that if they were picked up in the course of the next day or night they should not be upset because they would then be brought back to Wieringen."[15]

But instead of expediting the students' return, the Nazis used the addresses to round up these and other young Jewish men, ostensibly as a reprisal for recent bomb attacks by the Dutch resistance. Some of the Wieringen students, sensing danger, managed to elude capture, but fifty-seven of them were among a total of about three hundred young Jewish males arrested (mainly by Dutch policemen). In many cases, when police arrived to arrest the young Wieringers and found that they had gone away, they seized any other young men they could find at the same address, often members of families who had given the students hospitality. Those captured were sent to a concentration camp at Schoorl and from there to Mauthausen.

The leaders of the Jewish Council tried desperately to find out what had happened to the young men and to secure their release. M. L. Kan, an attorney and member of the council, sought the help of Hans Calmeyer, a German lawyer who had recently been appointed to a senior position in the occupation administration and who later acquired a reputation for being ready, in some cases, to help Jews.[16] (He was acknowledged in 1992 by Yad Vashem, the Israeli Holocaust remembrance authority, as one of the "righteous among the nations," though his role remains ambiguous.)[17] The matter, however, was beyond Calmeyer's capacity to intervene. A few days later, the first official notification arrived of the death of one of the students. It was accompanied by a form letter offering to return the ashes of the deceased upon payment of twenty-five guilders. Further such communications followed over the next few months.

Roland Marti, the Berlin delegate of the International Committee of the Red Cross, submitted a formal protest to the German government about Mauthausen in late 1941 and requested permission to visit "this notorious camp . . . where the Dutch Jews are taken." He said that "extraordinary, tragic rumours are rife: it is said that . . . out of 700 Dutch people who are thought to have been taken there [the 400 who had been arrested in February plus the 300 seized in June], only fourteen are alive."[18] By way of reply, Marti was told that "people could say what they liked." No visit would be permitted. In fact, the position was even worse than Marti thought. An internal German memorandum in December stated that only eight of the Mauthausen prisoners from Holland were still living.[19] By February 1942, death notices had been issued for all the missing Wieringen students.[20]

In her postwar memoir, Gertrude accepts full responsibility for the fateful decision to hand over the list of names, though, in fact, she did not take it alone: it was a collective decision in which Cohen and others had participated. When the Jewish Council met to consider the issue a few days later, Asscher suggested they should resign en bloc. As on countless occasions over the next two years, Cohen persuaded them to carry on lest even worse befall the Jewish community.[21]

Gertrude remained convinced to the end that Barbie had given his assurance in good faith but that "this intention was crossed by a new order for arrests received from the higher officials in The Hague."[22] The balance of evidence, however, points to deliberate deception by the Germans, anxious, no doubt, to avoid a repetition of the events of the previous February.[23] Gertrude was distraught at the consequences of her action. "It was then that I determined never again to give the name of any Jews to any German authority and never again to trust the word of any German."[24] This terrible event weighed heavily on her conscience for the rest of her life.

What remained of the *werkdorp* lingered until August 1941, when it finally closed on German orders. The Stichting Joodsche Arbeid, the foundation that ran the school, was taken over by the Jewish Council. The remaining pupils were sent to hostels in Amsterdam. There they attended some classes under the supervision of a new director, Jules Gerzon (brother of Mirjam Gerzon de Leeuw).[25]

Notwithstanding these grim events, Gertrude continued, with increasing desperation, to try to organize Jewish emigration. On

July 2, she wrote to Trone in New York: "At the present moment every emigration from Holland has been stopped and it is not certain whether and if so when exit permits will again be granted."[26]

Her efforts at this time were reinforced by a remarkable plot from within the German security establishment. G. Walter Schulze-Bernett—the head of the Dutch section of the Abwehr, the German Foreign Intelligence Service—had lived in Holland for many years before the war and was an anti-Nazi. Working together with a local German businessman, he concocted a scheme for enabling Jews to leave the Netherlands legally. They persuaded a senior official of the Sicherheitsdienst, Albin Pilling, working under Rauter, that the Jews' departure was necessary in order to smuggle Abwehr agents into the Americas. Official anxiety in Washington in 1941 about possible German infiltration of spies among refugees was thus not wholly off the mark. The head of the German military occupation force in Holland, General Christiansen, was party to the plan and added one or two Jews for whom he felt some personal sympathy. As a result of Schulze-Bernett's efforts, a total of 486 Jews left the Netherlands legally between May 1941 and January 1942, heading for Spain and the Americas.[27]

Was Schulze-Bernett's enterprise somehow connected with Gertrude's mission to Lisbon? In the absence of evidence, the possible link must remain speculative. Gertrude appears to have had some inkling of these behind-the-scenes intrigues. On June 23, she wrote to Troper that a small number of people had left "under quite special conditions." She added that "everything in connection with emigration is frightfully complicated at present."[28] After Schulze-Bernett's transfer to Ankara in July, legal departures wound down, though Pilling continued to help process the necessary paperwork so that two groups left in August and a final one in January 1942.

From August onwards, direction of Jewish policy in Amsterdam was entrusted to the newly established Zentralstelle. Lages, rather than the original nominee, Zoepf, was nominally in charge (Zoepf took overall charge of Jewish affairs, operating from the SD office in The Hague). Like Gertrude, Lages was a native of Braunschweig. In a postwar statement, he claimed to have joined the police out of "idealistic considerations."[29] Cohen found him "sly and untrustworthy."[30] Lages had a reputation for laziness and left day-to-day activities under the control of Hauptsturmführer Ferdinand Hugo aus der Fünten.

Although barely thirty years old, Aus der Fünten was one of the *alte Kämpfer* (old fighters) who had joined the Nazi party before Hitler came to power. His aristocratic-sounding name belied a quite humble background as a shop assistant in Cologne. A suave cynic, he had about him the shallow elegance of the floorwalker. Lackadaisical rather than rigorous in the performance of his duties, he had a liking for the good things in life, including wine, women, and song. He did not balk at the most ruthless measures against Jews, while often claiming that he took such actions with the utmost reluctance. Seated behind his desk, stone-faced, with lineaments that, in spite of his youth, already showed deep furrows, he seemed, to those who had the misfortune to be summoned into his presence, the ultimate killer-bureaucrat. "He knew only one god," a visitor later wrote, "a picture of whom hung alone on the wall: Heinrich Himmler."[31] Of the German war criminals in Holland, Aus der Fünten was among those most directly responsible for the mass murder of Dutch Jewry. Yet he was invariably polite to Gertrude when they met, and as will be seen, he saved her from deportation on two occasions.

A liaison bureau, the Expositur, handled relations between the Jewish Council and the Zentralstelle. Its head for most of its existence was Edwin Sluzker, a refugee from Austria who had arrived in the Netherlands in 1938 and subsequently worked for the Committee for Jewish Refugees. According to Gertrude, it was at her suggestion that Sluzker, a former lawyer, was appointed to this delicate position.[32] Somehow he retained the confidence of both Germans and Jews in his bizarre role as a go-between in the genocidal process.

Although not a member of the Jewish Council, Gertrude's importance in its organization was growing. While she was rarely invited to its meetings, she played a major role in the regular gatherings of the central committee, which brought together all the council's department heads.

On July 4, 1941, Gertrude celebrated her fiftieth birthday. The *Joodsche Weekblad* reported that she had wanted the date to pass unnoticed, but her colleagues insisted on publicly recognizing her long years of work on behalf of refugees and Jewish social causes.[33]

Meanwhile, the invasion of the Soviet Union on June 22, 1941, marked the start of genocide of Jews in eastern Europe, at first by mass shootings, and, at the same time, an intensification of anti-Jewish measures in the west. In August, Jewish emigration from German-occupied territories was prohibited, and on October 3, a decree was issued banning all further Jewish emigration from the Reich.

In the Netherlands, a new round of decrees effectively requisitioned most Jewish-owned property. Eventually most business enterprises, stocks and shares, real estate, bank accounts, vehicles, canal- and seagoing vessels, horses, art treasures, and jewelry were expropriated. Jewish children were excluded from public schools and herded into separate, all-Jewish schools with an all-Jewish teaching staff, under the aegis of the Jewish Council.

In October, the Germans extended the council's authority beyond the 79,000 Jews of Amsterdam to all Jews throughout the country. From being in charge of a committee concerned with helping Jewish refugees, Cohen and Asscher were thus installed as the unelected leaders of all 161,000 Jews (defined according to the Nazis' racist criteria) in the Netherlands. But they were figureheads of a puppet administration. The head of the occupation regime, Seyss-Inquart, in a secret document in November 1941, defined the council succinctly as a "body for the transmission of orders" (*Befehlsübermittlungsstelle*).[34]

As Jews were eliminated from Dutch cultural life, they were confined in a kind of cultural ghetto. In the autumn of 1941, the Hollandsche Schouwburg, a theater in the Plantage district near the Amsterdam zoo, was renamed Joodsche Schouwburg and set aside for dramatic, concert, and cabaret performances by Jewish thespians and musicians. A Jewish symphony orchestra performed works by Mendelssohn, Mahler, Offenbach, and other "non-Aryan" composers. Gertrude attended only once. "Hardened as I was, it gave me a lump in the throat to see some of those violinists, whom I had for many years seen playing prominently in the Concertgebouw Orchestra, back in such squalid surroundings."[35]

Gertrude's work as head of the council's emigration department dwindled as emigration opportunities shrank. In April, *Het Joodsche Weekblad*, in its second number, had published a long and optimistic article on settlement possibilities in the Dominican Republic.[36] Soon afterwards, the Republic issued several hundred "mercy visas" and expressed readiness to include settlers from Germany and occupied Europe. One hundred such visas were earmarked for applicants from Holland. Under pressure from the Joint, the U.S. State Department agreed in May to authorize the U.S. consul in Amsterdam to issue transit visas to twenty-five named emigrants from Holland. Trone (now in New York) cabled to Gertrude that this was seen as a "trial," which it was hoped would establish a precedent.[37] Elated, Gertrude went to see the American consul, "with whom," she said, "I am on very good terms," and in a long conversation tried to persuade him to issue further such visas. She told him that "there was a gentleman['s]-agreement . . . that these people will wait at Long Island." He was not prepared, however, to issue any further transit visas without specific instructions from Washington.[38]

That evening, as she listened to records of Brahms and Beethoven in her room in Amsterdam, Gertrude suddenly felt very lonely, missing her children dreadfully but still hopeful that some emigration might become possible.[39]

She pressed Trone to persuade the State Department to authorize the consul in Amsterdam to issue the full quota of one hundred visas to applicants she had selected.[40] But no such authorization was forthcoming, and even the first twenty-five settlers did not obtain exit permits from the German authorities. On June 18, Gertrude cabled to New York the names of fourteen who "cannot emigrate."[41] She did not give the reason. Probably she did not dare explain in an open telegram that twelve of them had been sent to Mauthausen.[42] The thirteenth, named Alfred Kanin, was presumably under arrest; he was "again in Amsterdam" (i.e., released) in early July. His fiancée, who was also on the list, married him shortly after. But both were later deported and murdered in Auschwitz.[43] On August 25, Gertrude wrote to the DORSA representative in Lisbon that "Peter Bielefeld, who was in possession of a Domingo visum, has died."[44] She did not give any details, but he was one of the Wieringers who had been killed at Mauthausen.

As for the remainder of the would-be settlers, any hope that they might still be able to leave soon turned to dust. In July, the U.S. State Department announced that it was "averse to having any of these people go to San Domingo" and refused to grant them U.S. transit visas.[45] American officials insisted that no immigration proposal was even to be taken up with the Dominican government until it had been cleared by the State Department.[46] The closure of the U.S. consulate in Amsterdam at the end of August rendered U.S. visas of any kind almost impossible to obtain. After the exchange of hundreds of letters and cables over several months, approval was finally secured in October for the admission to the Dominican Republic of a further group of refugees from Wieringen. DORSA later reported the outcome: "Dominican visas were secured. US transit visas were not secured, nor were exit permits ever granted. No one ever succeeded in coming from Holland."[47] Sosúa never fulfilled the ambitious hopes that had been vested in it. The peak population of the Jewish settlement there, attained in 1943, was a mere 476 persons.[48]

The Dominican failure showed how hard it was to find destinations for Jewish refugees. But before they could enter havens of refuge, they would have to secure exit permits from German-occupied territory. In August 1941, Gertrude reported, "We have already submitted a great number of emigration requests but are as yet unable to say when the first group will be able to leave."[49] She tried to get permission to go to Lisbon again for further consultations, but this time she was not allowed to leave. On September 12, the pendulum swung momentarily towards hope: she issued an announcement in *Het Joodsche Weekblad* inviting prospective emigrants to submit applications at the emigration bureau. The notice stressed that it applied to those who wished to leave "even if they are not yet in possession of a visa."[50]

The following week, Gertrude was invited to appear at a meeting of the Jewish Council, at which Cohen announced that it had been ordered to submit twenty emigration cases a day to the Zentralstelle, including those of persons who did not have visas but wished to leave. After "comprehensive discussion" on the basis of information provided by Gertrude, the council came to the conclusion that it was in the general Jewish interest to cooperate.[51] On October 9, Gertrude reported, "From all sides we are assured that exit permits will be forthcoming soon, but on the other hand none has actually been granted."[52] The consequent expansion of Gertrude's department meant that it occupied the whole of the large building on the Lijnbaansgracht.

The strain now overwhelmed Gertrude utterly. At the end of the month, she suffered a nervous collapse.[53] For a time she saw everything double or not at all. She missed her two children terribly. "In the past," she wrote to them, "I often struggled with an inclination (in large part inherited) to make an end of things. I would never do that any more now. . . . Whatever may happen, you may count on it that I shall try my best to stay alive and to live my life in such a way that others gain strength from it. . . . You must always think of me as someone who can live only if at peace with myself and my conscience. And if I am to have this peace I cannot abandon things here."[54] Her spirits were restored after several days of rest, injections of "arsenic" (probably an arsenic compound, at that period used in small doses as medication), and hours of reading and listening to music on her treasured gramophone.

While she convalesced, the Jewish position in Amsterdam took an ominous turn. On November 22, three Nazi security officers, including Aus der Fünten, met with the co-chairmen of the Jewish Council. They ordered that all German and stateless Jews, estimated to number twenty-five thousand, *must* apply for emigration. Forms were to be completed at a rate of at least two hundred a day. (As a concession, the required tempo was subsequently reduced to 100 to 150 registrations a day.) The chairmen insisted that there must be no compulsion. The Nazis guaranteed that, adding that it was a matter of "emigration, not deportation." As for those who declined to hand in forms, the chairmen were told vaguely that the German authorities would deal with that. Asscher and Cohen, well aware that opportunities for emigration to the free world were almost entirely closed, asked where all these registrants would be going? The answer was not reassuring: "We ourselves don't know."

They were told only that the destination would "not be Poland, but overseas." The council membership included no representative of non-Dutch Jews. Perhaps this made it readier to be satisfied with the further promise that, save in exceptional cases, no Dutch Jew would have to fill in the emigration forms.[55] Every one of these undertakings was subsequently to be broken.

Gertrude was momentarily encouraged. She wrote to her daughter: "The emigration dept. will have to be made much much bigger (and quickly too). . . . This does not necessarily mean that people will actually leave—but it might."[56]

In early December it was announced that all non-Dutch Jews, except those of European neutral states, should apply for "voluntary emigration."[57] Each person was required to fill in a thirty-five-page questionnaire, giving detailed personal information (physical description, religion, state of health) about the applicant and the applicant's parents, grandparents, and children; the quantity of baggage to be taken; an accounting of the applicant's means (bank accounts, cash, investments, promissory notes, insurance policies, real estate, patents and copyrights, debts, tax status, jewels, fine art); as well as lengthy additional forms about mortgages, foreign holdings, and so forth.[58] All applications had to be accompanied by ten passport-size photographs and other documents. The completion and submission of these materials constituted a formidable bureaucratic exercise. Once it was complete, the applicants were interviewed by a panel of Germans at the Zentralstelle, where (as one later recalled) they were "often treated to humiliating insults."[59]

Although the deadline for registration was set at December 15, it was far from finished by that date. Many German Jews were reluctant to come forward. The complexity of the process meant that each case took a long time. On January 12, Gertrude's department was obliged to publish a notice, covering the entire front page of *Het Joodsche Weekblad*. "To avoid a serious danger," it again

Office of the Jewish Council, Amsterdam, 1942 *(Jewish Historical Museum, Amsterdam)*

urged all those required to register to do so "in their enlightened self-interest." In a tone that sounded closer to a threat than a warning, the notice stated that anyone who did not register would be "held accountable."[60] Gertrude had been tipped off by Jacob Edelstein, one of the visitors from Prague the previous spring, that pending evidence that emigration was really in the offing, it would be wise to elongate these procedures as much as possible. She therefore procrastinated and tried to avoid filling the daily quotas. "My whole intention [she explained afterwards] was to prolong the registration and . . . instead of having this registration finished in about 4 months, which had been the intention of the Germans, it was not finished until June 1942 and not quite finished even by then."[61]

In reality, "emigration" was already, in Nazi minds, morphing into a euphemism for something much more sinister. On September 26, 1941, Seyss-Inquart visited Hitler, and it was agreed that "for the immediate future, it is intended to remove the approximately 15,000 Jewish emigrés from Germany living in the occupied Netherlands territories."[62] Where they were to be removed to was not specified in the written record of the conversation.

On October 20, the heads of the Jewish Council were ordered to prepare a *cartothèque* (card index) of all Jews on the basis of the information in the Population Registry. Twenty-five typists (later more) were assigned to prepare the cards, adding further detailed information, including current addresses. They started with the non-Dutch Jews. When finished, the cards were sent to the Jewish Council, where they were sorted and then delivered to the Zentralstelle.

Mistrusting official procedures for emigration, more Jews resorted to clandestine channels. Smugglers charged high fees to guide Jews across the frontier to Belgium, from where they hoped to filter through France to Spain and Portugal. A few found their way to Switzerland or Sweden. But most of those who escaped Nazi territory were unable to leave Europe. Hitler's declaration of war on the United States on December 11, following the Japanese attack on Pearl Harbor, brought passenger shipping from Lisbon to the United States almost to a standstill. Only a handful of neutral vessels still made the increasingly perilous voyage. Between January and May 1942, just thirteen ships, with five thousand passengers on board (not all refugees and not all Jews), sailed from Lisbon to the United States. Cooped up in Nazi Europe, the Jews awaited their fate.

There exists no written record, but it was most likely in November 1941 that Hitler issued the order for systematic mass murder of the European Jews. A few weeks later, mobile gas chambers were used at Chelmno to kill thousands of Jews. Meanwhile, permanent gas chambers were constructed at a number of other concentration camps in Poland. In January 1942, mass killing by gas began at Auschwitz, in Upper Silesia.

On January 20, Eichmann organized a conference of Nazi officials at a villa on the Wannsee, near Berlin, at which the logistics of genocide were discussed. It was probably immediately after this that instructions were issued for the deportation of all Jews, not just the German refugees, from the Netherlands to the east.[63]

In early 1942, Jewish men in Amsterdam began to be called up for work in labor camps outside the city. Large numbers of German Jews were sent to Westerbork, but the new orders affected some Dutch Jews too. The Jewish Council dispatched form letters to the conscripts, conveying German instructions to vacate their homes, hand over their keys, and present themselves, with their families, at the railway station.[64] They were permitted to take as much hand luggage as they could carry. The heads of the Jewish Council, after failing to persuade the Germans to rescind the orders, issued "urgent advice" to those called up not to "shirk" their "unavoidable duty" in order "to forestall worst measures."[65]

The involvement of the council in these proceedings aroused misgivings among many of its staff, including Gertrude. In a meeting of the central committee on February 13, several department heads expressed dissatisfaction and demanded an early discussion over "the fundamental question of how far the Jewish Council should continue to cooperate now that its work had taken on a different character from what had originally been promised."

Before any answer was given, the meeting was interrupted for a report from the two chairmen on their latest interview with Aus der Fünten and other Nazi officials. The news was bad. All remaining non-Dutch Jews would have to move to Westerbork. And more Jews from the provinces, where about one-third of Dutch Jews lived, would have to move to Amsterdam. There the council would be responsible for finding them accommodation in mainly Jewish districts in the center and east of the city. These were being turned into what Eichmann later called "*ein lockeres Ghetto*" (a loose ghetto).[66] The Germans told the chairmen that there was enough space there for the newcomers, provided people lived at a density of two or three to a room.[67]

The "fundamental question" was never considered by the central committee—or at any rate, such a discussion is not recorded in its almost complete surviving set of minutes. The council's submissive policy was by this time leading many Jews to see its leaders as complicit with the Nazis. Mordant wits complained that it was not a Joodsche *raad* (Jewish council) but a Joodsche *onraad* (danger) or even *verraad* (treason).

In spite of the virtual absence of emigration, the volume of work in Gertrude's office did not slacken. By February 1942, an average of 250 people a day were being registered, and the department was operating seven days a week to keep up with the Germans' demands.[68] Or so Gertrude reported to the central committee; in practice, she seems still to have been trying to stretch out the process. Gertrude faced difficulties on all sides. Some people refused to fill out forms properly or did not turn up to register for emigration when summoned. And she was obliged to fend off rabbinical displeasure with the department's breach of the law of Sabbath observance.[69]

Notwithstanding her qualms about the council's policy, Gertrude found herself compelled to serve as a transmitting agent for Nazi intimidation. "The German authorities," she wrote in a form letter sent out to non-registering alien Jews, would take "the sharpest measures" to deal with noncompliance with "the duty to obey the order to present an application for emigration."[70] What had originally been presented as an opportunity had thus been transformed into an order enforced by menacing threat. Some of the letters were sent by mistake to persons whose applications were already in process. They felt understandable distress and protested indignantly, necessitating the dispatch of several letters of apology.[71]

The refusal of about two thousand non-Dutch Jews to register led to a confrontation between Gertrude and Aus der Fünten. He summoned her to his office and demanded a list of all those who had not yet registered. Recalling the last occasion she had handed over such a list to the Germans, she refused point-blank. Aus der Fünten told her he could not accept such an answer and sent her away.

> The next day I was called again; he was not then alone but a secretary was sitting there taking a protocol of everything that was being said, and another SS man was also in the room. He repeated his request and I once more refused. He asked me why I did not want to give the list as nothing was going to happen to the people, and I then told him that, after the Wieringen incident . . . I had made a vow never to give the names of any Jews to any SS official. He repeated that he had to have the list. I was then again sent home and made some arrangements in the office and some private arrangements, fully expecting to be arrested soon. When I got a third call to see ADF a few days later, none of the few people who knew about this nor I myself expected that I would come back. The conversation was much as it had been the first time. . . . He then sent me home and that was the last I heard of the whole matter.[72]

Gertrude's assertiveness (according to her own account) in the face of the Nazi's intimidation must have contrasted with the obsequiousness to which he had become accustomed on the part of David Cohen. Perhaps for this reason Aus der Fünten seems henceforth to have held Gertrude in a certain respect, and at two critical junctures, he even went out of his way to afford her personal succor.

Gertrude felt once again close to the point of collapse. She wrote to Saly Mayer that she was suffering "even more than before from episodes of heart weakness arising from the incessant physical and psychological burdens." Since the German declaration of war on the United States, postal communication with her children had been severed, save occasionally through neutral intermediaries. By this time Gertrude had given up hope of being allowed to travel to Lisbon or Switzerland, as it was now "completely impossible to get a visa out of here."[73] She felt "like someone in a state of narcosis," she wrote, via Mayer, to her children. "Work, work and plenty of work again. I am reading a great deal. . . . I make myself strong and with iron discipline I shall try to hold out."[74] She was shaken to hear of the death in the Sachsenhausen concentration camp of Julius Seligsohn. "Every day now brings new problems here," she sighed to Mayer on April 1. That evening she attended the Passover seder at the hostel in Amsterdam, where many of the students who had been sent away from the Wieringen *werkdorp* were lodging. "We shall have to remember many who are no longer here."[75]

Over the previous few months, one of the few remaining outlets for Jewish emigration from Europe had seemed to be Cuba. Several thousand visitor's visas to the country had been issued to desperate would-be emigrants on payment of a visa fee of $250 plus bonds to the value of $2,500 per person. But it turned out that, as at the time of the *St Louis*, the trade was a scam. "Things in this respect as in everything else look blacker than ever," Gertrude wrote to her daughter.[76] On April 24, Gertrude's department announced that the president of Cuba had invalidated all visas issued to citizens of belligerent or occupied countries.[77] Now that faint hope too was extinguished.

A few days later, Gertrude was walking from her office to an emergency meeting of the council when she met her friend Max

Brahn coming in the opposite direction from the council headquarters on the Nieuwe Keizersgracht. "He walked and looked all of a sudden like the old man he really was. He seemed infinitely tired. I asked him what was the matter and he said: 'The Germans have just informed Cohen that all Jews will have to wear a distinctive yellow badge in future. You will hear details at the meeting."[78] Aus der Fünten had notified the two Jewish Council chairmen of the order that afternoon. They were at first "speechless." Cohen said it was "a terrible decree." Citing the famous headline in a German-Jewish newspaper in 1933, "*Tragt ihn mit Stolz den gelben Fleck!*" ("Wear it with pride, the yellow mark!"), he inquired "why the colour had to be yellow?" Was it deliberately designed to humiliate the wearers? Aus der Fünten responded, as if they were discussing a matter of traffic safety, that "the colour had been chosen for its clarity."[79] For all their protests, the co-chairmen, after they emerged from the meeting, promulgated their usual stern injunction to all Jews to comply.

That evening, Brahn came to visit Gertrude, who was living at the time in a boardinghouse on the Prins Hendriklaan.

> I was alone in the evening of this day in the beautiful room which was still mine, full of books and flowers, when suddenly Prof. Brahn came to see me. We saw each other practically every day but he had never yet come in the evening without first having telephoned to ask whether I was in. We just talked and when he left I went with him for a little way. He said, "If I had not come here tonight I would have committed suicide." I looked at him and asked "Do you think it is as bad as all that?" He simply answered, "Yes. They will hunt us now wherever they can find us. It is the beginning of the end.[80]

About this time, Gertrude, in common with a number of her close friends, began carrying a cyanide pill with her at all times. "This tiny yellow box," she later recalled, "gave me throughout, no matter what happened, a sense of freedom."[81]

On May 2, 1942, the wearing of the yellow "Jewish star," which had been made compulsory in Poland immediately after the German occupation in 1939, and in Germany in September 1941, became obligatory in the Netherlands. In the first few days, there were a number of demonstrative acts of sympathy by the non-Jewish Dutch population, but these were soon snuffed out by German threats.

Some fighting talk against the council leaders in the central committee soon sputtered out. In the end, staff worked overtime to issue enough stars before the deadline. Gertrude was closely involved in arrangements with the Germans on the subject. At a meeting with Aus der Fünten at 9:00 a.m. on May 7, she and Cohen were given detailed guidance for full implementation of the measure.[82] To add injury to insult, Jews had to purchase the stars at a charge of four cents each. Gertrude found this latest decree humiliating and deeply distressing (*erschütternd*), and she agonized about what might follow.[83]

Alongside the introduction of the star came a host of new restrictions and prohibitions: Jews were barred from the fish market and were forbidden to buy or consume fruit. All forms of outdoor sport were prohibited to Jews. They were excluded from a large number of further occupations. They had to hand over their bicycles (a requisition later extended to the entire Dutch population). They could no longer use any form of public transport, enter the homes of non-Jews, or shop in non-Jewish stores save between 3:00 and 5:00 p.m. Their telephone lines were disconnected, and they were barred from using public phones. They were subjected to a curfew from 8 in the evening till 6 in the morning (the ban extended to appearing on a balcony or even to leaning out of a window). And still more Jews were called up to work in labor camps.

Exemption from these regulations was limited to a few people, generally senior employees of the Jewish Council. Gertrude was among the relatively fortunate: she was allowed to go out during curfew hours, she was permitted to use public transport, and she could keep her telephone. These dispensations were granted on the ground that they were needed for her work.

Gertrude was now cut off almost entirely from the Joint. She received no letters from Lisbon, only occasional packets of coffee, tinned sardines, or dried figs. Her last link with the outside world was through Saly Mayer in St. Gallen. Communication between Switzerland and Holland, although difficult, was still technically possible: Gertrude and Mayer were able to correspond and to send and receive confidential messages through occasional Swiss travelers to Amsterdam. In their letters, Gertrude and Mayer addressed each other in the familiar German form of *du*, unusual in that period save among intimates. Correspondence through the regular mail was subject to censorship, and indeed one of Gertrude's earliest surviving wartime letters to Mayer, in June 1940, bears an indication that it had been opened by the German authorities.[84]

Mayer, like Gertrude, was not a paid employee of the Joint but was fully trusted by the organization's leaders. Switzerland at the time offered, it was said, a "*balcon sur l'Europe*,"[85] and Mayer, like other observers based there, had unusual opportunities to gather information about German atrocities against Jews in occupied Europe. He was able to make almost daily telephone calls to Lisbon, although these were often interrupted and disturbed by war conditions, and, of course, liable to be tapped by intelligence agencies. Mayer and his interlocutors often spoke in a mixture of Yiddish, Hebrew, German, and English, using code names for persons and countries, which they hoped would render the conversations barely intelligible to outsiders.[86] Through Mayer, the Joint maintained some limited contact with terrorized Jewish communities in occupied Europe, including the Netherlands.

In addition to acting as a transmission station for information and funds, Mayer helped Gertrude in other ways. For example, in May 1942, she sent him a list of medicaments that were urgently needed.[87] And in August, she asked for more medical items—or, if that were not possible, then at least ten kilograms of vitamin C tablets.[88] Mayer succeeded in getting some of the supplies through to Amsterdam.

At the beginning of June, Aus der Fünten ordered yet another registration of all Dutch Jews. This new round of bureaucracy was apparently designed to facilitate the sequestration of Jews' property prior to their deportation. The co-chairmen insisted that there must be no question of "emigration or transfer." Aus der Fünten responded that after all, in the case of the German Jews, it had amounted to no more than registration (though in fact many of those registered had been sent to labor camps). When the German demand was reported to council members, they insisted that it could have nothing to do with registering people for emigration or transfer. But after a lengthy discussion, the council decided, as usual, to cooperate. It stipulated only that the staff who registered the Dutch Jews must themselves be Dutch "or at least good Dutch speakers," a further indication of the tensions that prevailed between German and Dutch Jews, heightened by the disproportionate number of German Jews among the council's staff.[89]

Cohen considered resigning: "At first I refused, but later on I considered that if we should resign, the Germans would either undertake themselves the duties . . . with all the consequences of that, or leave them to the Dutch National Socialists with even worse consequences. Moreover, if we could act as intermediaries I hoped that we should be able to save many persons. Therefore I accepted the task and I believe to this day [he was writing in 1953] that we were right."[90] In explaining the council's new responsibility to a meeting of the central committee on June 5, 1942, Cohen assured his colleagues that this round of registration had nothing to do with emigration—which, it was now increasingly feared, would take the form of deportation to the east.[91]

Given the apparent efficiency with which Gertrude had registered the non-Dutch Jews, supposedly for emigration, she was an obvious choice to undertake management of the process for this larger population. Cohen invited her to assume this new responsibility but required that she replace most of her German-Jewish staff with Dutch Jews. She resisted this condition. Gertrude's own credentials as a Dutch Jew were called into question. Cohen defended her against those who suggested she should be dismissed on the ground that she was insufficiently Dutch to oversee their registration. After several days of ugly recriminations, she decided to resign.

Cohen told the central committee on June 12, "with warm words of appreciation for the standpoint of Mrs van Tijn, that she did not wish to be responsible for the direction of these duties."[92] At the next meeting of the central committee, almost unprecedentedly, a correction was inserted into the minutes prior to their approval. The passage beginning "with warm words of appreciation" was to be excised. In its place, Cohen was recorded as having stated that Gertrude had been advised by her doctor to take a few months' rest. Once she had recovered, she would resume work for the council but "in another position."[93] Quite why this emendation was entered into the record is not known. According to Louis de Jong, Gertrude had suffered a nervous breakdown.[94] In his postwar reminiscences, Cohen did not mention any policy differences, attributing her resignation to what he said was a widespread antipathy felt towards her because of her German origin and because "she always sought to thrust herself to the fore."[95] In any case, it is plain that a serious rift had opened between Gertrude and Cohen, with whom she had worked closely for the previous nine years.

Gertrude absented herself from meetings of the central committee from June 12 to August 5 (except for an emergency meeting on July 4). Yet she did not withdraw altogether from work for the council. Her reasons for not doing so at this critical juncture remain uncertain. She could no longer have any hope that the Germans would permit significant Jewish emigration. In a letter to her children in America on June 15 (sent as usual via Saly Mayer), she could only hint at the pressures under which she was operating: "You can naturally hardly have any conception of our life here and perhaps it is better thus. If we meet again, you will find me very much changed. . . . At work I have many difficulties at the moment. We have become a very big organization and many people now exercise influence who earlier hardly knew that they were Jews." Feeling exhausted, she was "pulling back a little." In a postscript to Mayer, she added, "David [Cohen] is well. My work with him will continue." But as if to pose a question mark against that, she added an ellipsis and a question: ". . . . When can I visit you?"[96]

CHAPTER SEVEN

Help for the Departing

In the summer of 1942, the Nazis began deporting Jews from the Netherlands to death camps in Poland. Eichmann had visited Holland in April, inspected Westerbork, and told Zoepf that transports would begin in the summer.[1] In early May, Heydrich and later Himmler came to discuss arrangements. On June 11, Eichmann presided at a meeting of SS officials from France, Belgium, and Holland to discuss the deportation of tens of thousands of Jews to the east, among them twenty-five thousand from the Netherlands. Following further consultations, Eichmann, on June 22, increased the projected size of the Dutch contingent to forty thousand.[2] Rauter, Wilhelm Harster (Rauter's deputy), and Zoepf were in overall charge, but close direction of the operation fell on the Amsterdam office of the SD, headed by Lages and, most particularly, Aus der Fünten.

Late on the evening of Friday, June 26, Aus der Fünten summoned the Jewish Council leaders and informed them that "police-controlled labor contingents" of Jewish men and women, aged sixteen to forty, were to be sent to Germany.[3] Supposedly as a concession, those with children could take them along. Cohen and Asscher protested "formally and emphatically," then kowtowed.[4] Again there was dissension in the Jewish Council, but again it decided to cooperate lest the Germans undertake the entire operation themselves, which, it was feared, would result in violence.

The Jewish leaders' acquiescence was eased by an assurance that members of the council and its employees, as well as staff of Jewish hospitals and welfare institutions, would not be deported, on the ground that they were already performing labor service in the Netherlands. Some additional categories of people were also granted certificates of exemption: Jews married to non-Jews, converts to Christianity, those with specialized industrial skills (especially diamond workers), members of the Portuguese Jewish community (who, it was argued, were ethnically "Aryan"), as well as a handful of Jews who were former members of the Dutch Nazi movement, the NSB, and vouched for by its leader, Anton Mussert. Initially, the Germans spared some other persons specifically nominated by the council, provided that the requisite weekly number of deportees was met.

Gertrude was invited by Cohen to participate in the emergency meeting of the central committee on July 4, even though she was supposedly on sick leave. Cohen outlined the Germans' plans, mentioning that they proposed to send whole families together to Germany "in order to avoid hardships." "The meeting became heated for somehow we all of us in our minds saw it as 'deportations,' different somehow from the way in which Dutch workers were sent to Germany to work (which was bad enough). Many of us felt that the J[ewish] C[ouncil] should not co-operate in what we rightly assumed to be the beginning of deportations." The objectors failed to make any impression on Cohen. Gertrude returned to her apartment, bedecked with flowers for her birthday, "and could hardly bear the incongruity of it all."[5]

The German authorities worked on the basis of the updated *cartothèque* (card index) at the Zentralstelle. Further information came from the lengthy forms that had been filled out by Jews with the help of the Jewish Council, all of which were cross-checked against lists of exempted Jews submitted by the council. The Zentralstelle then sent out call-up notices for "labor service in Germany." At first these were sent by registered mail; later they were delivered by the Amsterdam police. Those summoned had to report to the

Zentralstelle, where they completed more forms concerning their property and were instructed to report at a specified time to Amsterdam Central Station.

From there they were transported to Westerbork, which was to be used as a "transit camp" for the deportees. Barbed wire, watchtowers, and floodlights were installed around the camp, which was thus transformed from a refuge into a prison.[6] A German commandant took control. Dutch constables of the *Maréchaussée* continued to perform guard duty, but SS men prevented escape, and Jewish camp police ensured internal order.

Many Jews did not respond to their call-up orders. Consequently, on July 14, the Germans launched a raid on the Jewish quarter of Amsterdam, during which 300 men and about 240 women were seized in the street. A special edition of the *Joodsche Weekblad* carried an announcement from the German police that those arrested would be held until the first four thousand persons designated for deportation had surrendered to the authorities, failing which the hostages would be sent to a concentration camp. The intimidation seemed, at first, to work: more Jews turned up when summoned, and most of the hostages were released—for the time being.

On July 15, the first train left Westerbork, carrying Jews to "labor service in Germany," in fact to death camps in Poland. Two days later, the commandant of Auschwitz, Rudolf Höss, recorded in his diary that a distinguished visitor had watched the Dutch Jews being gassed. Heinrich Himmler "unobtrusively observed the officers and junior officers engaged in the proceedings, including myself."[7] Of 1,132 people on the first transport, 839 were former refugees from Germany, Austria, and Poland, and 51 were children from the Westerbork orphanage. A total of eight persons survived the war. The children were all among the dead.[8]

Over the next twenty-six months, 97 trainloads left Westerbork: 64 went to Auschwitz, 19 to Sobibor, and 14 to Bergen-

Belsen or Theresienstadt. Most of the trains to the first two destinations were sealed goods wagons without seats. Each carriage was supplied with one barrel of water and one barrel for toilet needs. The Reichsbahn charged a group fare (at half the price of a one-way ticket), which was paid for out of sequestered Jewish accounts. At first deportees had to walk with their luggage a mile or so to a station in the nearby town of Hooghalen; but between July and November 1942, a branch line was constructed into the camp, so that prisoners on later transports boarded trains in the camp itself.

A further raid on the Jewish quarter of Amsterdam on August 6 yielded another six hundred arrests. Aus der Fünten met Cohen that day and said, "Believe me, Herr Cohen, I don't want this." In a bizarrely melodramatic scene, Cohen took both the Nazi's hands in his and said, "Herr Hauptsturmführer, if you don't want it, then don't do it." Cohen recalled that Aus der Fünten then turned to the window, "as he always did when he was emotional and wanted to hide his tears." Then he said, "Herr Cohen, I have to. There is no other way."[9]

The next day, the German authorities issued a proclamation in a special edition of *Het Joodsche Weekblad*, in which they threatened consignment to Mauthausen for all Jews who avoided labor duty in Germany. For good measure, the same penalty would be imposed on Jews who were caught not wearing the yellow star or who left their homes without permission.[10] The Germans were aware that the very name "Mauthausen" struck terror into the hearts of Amsterdam Jews. Memories were alive of the fate of the prisoners in Mauthausen the previous year.

Although news soon seeped out that deportees were being sent to Auschwitz, realization of the even more terrible nature of that destination had not yet dawned. On August 13, the co-chairmen of the Jewish Council were informed that fifty-two letters had arrived from the "labor camp at Birkenau." The letters were dated between July 22 and August 3; all had similar contents. They stated that the journey from Westerbork had lasted "two to three days," that the treatment of passengers on the journey had been good, that they were being handled in a "correct" manner, and so forth. An official of the council commented that the families of the deportees had received these letters with joy.[11] After that, however, almost all was silence. By early October, only ninety-three letters and cards had arrived, whereas at least twenty thousand people were estimated to have been deported. Analysis of the communications by the Jewish Council was far from reassuring: their content was generally formulaic, and many had obviously not been written by the supposed senders. The absence of news from the rest of the deportees had disturbing effects on the remaining Jews in Amsterdam. The analyst noted that "no complaints were heard about treatment in the Birkenau labor camp."[12] Birkenau was, in fact, the site at Auschwitz of the gas chambers and crematoria, and by this time the great majority of the deportees had perished there. When some similarly unsettling letters and cards arrived a few weeks later, one of the recipients reported that a signatory had added the word "*sof*"—the Hebrew for "end."[13]

As time went on, fewer and fewer Jews turned up voluntarily when summoned for supposed labor service in Germany. Their reluctance reflected a dawning appreciation of what deportation really meant. The Germans therefore carried out further *razzias*, seizing Jews in the streets, in their homes, or at their workplaces. Those arrested were taken to a school or, from the end of July, to the Joodsche Schouwburg theater, which had been transformed into a short-term holding pen for deportees. Here they were registered by officials of the Expositur. They were then sent by tram (younger people had to go on foot) to Central Station. From there, special trains, generally departing between midnight and 3:00

a.m., took them to Westerbork. Dutch police, municipal transport employees, and railway personnel all helped ensure that these arrangements worked smoothly. The secretaries-general of the residual Dutch administration protested against the deportations but did not carry out an earlier threat to resign.

During these critical weeks, Gertrude wrestled with the question whether to sever her connection with the Jewish Council altogether. In the end, she adopted a semi-detached position. For a few weeks she worked as a volunteer in the Expositur, offering advice and comfort to those who had been summoned for deportation. As exemptions were being granted to persons who held medical certificates, she fixed medical or employment certification for as many of those who came to request it as she possibly could. From seven in the morning until seven in the evening she dealt with a stream of people clamoring for help. After eight, when the curfew for most Jews came into effect, she carried on, meeting "Aryan" friends of Jews who came to plead on their behalf.

> In the beginning, it was particularly the proletariat who came to see us and I had never realized to what degree a large part of the Amsterdam Jewry were paupers. Many families came with seven or even eight children, all of them feeble-minded. Numbers of families came of whom two, three, or more were suffering from trachoma. Since my work made it necessary for me to shake hands with them, I used to keep—although I am not by nature squeamish—a bowl of Lysol water under my desk, and I don't know how many times a day I dipped my hands into it, feeling absolutely contaminated.[14]

Gertrude's advice, she later wrote, often consisted of "giving people tips how to stay away" from the deportations. But this did not save many of those same people from being caught in the increasing number of arbitrary roundups.

Gertrude's work for the Expositur gave her access to the innards of the deportation machine:

> On transport nights we did not go home at all but worked in the gymnasium [i.e. high school] hall where the people were assembled. The "JR" [Jewish Council] employees who were allowed to work there wore white armlets with "JR" stamped on them. A few of us had drawers full of these armlets and whenever we saw somebody we knew or believed to be trustworthy and young enough to pass as such, we would quietly furnish him with an armlet, telling him where to return it and he would leave, pass the German guard, supposed to be on some errand in connection with "JR" work. Needless to say the Germans soon noticed all these tricks . . . so that this method of escape was barred. These nights at the [Z]entralstelle were like scenes of Dante's Inferno. Never as long as I live shall I be able to forget them.[15]

According to her later account, Gertrude volunteered to go with the deportees to Germany "on condition that I was allowed to work amongst our people as a social worker." A colleague (she continues) "discussed this with ADF [Aus der Fünten] several times and finally told me that ADF had plainly told him that this would not be allowed and that if I would go it would simply mean that I would be sent like everybody else."

In a letter to Saly Mayer on July 29, Gertrude came as close as the ever-present awareness of censorship would permit to disclosing the desperation she now felt: "From this end alas, as you know, there is nothing good to report. Everything here moves at a racing tempo and nobody could have dreamt that farewells would have to be made on such a scale as are now occurring. For us that naturally means that we are working day and night. You know, of course, how many years I've been engaged in this work, but I must tell you truthfully that I would never have thought possible anything like what we are now doing." She promised to convey his greetings to David Cohen (she called him "David" in her letters to Mayer, although it seems she never addressed Cohen directly by his first name), adding, "We are naturally still working on the same matter but our views on policy are moving very much apart."[16]

At the end of July, Gertrude, while continuing to direct the now practically redundant emigration department, took charge of a new department of the Jewish Council called "Help for the Departing." Its purpose was to assist in equipping deportees for the ordeal ahead. According to her later account, Gertrude laid down three conditions for her acceptance of the position: that it would be unpaid, that it would entail "charitable work only," and that she would not be "held responsible for any of the political decisions" of the council.[17]

The leaders of the council had collapsed into resigned helplessness. On the eve of the Jewish New Year in September, Cohen admitted to the central committee that the past year had been the darkest Dutch Jewry had ever endured. On the other hand, he said, Jews in other countries had experienced even worse things. He exhorted his colleagues to try in the coming year "to lighten the suffering of the remnant of Israel" and to "save what can be saved."[18]

Another meeting a week later recorded "the first report of a death in Auschwitz."[19] The deceased, Marcus Werkheim, a mat maker, had reportedly died on September 2.[20] By this time, 15,663 persons had been deported to Auschwitz from Holland, of whom the majority were killed on arrival. Evidently, so far as the Jewish Council was concerned, the fiction was still being successfully maintained that the Jews were being sent abroad primarily to work.

At the same meeting, on September 18, one member of the central committee (unnamed, but not Gertrude, who had only recently rejoined the group) again demanded a discussion of the general policy of the council and of the conduct of the co-chairmen. He asked what was the rationale for the council's policy of cooperating in measures against the Jewish community. The protester received some support from other department heads. Cohen responded from the chair that "it would be criminal to leave the community in the lurch in their hour of greatest danger. From this it followed that one must try to retain at least the most important people as long as possible." The exchange plainly went to the heart of the matter. But even this brief hint of opposition was excised from the final record of the meeting.[21]

A month afterwards, when news arrived of the arrest of two of its own senior officials, an unnamed committee member asked whether the moment had not at last come for the council to cease its work. The question was brushed aside. The arrests were, of course, regrettable, Cohen said, but it was impossible for the council to stop its work, which was indispensable for the Jewish community. Even if something happened to Cohen himself, he would insist that the work must go on. The minutes recorded that all present concurred in this view.[22]

Gertrude encountered initial difficulties in her new job. There were disputes over the degree of her financial independence.[23] She beat off attempts to encroach on her area of responsibility. Surviving correspondence shows that she was deeply preoccupied with decisions about hiring staff. Often, in order to save people from deportation, she employed them without salary or even reimbursement of expenses.[24]

Such decisions led to further conflict with Cohen. He told Gertrude that although he was willing to allow her to employ a few individuals with exceptional qualities, she could not simply give people a "free pass" (i.e., exemption from deportation) by allocating jobs in her department. For her part, she asserted that some of

Gertrude at her desk in her office at the Jewish Council, Amsterdam, 1942 *(Jewish Historical Museum, Amsterdam)*

the people who were receiving posts with the council had hitherto played scant part in Jewish communal life. Cohen admitted that this was so but maintained that it could not be the main consideration in hiring decisions.[25]

Gertrude's stewardship was at least partly vindicated in statistics of her department's activity. In its first three months of work, it supplied 1,000 blankets, 350 overcoats, 900 packets of sanitary towels, 4,000 plates, 500 sets of babies' underclothing, and 2,020 tubes of toothpaste, in addition to thousands of other garments, boots, towels, and medicines.[26] The department also organized the dispatch of food parcels to inmates of Westerbork and other camps as well as to Jews held in prison.

A leaflet issued by the department offered "practical hints" to deportees on what they should take with them. They were advised to carry rucksacks rather than suitcases and were given detailed suggestions about what and how to pack. The list of recommended items included a bread bag and water bottle (no thermos flask), soap, toilet paper, a toothbrush, a sponge or washcloth, hand towels, insect repellent, talcum powder (50 grams), aspirin tablets (20 half-gram pills), and 50 Norit tablets (against diarrhea). The bread bag and water bottle were to be placed in the middle of the rucksack. Deportees were told to bring food for three days (rye bread in cellophane wrap *without* butter or jam, a terrine of butter, a piece of cheese, tea, chocolate, chewing gum, condensed milk or milk powder). Approved clothing included winter jackets, work overalls, one pair of strong shoes "preferably with iron fittings," a pair of slippers, collars and cuff links, and more. Deportees were also told to pack two blankets, a penknife, writing materials, and a watch ("no silver"). It was also "perhaps necessary to take what German money you have." Among other suggestions were "a favourite book" and postcards with international reply coupons. The list went on and on. But the leaflet helpfully warned that it would be "unwise to pack the rucksacks *too full*."[27]

Eventually the task was simplified by prescribing minimal baggage items in the formal summons by the Zentralstelle.[28] As the number of Jews seized in their homes and deported at short notice increased, the council urged all Jews to keep a packed rucksack ready at all times.[29]

"We used to pack and unpack for hours, weigh our luggage, try to find out how it was easiest to carry, and when all was done, would never really be ready," recalled one deportee. "The mood of those uncertain days was dark despair lit up by faint glimmers of hope. Before the spectre of that journey into the distant unknown, life was under permanent high-tension."[30]

By November, there were 416 employees in Gertrude's department, all but 20 unpaid. They included accountants, lawyers, collectors, delivery-boys, sorters, "helpers," and over a hundred

Employees at a sub-office of the Help for the Departing department of the Jewish Council on Oude Schans, Amsterdam, 1942/1943 *(photograph by Joh. De Haas, Beeldbank WO2, NIOD)*

secretaries and typists, who assisted with forms and petitions. Gertrude instructed them to treat everyone "with the utmost goodwill and the greatest tact." She reminded them "that those needing your help for a couple of days generally are in a very nervous condition; be prepared, therefore, to *serve* selflessly and do not take it amiss if they forget to thank you." Where possible, families should be asked for a contribution to expenses. Staff members were to report on each case, including on any residual matters that might remain after each family had been deported. "Your work ends with the departure of the family."[31]

Actually, the department's work continued far beyond that point. In the Schouwburg detention center, the department provided food and drink to thousands of people and packed meals for the journey to Westerbork. Its reach also stretched into the camp. A sub-department, headed by Curt Blüth, sent large quantities of supplies to Westerbork, including food parcels donated by non-Jews, amounting sometimes to several railway wagonloads a week. The Jewish Council already maintained a branch in Westerbork, and it seemed natural that Gertrude's department would do the same. When word came that families were about to be deported from Westerbork "to Germany," their relatives in Amsterdam would be routinely notified and invited to supply three days of provisions plus "complete gear, maximum 15 kilograms."[32]

The department obtained permission from the authorities to enter empty homes of deportees in the company of security personnel to retrieve belongings and forward them to their owners. This procedure, however, brought the department into what, at least on the surface, appeared to be direct alignment with the Nazi authorities. On one occasion, Gertrude wrote to Cohen to complain about an incident in which "helpers" from her department, accompanied by an SS officer, had entered an empty apartment in order to take away luggage. When they arrived, neighbors told them that shortly before, someone else had taken away some suitcases. The SS officer said he suspected that a family member was responsible and announced that he would investigate the matter. He further warned that if such practices continued, no removal of belongings whatsoever from empty homes would be permitted. Gertrude begged Cohen to issue an urgent public warning that such private-enterprise removals must stop, as otherwise "our whole work will be endangered."[33] But Cohen replied the next day that orders had been received that entry to empty homes was henceforth forbidden altogether.[34]

In consequence, many deportees who, for one reason or another, had been unable to take luggage with them (presumably because they had been seized in street raids) found themselves in Westerbork without any belongings at all. Gertrude managed to get around this problem by establishing five depots where people could lodge their rucksacks or suitcases in advance of deportation. She got the Expositur to agree to a system of notification whereby such luggage would be forwarded to Westerbork as soon as the owner arrived there.[35] Of course, the procedure had the disadvantage that only those who had resigned themselves to eventual deportation were liable to take advantage of it.

In mid-November 1942 Gertrude herself was rounded up. At 12:30 a.m., two Dutch Nazis and an SS man came to the boardinghouse on Prins Hendriklaan where she was staying. They ransacked her apartment and escorted her, together with several elderly neighbors, to a collection point, where Jews were lined up to board trolleys to the station for onward transportation to Westerbork. "While I was standing almost at the end of the queue, the door opened and Aus der Fuenten came onto the street. When he saw me, he said: 'Frau van Tijn, was tun Sie hier?' (Mrs van Tijn, what are you doing here?). I answered, 'Man hat mich geholt.' (They fetched me.) He opened a door marked 'doctor' and said 'Kommen Sie hier herein (Come in).'" Gertrude grabbed the housekeeper of the boardinghouse, Lucie Ascher, "a perfect saint of a woman," who was standing beside her, "and the next thing we knew, both of us were told to go home. All the others were sent to Westerbork."[36]

Why Aus der Fünten spared Gertrude remains a matter for speculation. Gertrude's later account does not even speculate: "I had not seen Aus der Fuenten since I had refused to give him the list. He not only recognized me but really saved me, for once in Westerbork it would have been almost impossible to get me back.[37]

The two women returned to the now-empty house. A few days afterwards, they moved into an apartment above a bank at 32 Nieuwe Amstelstraat, in the heart of the Jewish district of central Amsterdam. "From my windows I had a perfect view of the Waterlooplein with its ancient buildings and large trees. Beyond I could see the river Amstel and some of the old drawbridges. All day long, gulls were flitting past, giving an illusion of freedom and joy. Once I had arranged my books and other belongings the place looked as though nothing bad could ever happen there."[38] This was to be Gertrude's last home in Amsterdam. Lucie Ascher, who had come to Amsterdam as a refugee from Nazi Germany in 1933, worked as Gertrude's housekeeper for the next six months, and Gertrude found her a nominal position with the Jewish Council.

Photographs of the activity of the Help for the Departing department, taken in late 1942, were included in a congratulatory album presented to David Cohen at a party in celebration of his sixtieth birthday in December. The photographs show cheerful council workers organizing the distribution of supplies, rather as if they were charity workers sending aid to victims of some natural disaster, such as a flood or an earthquake.

Most of what the department disbursed came in the form of donations from Jews themselves. By the end of 1942, however, Jews in the city had been driven into total destitution by German sequestrations. Thereafter, the activities of the council, including those of Gertrude's two departments, were largely financed by German-sanctioned withdrawals of funds from confiscated Jewish bank accounts. In effect, therefore, the Jews themselves were made to pay the ancillary expenses of their own destruction.

Some, no doubt, derived temporary benefit from the council's aid and may thereby have been helped to survive the ordeal of transportation to the east. On arrival in Auschwitz, however, any goods they still carried were confiscated with a view to servicing German needs.

Gertrude records that she was able to help some individuals escape from the Schouwburg detention center, an effort in which several council employees cooperated. Walter Süskind, who worked in the Schouwburg as an employee of the Expositur, was a central figure in the escape effort. He worked with a number of resistance groups, as well as with employees of Gertrude's Help for the Departing department, in facilitating the escape of children from a crèche across the road from the Schouwburg. This institution held orphans and young people who had been found in hiding, as well as children who were separated from their parents when they arrived at the Schouwburg. When the parents were sent to Westerbork, a colleague of Süskind would ply Aus der Fünten with liquor while a fellow resister interfered with the card registry, so as to conceal the absence of the children, who were meanwhile being spirited away from the crèche to safe hiding places with Dutch, non-Jewish foster families.[39] Several hundred children were saved in this way. Süskind was subsequently deported to Auschwitz, where he died in early 1945. Among those who organized the escapes of these children were David Cohen's two daughters. In his posthumously published memoirs, he claimed to have known about and encouraged their activity at the time.[40]

Mistrusting German assurances that the deportees would merely be set to work in Germany, Jews desperately sought exemption from deportation by any means. The most promising expedient was to secure employment with the Jewish Council. From an original staff numbering twenty-five, the workforce proliferated and spread to different parts of the city. The building on Lijnbaansgracht alone held eight hundred employees by November 1942 and no fewer than twelve hundred a few months later.

An elaborate system developed of special stamps in identity documents that supposedly guaranteed various levels of personal security, most notably immunity from "labor service." Eventually the council was allowed 17,500 such exemptions (it had asked for double that number). A large minority of Amsterdam Jewry thereby gained a temporary respite by helping to organize the deportation of the majority. The council's leaders persuaded themselves that this was necessary, in order to "preserve a core" of the community—though since that core included themselves and their families, they laid themselves open to accusations of self-interest.[41]

The council's ability to grant exemptions opened the door to favoritism. Almost inevitably, council members tended to protect relatives and close friends. In the atmosphere of collective panic, allegations of corruption would have been natural even if there had been no basis for them in reality. Suspicion of the council also had a class element, since its members were mainly bourgeois whereas those deported came disproportionately from the working class.

In September 1942, Rauter wrote to Himmler that the roundup of the Jews was causing his staff huge vexation. "On no account do I want a single train to drop out, since what is gone is gone (*was weg ist, ist weg*)." The evacuation of the Jews, he admitted, had given rise to "quite a lot of disquiet." A great number of Jews had fled to Belgium and a few to Switzerland.[42]

Two weeks later, Rauter submitted another report. So far 20,000 Jews had been sent to death camps; a further 120,000 awaited deportation. Rauter said he would try to run three instead of two trains a week. He expected that by Christmas, half the Jews in the country would have been disposed of.[43] This objective was not attained quite so fast. By the end of the year, forty-two trains from Westerbork had taken 38,606 Jews "to the East."[44] In March 1943, Rauter told an official meeting that 55,000 Jews had so far been deported, and a further 12,000 were in camps in the Netherlands. But he now planned to send off 12,000 Jews a month so that soon Jews would no longer be "walking about in Dutch streets."[45]

CHAPTER EIGHT

Trading with the Enemy

In addition to her new position, Gertrude still operated as head of the council's emigration department. Its workload had diminished, as innumerable barriers now faced Jews who sought to leave. An office memorandum in November 1942 noted that over the previous three months, only about forty people had been able to emigrate. Presumably this referred only to legal departures.[1] Gertrude, however, declared it "an error to suggest that this department is now dormant."[2] The numbers were small, but she worked with almost frenetic energy, conscious that behind the statistics were human souls being rescued, one by one, from mortal danger.

Some examples illustrate her modus operandi and the difficulties with which she had to deal. In December 1942, she wrote to Saly Mayer about the case of Eli Dasberg, a religious Zionist and member of a prominent rabbinical family, who had been involved for many years in the Wieringen project and was now an official of the Jewish Council. Dasberg was one of a group of Jews from Holland who had been given permission to go to Lyons, where they had been promised delivery of Swiss entry visas.[3] For unknown reasons, the plan misfired. Dasberg remained in Amsterdam for several months. Perhaps he was, after all, fortunate not to go to Lyons just then: a few weeks earlier, following the German occupation of Vichy France, Klaus Barbie had arrived there to take charge of Nazi security police operations in the city.

In September 1942, Gertrude had written to Mayer about another friend, Abel Herzberg—the well-known Amsterdam lawyer, journalist, and Zionist, who had served for a time on the board of *Het Joodsche Weekblad*. For a brief period, as we have seen, he had directed the Wieringen *werkdorp*. Herzberg, together with seven members of his family, had been granted an official exit permit "but unfortunately has only an expired visa for Cuba." Gertrude asked Mayer whether it might be possible to arrange a visa for the family to another country. Perhaps "Richard" at 52 rue Paquis in Geneva might be able to help?[4] "Richard" was Richard Lichtheim, the representative in Switzerland of the Jewish Agency. His initial reaction was discouraging.[5] Nevertheless, Herzberg was later placed on a list of persons who might be exchanged for Germans in Palestine. He was not actually exchanged, but his presence on the list afforded him some protection against deportation to the death camps, and he survived the war.

Several exchanges of Allied for Axis civilians took place during the war, including a few of Jews (Palestinian citizens and others) for German residents of Palestine. In an initial such transfer in Turkey in December 1941, sixty-seven Germans were exchanged for forty-six Palestinians Jews from Poland.[6] The episode suggested that this might be a viable method of extricating more Jews from Europe.

"This Palestine exchange idea was really my work," Gertrude later wrote—an unusual claim for someone who rarely sought individual recognition.[7] In fact, as she went on to say, the initiative was taken by Helmuth Mainz, a German-Jewish banker who had come to the Netherlands in 1933. Mainz served as a financial adviser to the Swiss consulate and engaged the support of Ernest Prodolliet, the Swiss consular agent in Amsterdam.

Prodolliet was deeply sympathetic to the cause of Jewish refugees, but he had to tread carefully. As a staff member at the consulate at Bregenz in Austria in 1938, he had taken illicit steps to help refugees escape the country. When these came to the attention of his superiors, he was subjected to disciplinary proceedings, reprimanded, and for a time suspended from duty.

Mainz at first found it hard to persuade the Jewish Council that there was a serious prospect of arranging any further exchange. According to his later account, it was only when he invited Gertrude to tea with Prodolliet that she was persuaded that the Swiss diplomat was both willing and able to help.[8] Gertrude's version was more self-congratulatory: "He [Mainz] came to me with this information and I had the vision *and* the connections to take it up."[9] Prodolliet undertook to arrange for the forwarding to the German and British authorities of a list of Jews in Holland who were Palestinian citizens and therefore potentially eligible for exchange. This conversation broke the ice, whereupon Gertrude assumed prime responsibility for compiling the list.

Very few Palestinian citizens were to be found in Holland at this time, but the concept was soon stretched to include a broader range of people who might be eligible. On October 30, 1942, a notice appeared in *Het Joodsche Weekblad* inviting three categories of persons to register at the emigration department for possible departure to Palestine: (1) possessors of an immigration certificate for Palestine issued before the outbreak of war, (2) children whose parents were resident in Palestine, and (3) parents of children resident in Palestine who had been promised a certificate. "In order not to create any false hope," the notice emphasized that only these categories should register, and that this would be merely a provisional registration that would not guarantee departure to Palestine.

A second exchange, on November 12, 1942, again in Turkey, saw 301 Germans and 4 Italians handed over in return for 137 persons, of whom 78 were Jews (69 of them Palestinians). About a dozen of these were from the Netherlands.[10] The disparity in number of exchangees between the two sides occasioned some complaint. The Germans explained that they had had difficulty in finding suitable candidates (in itself an ominous admission). After conducting a three-month search of ghettos and concentration camps in Poland, they produced a further three women and a dozen children, all from Westerbork.[11]

On November 15, at German insistence, the consulates of neutral states in Amsterdam, including that of Switzerland, closed. Using a Swiss protection document issued to him by Prodolliet, Mainz managed, in early December, to secure an interview with Ferdinand Berttram, an assistant to the German Foreign Office representative at The Hague, Otto Bene. "I was not received in an excessively friendly fashion," he recalled. Bene was known to be close to high SS dignitaries in the occupation administration. Mainz nevertheless found in Berttram a receptive ear. Mainz asked him what, in his opinion, the attitude of the German government would be to another exchange, this time involving Germans from Palestine and the British Empire in return for non-Palestinian Jews from Holland. The diplomat responded that in his opinion, the German government would be very interested in such an exchange, since there were far more *Volksdeutsche* (the Nazi term for Germans living outside the Reich) than there were *Englische Austauschobjekte* (English people available for exchange) in Germany or the occupied territories. "Satisfied with this information, I travelled back and immediately reported to Frau van Tyn on my conversation."[12] On this basis, Mainz and Gertrude attempted to broaden the eligibility of people placed on lists, so as to embrace Jews who were not Palestinian citizens.

In addition to the categories already mentioned, four more were opened for application: women with husbands in Palestine, immediate blood relatives of Palestine residents, "veteran Zionists," and persons qualifying for special immigration certificates (rabbis, Youth Aliya, and so on).[13] In a letter to the Jewish Council's

Jews at an assembly point in Amsterdam, awaiting removal to Westerbork, May/June 1943 *(Jewish Historical Museum, Amsterdam)*

department in Westerbork, Gertrude tried to damp down exaggerated hopes, pointing out that the number of persons likely to be involved in any exchange would be small.[14]

Mainz and Gertrude were aided by the activity in Palestine of an association of Dutch Zionist immigrants, headed by her old friends Leib and Mirjam de Leeuw. The group stepped up its efforts after news percolated through to Palestine of Nazi mass murder of Jews in eastern Europe. Many of the exchangees who arrived in Palestine in November 1942 had brought horrific, eyewitness accounts of German crimes in eastern Europe. These were officially confirmed a month later in a simultaneous declaration by eleven Allied governments (including the Dutch), denouncing the Nazi program of systematic extermination of the Jews of Europe.[15]

Upon receiving news of the acceleration of deportations from Holland in the summer of 1943, the Jewish Agency urged the British and American governments to move ahead to a third exchange. The Zionists pressed the British authorities to be more liberal in granting Palestine immigration certificates. The British were very reluctant to signal any change in the White Paper policy, but they eventually relaxed its implementation slightly. The overall limit on Jewish immigration set in 1939 was to be maintained, but the absolute bar on refugees from territories occupied by the enemy was removed. In addition to Palestinian citizens, "veteran Zionists," and others whose bona fides was guaranteed by the Jewish Agency became eligible for exchange. Meanwhile, the Jewish Agency had discovered that mere placement on a list of potential exchangees often gave holders some degree of protection against deportation to death camps. As a result, there was great competition to secure certificates and places on exchange lists. Such lists proliferated in Jerusalem, Istanbul, Switzerland—and Amsterdam. By June 1943, Gertrude had registered at least 798 potential exchangees.[16]

In view of later controversy over Gertrude's role in drawing up these lists, it should be noted that she did not do so alone. She formed a committee of veteran Zionists, representing various parties and groups, which took responsibility for determining whom to include. One of the members was Eli Dasberg, who represented the Mirachi (religious Zionist) Party. "This committee," Gertrude recalled, considered every single case, sometimes for hours, sometimes three or four times, before deciding. . . . Although, naturally, we had to disappoint many people in not being able to consider the whole NZB (Netherlands Zionist Federation) as eligible, it was generally recognized that the committee's decisions were honest and not influenced by nepotism."[17]

Two cases of Jews afforded at least temporary protection by inclusion on exchange lists were Edith Landwirth and Maurice

Hirschel. Landwirth, the daughter of a Viennese Jew, had been brought to Holland in early 1939 with the Kindertransport. Aged fourteen in 1943, she was living with a Dutch Jewish family in Amsterdam. Her parents had found refuge in Palestine, albeit as illegal immigrants, and Edith applied to join them there. In May 1943, Gertrude informed her that she had been registered for exchange.[18] In the end, Edith was not exchanged, but she was not deported either. Later she went into hiding and survived the war.[19]

Hirschel, a young medical orderly, worked as an assistant to one of the doctors in the Schouwburg detention center. In that capacity, he had access to the neighboring crèche and participated in Süskind's operation to save children by smuggling them from there. Hirschel was approved for exchange in early September 1943.[20] He too was not exchanged but also not deported. Like Edith, he went into hiding and survived the war.

Through the International Red Cross, Gertrude's office was able to maintain a line of communication with the Jewish Agency representative in Geneva and its head office in Jerusalem, seeking letters of confirmation that applicants were related to residents of Palestine or had some other qualifying status. Upon receipt of a suitable response, Gertrude's assistant, Curt Albersheim, would write a letter certifying that the applicant had been "registered for eventual exchange to Palestine."[21] Subsequently, Gertrude herself would sign a letter stating that the recipient had been placed on a list submitted to the Swiss Legation in Berlin, which was handling arrangements for exchanges.[22]

All this took some time, especially as there were often delays in securing "clearing" authorization for payments for telegrams. Pending receipt of a Palestine immigration certificate, however, possession of a so-called Albersheim letter seemed to afford some measure of protection to the holder. In particular, prisoners interned at Westerbork who held such documents were generally safe, at least for a while, from deportation to the east.

The Dutch colonial empire provided another long-distance safety valve. Although passage to the East Indies was impossible after December 1941, a few Jews were able to make their way to Dutch colonies in the Western Hemisphere. In December 1942, after waiting two years in France, Spain, and Portugal, a group of 122 refugees, of whom 104 were Jewish, reached Paramaribo, the capital of Surinam. Another group of 25 refugees in Surinam, according to an internal report of the Joint, had "turned over substantial sums of money to Mrs van Tijn in Holland on the understanding that their transportation would be provided after they left Holland and additional needs would be met."[23] The Joint again showed its confidence in Gertrude by honoring these commitments. Since the colony remained under the control of the Dutch government in London for the duration of the war, the refugees' safety was guaranteed, though most of them regarded Surinam as no more than a way station to somewhere else and left as soon as they could. In the course of 1943, several hundred further Dutch refugees, not all of them Jews, traveled from Spain and Portugal to the British West Indies, and from there most proceeded to Surinam.[24]

A small number of Jewish refugees reached Curaçao between 1940 and 1944. At least 125 of these fugitives were Dutch citizens, but the governor, Guilliam Wouters, was unsympathetic, and the Germans and Austrians among them were interned. In November 1941, when 86 more, who had arrived with visas for Uruguay, sought temporary admission, he cabled to the London government opposing their admission, as it was "all too clear [that] they would never leave the island."[25] Eventually, after the Joint guaranteed that it would cover the costs of their internment, they were admitted by order of the Dutch minister for the colonies. Following Wouters's replacement in 1942, they were released from detention. They remained, however, subject to restrictions, such as a ban on possessing a radio or entering places of public entertainment—prohibitions that strangely echoed the German-imposed anti-Jewish laws that were being enforced at the same time in Holland.[26]

Prospective emigrants from Holland grasped at another straw: they tried to secure the passport of a neutral state. For all their contempt for international law, the Germans were generally punctilious in observing the immunity from persecution of citizens of neutral states. Such papers therefore offered not merely the prospect of exit from occupied Europe but some security in the interim. Documents of Latin American states were particularly attractive, since, unlike the few remaining European neutrals, these states were not threatened with invasion by the Axis. Many passports were sold by venal consular representatives. Even after most Latin American states broke off diplomatic relations with Germany and, in some cases, declared war on her, possession of such documents remained valuable, since their holders could hope to be regarded by the Germans as suitable material for exchange in return for the large number of German nationals in those countries.

In Amsterdam, a market in forged documents of all kinds developed. The Dutch resistance manufactured identity cards and other papers that enabled some Jews to escape the rigors of the anti-Jewish laws. Racketeers sold these and other documents, including false passports of neutral states.

The purchase of such documents, of course, crossed the line into illegality. But in a few cases, money could also buy quite legal exits. Thanks in large measure to her connection with Saly Mayer, Gertrude became involved in efforts by Jews in Holland to buy their way openly out of the country and into Switzerland.

Though neutral throughout the war, Switzerland—with its large German-speaking population, surrounded by Axis and pro-Axis neighbors, and fearful of possible Nazi invasion—had never been particularly friendly to refugees from Nazism. From August 1942, the Swiss specifically prohibited the admission of "refugees who have fled purely on racial grounds, e.g. Jews."[27] As a result, many were refused visas or turned back at the border. But there were exceptions as well as twists and turns of policy.

Until the closure of the Swiss consulate in Amsterdam in November, Ernst Prodolliet, ignoring official guidelines, issued a number of Swiss transit visas to Jews. When the consulate closed, Prodolliet provided Gertrude with the equivalent in guilders of 37,500 Swiss francs, representing his entire available consular funds (about $13,000 at the then rate of exchange, or about $180,000 in 2014 dollars).[28] The money was repaid by Mayer to Prodolliet in Switzerland, upon production of a receipt signed by Gertrude.[29] The value of this money was enhanced by the fact that the Swiss franc was at the time the only European currency, apart from the Portuguese escudo, that was freely convertible. Gertrude was able to use these funds for local relief purposes in Amsterdam and to help more Jews escape the country. Altogether, about twenty-one thousand Jews (or persons of Jewish origin) from Nazi-occupied Europe found refuge in Switzerland between 1939 and 1945 (in addition to the seven to eight thousand who had arrived before the outbreak of the war).[30]

A handful of these were Dutch Jews, who managed to bribe their way out of the Netherlands. The main reason they succeeded was a decision by the German authorities, who urgently required foreign currency, to permit very wealthy Jews to ransom their way to freedom. In the summer of 1941, discussions began in Berlin on the scheme for "the ransoming of Dutch Jews against payment of a fine (*gegen Zahlung einer Busse*) in Swiss Francs"—as an official of the Dresdner Bank described it.[31] A memorandum by Himmler in December 1942 recorded that Hitler had "approved the release of Jews against a considerable ransom in foreign currency" and had accorded Himmler full authority to decide on such cases.[32] Holland was not the only country where such transactions were approved by the occupying authorities: in Hungary and Romania too a few very wealthy Jews were able to buy their way to freedom by surrendering money or industrial plants.

Among those who succeeded in escaping by this means was Jacques van Tijn's former employer, the businessman and philanthropist Bernard van Leer, who transferred ownership of his entire enterprise to the German Mauser and Mannesmann companies and to a Dutch "Aryan" concern at a rock-bottom price. In return, he was permitted to leave the country. In June 1941, he traveled to the United States via Spain, accompanied by fourteen family members and associates. He was able to take with him $3,000 in cash, two cars, nineteen horses, a large quantity of jewelry, and a Stradivarius violin. The greater part of what remained of his Dutch fortune, after the Germans had stripped him of the bulk of his assets, was placed at the disposal of the Jewish Council, to be used for cultural purposes.[33]

Negotiations for such departures were complex, and often dragged on for months or even years. Typical ransom amounts for families seeking an exit permit from Holland to Switzerland ranged from 10,000 to as much as 100,000 Swiss francs (then about $35,000, or nearly $500,000 in 2014 value).[34] By November 1942, eight permits, allowing the exit of thirty-six Jews, had been granted for a total of SF 1,290,000 (about $450,000). The proceeds were retained by the SS and the German police "for their own purposes."[35]

An American diplomatic report from Switzerland in October 1942 described the mechanisms by which ransoms were generally paid. Relatives in the United States or a neutral country would transfer money to a Swiss bank, from which it would be deposited in a German-controlled account. A number of shady intermediaries handled these transactions.

Arthur Wiederkehr, a shady Zurich attorney, was said to be "very well known in Holland as the man who can get refugees into Switzerland at a price."[36] Wiederkehr was also mixed up in the lucrative trade in looted art, some of which figured in ransom negotiations. He was accordingly placed on an Allied "black list." Towards the end of the war, seeking to have his name removed from the list, he made a statement to the British authorities in which he declared his "desire to tell the whole truth." He portrayed his actions not as participation in extortion but as an effort, in conjunction with the former Swiss consul in Amsterdam, Otto Lanz, to help "in connection with emigration permits for various Jewish clients." Wiederkehr stated that he had visited Amsterdam on several occasions in 1941 and 1942 and arranged for paintings—including a Van Gogh self-portrait, five Cézannes, and a Jan Steen—to be "smuggled into Switzerland by diplomatic bag." Wiederkehr held the pictures for a German client, "a great friend of Goering," from 1942 to 1944. A little implausibly, the attorney claimed that he had acted as custodian of the paintings "without knowing their value."[37]

The paintings had been looted from Jewish owners, including an Amsterdam art dealer, Jacques Goudstikker, who had owned one of the most valuable collections of Dutch old masters before the war. In May 1940, he was one of the refugees who fled IJmuiden on the SS *Bodegraven.* On the ship, however, he slipped and fell to his death. The greater part of his collection fell into the hands of Göring, whereupon Wiederkehr and others sold them on the international art market.

At least four hundred Jews in the Netherlands escaped from the Nazis by means of payments through such squalid Swiss person-traffickers. The total paid amounted to at least 35 million Swiss francs (about $12 million in 1943, or $170 million in 2014 value).[38] To these sums must be added paintings, precious stones, shares in companies, and other items turned over to the Nazis. By the very nature of the trade, much of it was never documented. These figures must therefore be regarded as conservative estimates.

One of those who bought his way out of Amsterdam with Gertrude's help and using the services of Wiederkehr was a German-Jewish banker, Hans Kroch. Wiederkehr spoke personally to Eichmann in order to obtain Kroch's exit permit. Wiederkehr was not, however, able to secure the release of Kroch's wife, who was a prisoner in the Ravensbrück women's concentration camp. In August 1942, Kroch traveled via Spain to Argentina, together with four members of his family and another family. The price was 100,000 Swiss francs, apparently paid through Wiederkehr to the SS. Kroch also paid $9,000 to Gertrude to cover the cost of trans-Atlantic transportation for nine persons; the passages were purchased by the Joint. Gertrude applied Kroch's money in Amsterdam, "for the relief program conducted in that country."[39]

As soon as Kroch was out of reach of the Nazis, he contacted the Joint and Wiederkehr in the hope that more Jews might be able to get out of Holland. He sent Wiederkehr a list of 126 persons or families whose freedom might be purchased by themselves or by relatives in the United States or elsewhere. Gertrude's name was among those on Kroch's list.[40]

Gertrude met Wiederkehr in Amsterdam on at least one occasion, in July 1942. It seems he introduced himself as an acquaintance of Saly Mayer. Wiederkehr told her that he was arranging for the departure of several families from Holland to Switzerland and apparently offered to organize a visa for Gertrude too. In mid-August she wrote to Mayer, "I shall probably not be here much longer."[41] From the context it is possible, however, that she was alluding to her likely removal not to Switzerland but to Westerbork and the east. A week later, Mayer spoke by telephone from St. Gallen to Joseph Schwartz, who had succeeded Troper as the Joint representative in Lisbon. They discussed arrangements for getting Gertrude as well as others out of Holland:

MAYER: I have been able to let them know that we are willing to pay 5,000 S [dollars or Swiss francs] to get them out.
SCHWARTZ: OK, do you think they can leave Holland?
MAYER: Well, we have them [*sic*] at least a chance as they of all people deserve it best.
SCHWARTZ: Yes, you are right.[42]

Perhaps because they were probably being overheard, they did not go into further detail.

From subsequent correspondence, it emerges that Mayer was at this stage seeking to organize the departure of four persons: Abraham Krouwer (a prominent businessman, a member of the Jewish Council, and an old friend of Mayer), the two daughters of David Cohen, and Gertrude. The difficulty seemed at first to be with Swiss entry as much as with Dutch exit, as the Swiss federal authorities informed Mayer that no canton was willing to admit Gertrude. Mayer persisted, however, and in January 1943 obtained entry authorization for Gertrude.[43] But by the time Gertrude was notified of this in early February, departure from the Netherlands had become impossible. Shortly afterwards, Roger Brunschvig, a Swiss citizen, visited Amsterdam and called on Gertrude on behalf of Mayer. On his return, he told Mayer that Gertrude had said that even if she was unable to secure permission to leave Holland, the fact that she held a Swiss entry permit would still be "a great help" to her.[44]

Gertrude's role in the trade in exit permits, as both an intermediary and a potential beneficiary, was fraught with danger from many angles. The Allied governments strongly opposed any such dealings with the Nazis. The Dutch government in London denounced the practice as a racket.[45] The British, in particular, sought to stem any leakage through the economic blockade of Nazi Europe. In November 1942, the British minister of economic warfare, Lord Selborne, announced in the House of Lords that the government would henceforth regard all persons involved in the trade, "furthering it or facilitating it in any way, as being engaged in transactions for the benefit of the enemy."[46]

As time went on, Allied opposition to ransom efforts hardened further. Efforts in 1944 to purchase the release of large numbers of Jews from Hungary, Romania, and Bulgaria mostly foundered on the rock of the economic blockade. "Trading with the enemy," by Gertrude and others, saved a small number of lives but could not be allowed to interfere with the overriding Allied objective of winning the war.

CHAPTER NINE

To the Bitter End

By late 1942, the machinery of mass murder was operating at full throttle. Initial limitations based on age, sex, or state of health had been set aside: children, the elderly, and invalids were all dispatched for "labor service in Germany."

On January 21, 1943, a police unit, commanded by Aus der Fünten, raided the Jewish mental hospital at Apeldoorn and hurled hundreds of patients pell-mell onto trucks. At Apeldoorn station, Zoepf supervised the loading of prisoners, some of them in strait-jackets, in nightgowns, or naked, onto goods wagons. Fifty-two nurses volunteered to go along to look after them. Patients and caregivers alike were transported to their deaths.

Next came the orphans. By this time, Gertrude later wrote, "the Jewish orphanages were . . . all crowded because in many cases where parents were deported and for some reason or other children stayed behind, the 'J.R.' [Jewish Council] was wont to put them into orphanages."[1] Among the children were some who had come to Holland with the Kindertransport.

Gertrude was living at the time within direct sight of the Jewish boys' home, Megadle Jethomiem, on the other side of the Water-looplein. She must have felt an additional personal involvement, as a friend and senior member of her department, Sam Roet, was a director of the institution. Members of her staff helped the children pack.[2] On February 10, German police surrounded the building. Nearly one hundred children were taken away. Three members of the staff volunteered to accompany them.[3] The boys were removed to Sobibor and Auschwitz and killed.

At the end of February, the German authorities told the co-chairmen of the Jewish Council that most Jews still at liberty would be sent to the camps at Vught and Westerbork, where the Jewish Council itself was to be installed. Only a small council apparatus would remain in Amsterdam. Jews capable of work would be concentrated at Vught. Pathetically seeking grains of comfort, the Jewish leaders opined that this might mean that fewer Jews would henceforth be sent to Germany, and perhaps the deportations might even stop altogether.[4]

On March 3, Gertrude's Help for the Departing department was abruptly informed that the Germans had forbidden any further collections of clothes and goods for deportees.[5] When the decision was appealed to Aus der Fünten, he said that the prohibition must be maintained, providing only a vague assurance that he would try to find some other way of supplying the necessary materials.[6] As a large part of the personnel of Gertrude's department was devoted to such collections, the new rule threatened to render many of her staff redundant and likely to be deported. She therefore reorganized their work, assigning more employees to help people in their homes prepare for departure.

The department also took on the delivery of messages for the Expositur—more than 8,800 in March 1943 alone.[7] This task, however, moved Gertrude's department, like the rest of the Jewish Council apparatus, closer towards collusion in the process of destruction. Such messages often contained declarations exempting recipients for one reason or another from deportation, but sometimes they carried less welcome news.

Soon afterwards, Gertrude was brought up against another hard decision when the Zentralstelle demanded that she identify donors of gifts to her department from three specified addresses. On the face of it, this was a simple request for information. But Gertrude's response might have terrible consequences. Her dilemma was similar to that of two years earlier, when Barbie had required the addresses of the Wieringen students in Amsterdam. The reasons for the inquiry by Aus der Fünten's office were not stated, but it could be presumed that the underlying intention was not benevolent. Gertrude seems to have contrived some way of failing to reply: the letter is stamped as having been received on April 1, but the space for the date when it was answered remains blank.[8]

The subsequent fates of residents at all three addresses are known. In the first case, that of the family of Salomon Witteboon, a tailor, they appear to have moved elsewhere in Amsterdam before the date of the inquiry. Witteboon, his wife, and their fifteen-year-old son were located and deported a year later. In the case of the second address, that of a divorced woman named Rica Naarden, the Germans had been given the wrong house number. She was tracked down and deported to Sobibor in June. In the third case, the name of the resident, Izak Pezon, a thirty-three-year-old male nurse, had been wrongly rendered as "Petson." He was deported in March 1944.

In May 1943, the Germans began requiring Jewish partners in mixed marriages to choose between sterilization or deportation to Poland. Most opted for sterilization. Representatives of all the main churches in the country protested against this "shameful practice"—but to little avail. Many Jewish and non-Jewish doctors refused to cooperate or avoided doing so, but 2,562 such procedures were performed over the next thirteen months.[9]

The numbers of people transported from Amsterdam to Westerbork and from there to the east reached unprecedented heights in the spring and summer of 1943. On some occasions, over two thousand left for the death camps on a single day. In March, when four of her employees were threatened with deportation, Gertrude wrote to Cohen appealing for exemptions. Cohen's reply has not been found. Her intervention may have won them temporary reprieves: one was deported to a death camp in May 1943, two were deported in 1944, and one survived the war.[10]

It became known in March 1943 that department chiefs would have to supply a list of all their "real employees" (presumably as distinct from those who had purely fictional positions as a protection against deportation), ranked according to their degree of importance. The chiefs were assured that lists could be submitted either ranked or in alphabetical order, as they preferred.[11] When the rumor spread a few weeks later that, after all, the lists would have to be ordered according to degree of dispensability, Gertrude protested to Cohen, pronouncing herself "flabbergasted."[12]

In May, Gertrude submitted one of her last reports on the work of the emigration department. It was still active, dealing with hundreds of visitors and letters of inquiry, and it continued to seek Palestinian immigration certificates. Actual Jewish emigration, however, save to the death camps, had come to an almost complete stop. In the previous month, the only recorded (i.e., legal) departures of Jews from Holland were sixteen persons who had been "repatriated" to Sweden, Denmark, Italy, and Hungary, and one Englishwoman who had been exchanged.[13]

Meanwhile, on May 10, Zoepf sent a cable to Westerbork, drafted by his assistant, Gertrud Slottke, stating that on orders from Berlin, the number of deportees that month would have to be increased. As the available stock of Jews was insufficient, new measures would be required. One possibility would be a further *Erfassungsoperation* (*razzia* or raid) in Amsterdam in the last week of the month.[14]

On the morning of Friday, May 21, Aus der Fünten told Cohen, Asscher, and Sluzker that the council must furnish the names of seven thousand of its own employees for deportation. The co-chairmen said that this would render the work of the council impossible. Aus der Fünten said that if they failed to make the selections, he would choose random letters of the alphabet and take away those whose names began with those letters. After an anguished debate the same day, the council unanimously authorized its co-chairmen to "negotiate" with the Germans in the hope of modifying the order. Asscher and Cohen were given a free hand, however, to comply if necessary. As usual, the decision was justified as an effort to avert "an even worse disaster."[15]

At a meeting of the central committee, Gertrude was one of four department heads who objected.[16] She submitted her resignation, which Cohen declined to accept. As she persisted in her refusal to select those of her staff who were dispensable, he told her she could submit a list of them all in alphabetical order, which she did. In a letter to Saly Mayer that day, Gertrude did not mention these events. She confessed that she felt "very lonely" but wrote that she was extraordinarily busy, "which is the best thing for me."[17]

The next day, Saturday, Cohen gathered his most trusted associates at the council's headquarters in an old patrician merchant house at 58 Nieuwe Keizersgracht. As only a few department heads had, in the end, submitted lists, Cohen and his colleagues began the work of selection themselves. They conducted a systematic examination of the card indexes in order to sift essential from nonessential employees.

A witness described the scene. The whole building "was lit from top to bottom as if it were a feast day." People scurried around as heads of various departments came to plead for their people. Some discussed the possibility of burning the entire *cartothèque.* One department head removed the cards of all his staff. A scheme was devised whereby the names of three thousand people, known already to be in hiding, would be sent up first to the "holy of holies," where the council leaders were choosing those to be summoned for consignment to Westerbork. "I can still see them sitting there in the front room . . . with the big card index boxes in front of them, as people went to and fro bringing in new boxes and taking out others with the cards of the doomed." Another room was set aside for typists to fill out forms containing summonses. Relays of messengers carried lists from room to room. One boy, encountering his own name on a list, ran away in terror. The work went on all night and into the next day. Asscher appeared only briefly, clutching a bottle of brandy, "like the chairman of a board . . . who did not want to soil his hands with such sordid machinations." On Sunday, the typed call-up notices were delivered by registered mail. Recipients were ordered to appear at the departure point on the evening of Tuesday, May 25.[18]

On Monday, the council building was besieged by frenzied crowds of people desperately beseeching exemptions. On that day, Gertrude wrote two letters to Cohen to complain that the call-up of a huge number of people from her department was preventing it from doing its work effectively. She asked that no more be summoned and that call-up notices to two specific staff members be withdrawn, as they were indispensable.[19] No replies have been found.

"With artifice and acrobatics" Cohen and his colleagues completed their selection by Monday evening.[20] According to Cohen's postwar account, no more than fifty-seven hundred summonses were sent out.[21] As no list was submitted to the Germans, the hope was that they would not realize the discrepancy. In the meantime, a zealous postal official had brought back a large pile of letters marked for return, as the addressees had gone into hiding or were otherwise not to be found. By then, according to a description given to Gertrude, "the place looked like a battlefield, all card indexes having been pulled to bits, cards lying on the floor everywhere and people dropping with fatigue and excitement."[22]

View of Gertrude's last home in Amsterdam, 32 Nieuwe Amstelstraat, in 1943, showing the sign, near the Blue Bridge, marking the entrance to the "Jewish Quarter" *(Amsterdam City Archives)*

As fewer than seven thousand had been called up and so many had disappeared, only a small part of the required number appeared at the assembly point. The Germans decided to make up the shortfall by launching a new raid on the Jewish quarter. Jewish policemen from Westerbork were deployed as auxiliaries in the operation.[23] Gertrude's apartment provided her with a grandstand seat from which to watch the *razzia* on the night of May 25–26. From her window at the corner of the Waterlooplein, she had a panoramic view over the surrounding area. She later recalled what she had witnessed:

> The first warning I had that something was afoot was when, around 12 o'clock that night, I began to hear the by then

> familiar noise of the battering of doors. . . . Soon after that I heard cars with loudspeakers rushing through the streets giving the order for non-Jews to remain in their houses and for all Jews indiscriminately to get themselves ready to leave. The faithful Lucy Asser [Lucie Ascher], who had been saved together with me in November 1942 and who had kept house for me since then, was also awakened and we both proceeded to get ready. We looked out of the window and saw by the bright light of the searchlights that the Blue Bridge across the Amstel as well as the Waterloo Plein were crammed with police and soldiers in SS uniform with steel helmets, mounted bayonets, heavily armed, not as if they were going to proceed to take Jews from their houses but as if they were to meet the enemy in battle; machine guns were mounted on the houses commanding the Amstel and the Waterloo Plein and that part of the town looked like a place where battle was about to commence.

At 3:00 a.m. there was a knock on Gertrude's door. "When I opened it, immediately two SS soldiers, armed to their teeth with pistols drawn, entered the flat." After searching the apartment, the men ordered the two women to follow them.

> We took our rucksack, breadsacks and roll of blankets and proceeded to the Waterloo Plein where all the people in that part of the town were being collected. . . . After some hours when hundreds of people were collected, we were marched to the Great Synagogue which was used as a registration office. . . . We were supposed to give up the keys to our dwellings there but I managed to retain mine. . . . After that we were again made to wait outside on the big square in front of the synagogue. Fortunately it had been a beautiful night. At about 8.00 o'clock in the morning my name was called by an SS man and I was told to come to the synagogue. . . . Aus der Fuenten was there, looked at me and said, "Go at once to the 'Expositur'

> and don't show up anymore today otherwise you might be taken again." Before I could even grasp what he had said I was literally thrown into a lorry and driven off at an extraordinary speed to the "Expositur." I remember this because the lorry being empty I was thrown from one side to the other continually and bruised all over when I finally got out.

It soon emerged that Gertrude was the only person to have been liberated after the roundup.[24]

During an air-raid alarm in the later stages of the operation, a few people took the opportunity to flee. A doctor who attempted to take cyanide was prevented from doing so by policemen and delivered alive for transportation to Westerbork.[25] By the time the raid was over, hardly any Jews were left in the district. Among those arrested were Helmuth Mainz and his family as well as about fifty former pupils of the Wieringen *werkdorp*.

A German report noted that "the potentially very pro-Jewish population behaved in a reserved manner." It added that very few members of the Jewish Council had been arrested. "On that account the bitterness among other Jews had grown ever stronger, as the Jewish Council was largely blamed for the fact that better placed Jews allegedly remain unmolested."[26] Gertrud Slottke, Zoepf's assistant, who had been present during the roundup, noted that all had gone smoothly, apart from a few women who burst out in hysterical screams during the registration in the synagogue.[27]

From Westerbork, 3,006 people were sent to Sobibor on June 1. Among them was Lucie Ascher who was killed there three days later. Only one of these deportees was still alive at the end of the war. A further 3,017 Jews left Holland the following week.[28] None survived. These were the largest numbers deported on single days in the course of the Dutch-Jewish genocide. Further raids in the course of the summer reduced the number of Jews remaining in

Amsterdam to just a few thousand, not counting *onderduikers*—literally, people who had gone "under water," or into hiding, often outside the city. Friends urged Gertrude to go "under water" too, even offering her forged papers, but she refused.

The arrest of many of her employees had left her department short of staff. Of course, it also had less work, now that so many Jews had been deported. But Gertrude persisted in trying to employ more people, as this might yet be the one way to save them from deportation. On June 4 she appealed urgently to Cohen and Asscher to authorize her to make appointments to 121 vacant positions in her department, as typists, "helpers," porters, messengers, night watchmen, and so forth.[29] No reply has been found, but the appointments, if they were ever authorized, did not grant many even a temporary reprieve: staff numbers continued to fall.

Later that month, Gertrude, together with other council staff members, was given a certificate, signed by Aus der Fünten, stating that she was active in the service of his office ("*ist im Auftrag der Zentralstelle für jüdische Auswanderung tätig*") and therefore excluded from arrest.[30] On July 29, she received a much-coveted "120,000" stamp on her identity card, which supposedly protected the holder with absolute assurance from any danger of deportation. Among the fifteen hundred or so favored persons who received this stamp were the families of Asscher and Cohen, senior officials of the Jewish Council, and certain Jews with special skills in the diamond industry.

But even these certificates soon proved of dubious value. On August 5, twenty-eight of the council's senior officers sent a collective protest to the cochairmen, recording their "great anxiety" that certificates that had hitherto protected them seemed no longer to be recognized by the Germans. The letter cited cases of recently arrested persons who had been in possession of certificates that were thought to be in the highest exemption category. This

Max Brahn *(Leo Baeck Institute, New York)*

was the only recorded instance of such a collective protest in the history of the council, but it had no effect. Gertrude, perhaps sensing the self-serving nature of the complaint, was not among the signatories.[31]

The workload of both of Gertrude's departments had, concertina-like, subsided again, since the Jewish population of Amsterdam had been reduced to a fraction of its former size. She was therefore able to relax a little and enjoy such social and cultural amenities as were available in the restricted environment of the quasi-ghetto. Among those whom she met regularly were two men, both of German-Jewish origin: Max Brahn and Ernst Laqueur.

Brahn, aged seventy in 1943, was an educational psychologist who had studied philosophy at Heidelberg and edited some writings of Nietzsche for publication. Although he had lectured and directed an institute at the University of Leipzig, he was passed over for a professorship. Between 1914 and 1918, he had worked for the German war effort, developing aptitude tests for pilots. In the Weimar period, he was employed as an arbitrator by the Ministry of Labour.[32] Following the Nazi seizure of power, he moved to the Netherlands, where he was known as "Professor" Brahn.

Widely respected for his integrity and dignity, Brahn was commended by David Cohen as "an extraordinarily gifted man."[33] After the German invasion, he served as head of the *Beirat*, an advisory body to the Jewish Council, representing non-Dutch Jews (mainly German refugees). Given the acrimonious relations between German and Dutch Jews, this was a delicate position. Although Brahn was eventually allowed to attend meetings of the council, he had no vote and could exercise next to no influence over decisions.

Brahn was allocated an office in the same building as Gertrude, and by 1942, their friendship had blossomed into love. Gertrude wrote later that of all the people she ever met in her life, Brahn was "certainly the greatest." She called him "infinitely wise, gentle, and resigned."[34] Their relations seem to have been in no way inhibited by the fact that Brahn was married (his wife lived with him in Amsterdam).

Gertrude's second friend, Ernst Laqueur, had been professor of pharmacology at the University of Amsterdam since 1920 and served as Rector Magnificus in 1936. Laqueur came from a similar background to Gertrude. Born near Breslau, he was of Jewish origin but converted to Christianity as a young man—apparently a *Karrieretaufe* (career baptism). During the First World War, he conducted research in Berlin into gas warfare and treatment of

Ernst Laqueur *(photograph by Gert Jan van Rooij of painting by Wim Schumacher)*

victims of gas poisoning.[35] This seems to have become generally known, and in a diary entry in 1942, Etty Hillesum, a young typist in Gertrude's department, jokingly called him "the poison gas gangster."[36]

Laqueur was generally credited as the discoverer, in bulls' testicles, of the hormone testosterone—a term he coined. (The discovery was actually made by a researcher working under his direction.) Laqueur next sought to synthesize and produce testosterone commercially. In 1923, in partnership with a Dutch-Jewish businessman, he founded the pharmaceutical company Organon. Using bovine carcasses provided by his partner's slaughterhouse, he sought to manufacture testosterone on an industrial scale. He mistakenly believed that the hormone could be administered to treat enlarged prostate glands in elderly men.[37] The possibility of artificial production of testosterone was held (as the *New York Times* put it in 1935) to open the way to "a vast field of biological and physiological investigation into theories about rejuvenation, postponement of old age and atrophy of the glands, kidneys and other organs."[38] Organon made Laqueur a wealthy man.

In spite of his conversion, Laqueur identified closely with the Jewish plight in the 1930s, serving as treasurer of the Academisch Steunfonds, a body that sought positions for academic refugees from Germany. On April 30, 1940, he was due to leave for a lecture tour of the United States but decided to stay. He remained in Holland throughout the German occupation. The Nazis removed him from his university chair but, interested in the possible utility of his research, permitted him to remain at liberty, provided he continued his work for Organon. Of course, his baptism was of little help to him in dealing with the Nazis, given their racist conception of Jewishness. In 1942, he was denounced to the SS as a "great German-hater."[39] After investigation, however, the Germans decided that there was no evidence to support the charge.[40] When Laqueur's application for permission to emigrate, in return for handing over his shares in Organon, reached the desk of Eichmann in Berlin, he ordered a further investigation.[41] Laqueur, his wife, and a daughter were arrested in 1943 and briefly sent to Westerbork. After a few days, they were allowed to return to Amsterdam, where Laqueur resumed his scientific work. The three were even excused from the requirement to wear the "Jewish star." Two other daughters, however, together with their families, were later sent to concentration camps for the duration of the war (one died of typhus in April 1945).[42]

Laqueur's marriage had long been strained: he and his wife (a cousin) "could not live together and they could not live apart," as his biographer puts it.[43] Laqueur, who had a reputation as a womanizer, had several affairs. In her diary, Etty Hillesum refers to a "nurse led astray" by Laqueur.[44] This woman, a gentile, wrote letters to Reichskommissar Seyss-Inquart, pleading for Laqueur not to be deported.

Even while Gertrude maintained an intimate, if platonic, friendship with Brahn, she became Laqueur's lover. For Gertrude, these were both intense, romantic entanglements; we have little evidence of how the men felt about it. Brahn and Laqueur used to call at Gertrude's flat daily, "sometimes alone, sometimes together"—as she later told her daughter.[45] Brahn, she recalled, "never asked me about my relationship to Bob [her pseudonym for Laqueur], but I felt sure he knew we were lovers. Both men answered a different need in me."[46]

On Sunday mornings, the two would come to Gertrude's apartment for coffee—not the locally available *Ersatz* substitute but the precious real thing, made from genuine coffee beans that she received from time to time from Joseph Schwartz, the Joint representative in Lisbon. Sometimes, other friends would join them. They would listen to gramophone records of Beethoven and Mozart and talk about literature, Zionism, painting, travel—anything except current events in the Netherlands. She valued not only the emotional closeness but also the intellectual fellowship they offered. "Particularly Brahn was a marvellous man to clear up one's muddles."[47]

With the threat of deportation hanging constantly over her head, Gertrude feared she would never see her children again. She had been living alone, starved of companionship since the arrest of her housekeeper, Lucie Ascher, in the midnight *razzia* of May 25–26. Laqueur and Brahn filled the deep void in Gertrude's heart that had been left by the death of Pieter Vuyk, the betrayal of her husband, and the departure of Curt Bondy.

The summer of 1943 was, for Gertrude, the worst of times and yet the best of times. She experienced an exalted happiness in her private life that did not so much compensate for the unending grief of her work as complement it. As often happens in wartime, the atmosphere of relentless danger heightened all feelings, whether of pain or joy. During those months, her life attained an emotional pitch that she had never known before and that she would never know again.

By the beginning of September, the number of council employees had fallen to 956 (107 in Gertrude's department), of whom two-thirds were working without pay. The education department now employed just fourteen people, as most of the children had been taken away.[48]

On September 3, the commandant of Westerbork announced to senior staff of the camp that Himmler had ordained that the whole of western Europe was to be made empty of Jews ("*judenrein*"). Various groups of Jews who had hitherto been exempt from deportation, including those in Westerbork itself, would now have to leave. This news was freely disseminated in the camp, and word quickly spread to Amsterdam.[49]

A momentary spark of hope was kindled on September 21 by a telegram to Gertrude, transmitted through the Red Cross, from Henrietta Szold in Jerusalem. Szold indicated that the Palestine government had agreed to make five hundred Youth Aliyah certificates available for children from Holland.[50] But like several others around this time, this initiative, designed to extricate children from the inferno, came to nothing. The Nazi authorities were now completing plans for a final roundup of Jews in Amsterdam, including children in the last remaining Jewish orphanage in the city.

Gertrude realized that her turn must come soon. She wrote a farewell letter to her children and gave it to a friend, who promised to dispatch it whenever that became possible. The letter, which Gertrude intended as a personal testament, was returned to her unopened after the war.

It is plain from what she wrote that her overriding concern was that her memory should not be sullied by association with those responsible for the decisions taken by the Jewish Council. The self-dramatizing tone may be excused by the constant nervous strain to which she was subject and the scale of the human tragedy to which she was witness:

> My darling children,
> This year has been one of unprecedented suffering, worsened by internal strife; if I should not live to see the end, there are several people who possess my political testament, and who can bear witness that I have had nothing to do with the Jewish policy here from the moment the deportations started. If I should live to see the end, I know that this will be fully recognized, and that I shall be able to look people into the face and to continue serving anywhere, in any capacity. This to me is tremendously important. You must know that, whatever happens, I am leaving you an untarnished name.
>
> The personal side: my dears, I do love you more than anybody in the world. . . .
>
> My life: it is hard to give you an idea of it. My flat is a centre of peace for the few very good friends I have made. . . . And yet though I have kept all this up for myself and my friends, it

has been a dreadful year. 87,000 people have been sent away; 13,000 are in camps; to-day even the news has come that the rest will have to be liquidated quickly.

Great pressure is put on me to try to save myself; but somehow, I cannot do it. For many I have become a kind of symbol. And though I have little to do these last 3 weeks (and the work is likely to diminish) there is a feeling I somehow have, of sticking to my guns to the last. I don't think I could live at peace with myself if I now saved myself, even though many think I shall be very much needed after the war. I shall be of no use to anybody [if] I have no peace with myself; and I fear I would not have this, if I did not stick it out to the bitter end.[51]

CHAPTER TEN

Last Exit from Amsterdam

On September 29, 1943, the eve of the Jewish New Year, nearly all surviving Jews in Amsterdam, including the leaders of the Jewish Council, were rounded up and sent to Westerbork. Aus der Fünten informed Cohen and Asscher that the council, having fulfilled its purpose, was now dissolved. A residual office remained in Amsterdam for a year, whereupon its handful of remaining employees went "under water." The one department of the council that continued to perform some useful function was Help for the Departing, which dispatched parcels containing food and other aid to inmates at Westerbork for another eleven months.[1]

Richard Lichtheim, the Jewish Agency representative in Geneva, reported to Jerusalem on September 29 that "the total destruction of the Jewish communities in Belgium and Holland is nearly completed." "Professor Cohen and Mrs van Tijn are still there but for how long? The leaders of the community seem to have given up all hope. Some are now trying to escape. . . . The arrests and deportations are made with the usual brutality. Everything the Jews possess is taken away from them. 40 or 50 persons are herded together in one carriage, otherwise used for cattle, and then they are sent to their 'unknown destination.'"[2] Four weeks later, Pieter Gerbrandy, the prime minister of the Dutch government-in-exile, announced in a broadcast from London that the last Jews from Amsterdam had been deported from Westerbork to an unknown destination. "Although there are hardly any Jews left on Dutch soil, the Jewish section of our people will resume one day its place in the Netherlands," he declared. He then uttered an equivocal tribute: "I am moved by the tragic fact that Jewish leaders were forced to help organize the expulsion of their brethren. The Jewish Council accepted the offer to assist Jews in their misfortune and it performed its task with love and devotion. But the oppressor used and misused even this Council. When victims for deportation were no longer available, the members of the Council suffered the same fate [as] all the Jews of Holland."[3]

Gertrude had been alerted the previous day that a raid was impending. She discussed the danger with Brahn and Laqueur. Such warnings had previously turned out to be false alarms. They considered whether to "go under," but the three of them decided not to do so.[4]

When the knock came at her door, Gertrude was alone in her apartment reading the *Stundenbuch* (*Book of Hours*) of Rainer Maria Rilke. She had to leave behind most of her belongings—books, records, and papers. Her rucksack was very heavy, and her guard carried it for her to the Amstel station. Laqueur rushed there but could not extricate her from the group awaiting transportation. After saying good-bye to him, Gertrude went to collect her luggage and encountered Aus der Fünten standing next to it. This time there was to be no reprieve. "Mrs van Tijn," he said, "everybody has already been asking for you." "I did not say anything to him and took my luggage and somehow or other managed to struggle up the stairs, almost collapsing under the weight."[5]

On their way to Westerbork, the prisoners were guarded by Jewish Ordedienst men from the camp, who had been sent to Amsterdam in trucks for the purpose. These were mainly German-Jewish refugees, who acted as auxiliaries to the German security personnel. Their chief task was to preserve order in the camp. They accompanied prisoners to the weekly trains heading for the death camps, loaded the wagons, and sealed them. Occasionally, as we have seen, they were deployed elsewhere—for example, in raids on the Jewish quarter of Amsterdam and in the assault on the Jewish mental hospital at Apeldoorn in January 1943.

Westerbork, when Gertrude arrived there, was "a village of wooden barracks, set between heath and sky, with a glaring yellow lupin field in the middle and barbed wire all around"—the description of Etty Hillesum, who spent three periods in the camp in 1942–1943.[6] Situated on a desolate, windswept peat bog, Westerbork consisted of rows of huts, with a central thoroughfare that came to be known as the "Boulevard des Misères." Alongside this ran the railway track where trains came and went. From its original conception as a camp for German-Jewish refugees, Westerbork had slowly evolved into an antechamber to mass murder. Since its designation as a *Durchgangslager* (transit camp) in July 1942, the greater part of Dutch Jewry had passed through it on their way to death camps in the east.

The commandant of the camp, Albert Konrad Gemmeker, had served there since October 1942. Just thirty-five years old at the time of his appointment, he was a gentleman murderer. He did not soil his own hands with blood. More than one inmate recalled his "singular charm."[7] Etty Hillesum recorded that at deportations, Gemmeker appeared "at the end of the asphalt path, like a famous star making his entrance during the grand finale. . . . He walks along the train, his gray, immaculately brushed hair just showing beneath his flat, light green cap. . . . And there is something else about him, halfway between a dapper hairdresser's assistant and a stagedoor Johnny."[8] Gertrude noted that he lived in great luxury, but she added, "Contrary to other German commandants of concentration camps, he did not allow any of his subordinates . . . to commit brutalities. No Jews were ever ill-treated in Westerbork."[9] He was "invariably courteous," she wrote, and "it was said of him that he sent people on transport with a smile."[10]

In several respects, Westerbork was unlike any of the hundreds of other camps in the Nazi prison system. Vestiges of its origins as a refugee camp were still visible in the camp's organization. Although most of the hundred thousand Jews who arrived there as prisoners stayed only a short time, sometimes only a few hours, before onward transportation to their deaths, a nucleus remained as semi-permanent residents. The Germans had continued their Dutch predecessors' practice of allowing inmates to organize the internal government of the camp, thereby sparing themselves manpower and inconvenience.

Long-established German-Jewish residents, as a result, had come to dominate the camp administration. Their position was analogous to that of the Jewish Council in Amsterdam, with the difference that here, German rather than Dutch Jews ruled the roost—or gave the appearance of doing so within the barbed-wire coop. The official language of the camp remained German even after Dutch Jews outnumbered the original inhabitants. The German Jews were accused of behaving like an oligarchy, of acting as slave drivers, and of selecting prisoners, generally Dutch Jews, for the deportation trains. According to Gertrude, these *alte Kampinsassen* (veteran camp inmates) "were embittered to an incredible degree against members of the old refugee committee and—later—the Jewish Council."[11] Many of them held the Dutch Jews responsible for their initial internment, "suffered from camp psychosis" after spending several years of confinement, and rejoiced now that the tables were turned. German Jews appropriated superior accommodations and secured minor perquisites. By the time Gertrude arrived, the latent aversion of Dutch Jews towards their German coreligionists had developed in many cases into fierce hatred. Gertrude found that she and former colleagues were particular targets of venom, since some German-Jewish refugees held the Committee for Jewish Refugees and the council responsible for failing to arrange their emigration before it was too late.

The *Oberster Dienstleiter* (head of the camp administration) was one of the veterans, Kurt Schlesinger, of whom Gertrude painted an unflattering portrait: "Dr Schlesinger looked and behaved like an SS man. . . . He was corrupt and used the influence he had to enrich himself and to protect those with whom it seemed advisable to keep on good terms. If a girl was pretty and Schlesinger happened to come into contact with her, there was a way for her to be saved from transport. If she remained unwilling to give in to him, she was sent to Poland. His vanity was excessive; he wanted to be asked and to distribute favours."[12] For a time, she wrote, Schlesinger "took the most prominent part in the making up of the transport lists." Later that task was assigned to three other Jews (one Dutch and two German). From late 1943, however, the Germans, she reported, took over complete control of the lists.[13]

Astonishingly, a few privileged inmates were occasionally allowed to go home, to Amsterdam or elsewhere, on short periods of leave. The Jewish Council maintained an office in the camp, and its representatives were for a while permitted to come and go. The celebrated Dutch-Jewish singing duo Johnny and Jones, who performed in cabaret shows in Westerbork, were granted leave to return to Amsterdam briefly in the summer of 1944. During their visit to the city, they recorded "The Westerbork Serenade" and other songs. They then returned to the camp, from which they were later deported to Theresienstadt and Bergen-Belsen, where both died in the spring of 1945.

Westerbork boasted a well-equipped hospital, with 1,725 beds (more, according to Gertrude, than in any other hospital in Holland) and 120 doctors. There were frequent musical and cabaret performances by artists who had earlier appeared on the stage of the Joodsche Schouwburg. Gertrude, appalled by such jollifications, never attended. On the other hand, Hauptsturmführer Aus der Fünten was so impressed by these shows that he made several trips to the camp specifically for the purpose of joining the audience.

Albert Gemmeker (right) with Ferdinand Hugo Aus der Fünten and two women friends at Christmas party, Westerbork, Dec. 19, 1942 *(Beeldbank WO2, NIOD)*

His visits seem to have been convivial occasions. On December 19, 1942, he was the guest of honor at a Christmas party hosted by Gemmeker. On October 17, 1943, a fortnight or so after Gertrude's arrival, Aus der Fünten visited again, this time to watch a cabaret performance featuring the "Westerbork Girls." In December he went on a shooting expedition for hares and partridges, using guards from the camp as beaters.[14]

By comparison with other Nazi prison camps, escape from Westerbork was relatively easy. Yet a total of only 210 Jews ever escaped.[15] Whether out of obedience, despair, lingering hope, or fear of reprisals that might be wreaked on loved ones, few others even tried to do so.

When Gertrude arrived in Westerbork, there were seventeen thousand people in quarters that had been designed for five thousand. The barracks were packed with beds arranged in three tiers. She was assigned to barrack 61.[16] Also living there was Fré (Frederika) Tal-Vaz Dias, who had worked as Gertrude's secretary since 1938. Together with her husband and children, she had been registered for exchange to Palestine. There seemed little prospect of that now.

From her bunk on the topmost tier, Gertrude "could see the rats scuttling along beams at night."[17] Sometimes they scrambled over her as she tried to sleep. At first she was assigned work in the camp library. When that was taken away, she had to sort peas. After a short time, she developed jaundice and spent several weeks in the hospital. Then she returned to pea sorting.

Above the surface normality of the camp hung a lowering cloud: the menace of deportation. Every Tuesday morning at 11:00 a.m., with almost metronomic regularity, a train, generally composed of cattle trucks or goods wagons, would depart for Auschwitz or Sobibor, laden with one thousand Jews. A prisoner in the camp recorded the dread that prevailed as people waited to learn whether their names were on the deportation lists: "There is a sulky, sombre atmosphere; everybody trembling in terror and dreadful anticipation; people racing about like madmen; everybody trying to get for himself some sort of deferment. Sometimes frenzied entreaties do avail, but then some other Jew has to go instead—the transport has got to be complete. The faces of those about to be deported are hardly to be recognized."[18] Jewish Council personnel did what they could to secure exemptions from deportation and devoted hours to registering arrivals and departures. Etty Hillesum wrote of "the unremitting clatter of a battery of typewriters: the machine-gun fire of bureaucracy."[19]

Did the deportees know where they were really going? The fiction of "labour service in the east" was maintained to the end. But

Train to death camp being loaded at Westerbork *(watercolor by Werner Löwenhardt, an inmate of Westerbork, Beeldbank WO2, NIOD)*

many sensed something much more sinister. Gertrude described the panic that preceded the departure of every train and the desperate efforts of those on the deportation lists to secure last-minute exemptions. Yet she observed that "as a rule, people left with utter docility and—even for Dutch Jews an almost incredible feeling of optimism. They left with shouts of 'We'll come back. . . .' 'See you soon'. . . . or, 'Don't forget to fetch us after the war.' It seemed incredible that by that time the truth about these transports, destination gas chambers, had not leaked out."[20]

Immediately after her arrival, Gertrude was able to get a message out to Saly Mayer in St. Gallen, informing him that she had been arrested and asking him to forward the news to her children.[21] He sent her a sympathetic and supportive reply: "I hope you have the strength to bear it all, for your clear conscience is your greatest comfort in these times. I will pray with you to dear God that all will end well."[22]

A few weeks later, Eichmann issued strict instructions limiting communication by Westerbork inmates to one censored postcard a month.[23] But Gertrude found it possible to conduct clandestine correspondence with a few close friends, notably Brahn and Laqueur, both still in Amsterdam. Brahn's letters were pessimistic, "saturated by an immense sadness." He was thinking of Gertrude all the time. "There are days when I feel I would prefer to be near you even in camp, for without you life is too lonely. There is nobody who can ever take your place." He sent her some translations he had made for her of poems by Horace—"but I realize," he wrote, "that all our *Lebenskunst* [literally "art of living"] cannot help us when there is no freedom." Laqueur's letters were brighter, and he expressed confidence that they would meet again in freedom. He sent her sleeping powders that helped her get through the terror-laden nights. "As a doctor, he objected to my heavy smoking; yet, he saw to it that in Westerbork, where we were allowed to smoke, I was never without cigarettes."[24]

On December 24, as she was doing her laundry, Gertrude was told that a new trainload of Jews had arrived from Amsterdam and that among them was Brahn: "I rushed out to find him. Not caring what anybody might say or think, I rushed straight into his arms. I was deliriously happy to be near him, and yet heartbroken. When I could actually touch him and talk to him, I realized how much I had missed him. Yet I would have given anything to still have known him safe in Amsterdam." He spent as much time as possible with Gertrude. "Notwithstanding the bitter cold, we walked to the end of the camp, where we could be alone together."[25] But after two days, he was deported to Theresienstadt. They never saw each other again. Gertrude was distraught. Yet she later recalled, "Maxim's infinite wisdom, and his capacity to be himself, no matter what the outer circumstances, renewed in me a courage I had all but lost."[26]

Soon after Gertrude's arrival, rumors spread in the camp that the Germans were finalizing lists of Jews eligible for exchange. "The word 'exchange' had a magical sound to it, since it promised freedom," recalled one prisoner.[27] Some viewed the rumors skeptically, calling them a mere *Austauschwitz* (exchange joke), which, as another inmate noted, "sounds so very like Auschwitz."[28]

The latest lists were based on drafts prepared by the Jewish Agency in Jerusalem. They, in turn, were drawn from the lists provided by Gertrude and others, including the association of Dutch immigrants in Palestine. The Agency's lists, sometimes shortened at the insistence of mandatory government officials, were forwarded by the British through the Swiss Foreign Ministry to the Germans. By this time, there were thousands of names on paper—though in many cases the persons named were already dead.[29]

Gertrude's name had appeared on a list of forty-five Zionist activists from Holland that was submitted to the Jewish Agency in March 1943 by the Dutch Immigrants' Association in Palestine, in which Mirjam de Leeuw played a key role. Others on the list included David Cohen, Abel Herzberg, and Eli Dasberg. The association came under pressure to indicate priorities. Cohen, Herzberg and Dasberg were all placed in the first twenty. Gertrude's position was 39, later revised to 42, out of 45. Mirjam de Leeuw did not decide alone on the recommended priorities but as a member of an eight-person committee that was subject to enormous pressure from all sides. The criteria according to which this "strictly confidential" ordering was decided were unstated, although most of the persons named had held office or played a role in Zionist organizations. In the end, only thirty-five names were transmitted to the Jewish Agency on March 19, 1943; Gertrude's was not among them.[30] Why Gertrude's name drifted so far down the list and then dropped off altogether remains unclear. Whatever the reason, the omission marked the start of bad blood between the two old friends.

In May, news reached Amsterdam that the names had been "registered" by the Jewish Agency, but Gertrude wrote to Saly Mayer that "inexplicably, my name does not appear on this list."[31] Gertrude's friend Jules Gerzon (whose own name appeared on the list) cabled from Amsterdam, through the Red Cross, to his sister, Mirjam, in Jerusalem: "Omission Gertrude Vantyn first veteran list inexplicable please rectify immediately."[32] When a Swiss emissary from Saly Mayer visited Amsterdam that month, Gertrude again asked for help. Mayer raised the matter in a telephone call to Joseph Schwartz at the Joint office in Lisbon, but he responded, "I cannot do anything from here."[33] Fortunately for Gertrude, however, her name had been restored to an expanded list of 170 exchange candidates—comprising "veteran Zionists, rabbis etc. from Holland"—that the Jewish Agency sent to the government of Palestine.[34] In mid-August 1943, she received a letter from the Palestine Office (i.e., the Jewish Agency representative) in Geneva informing her that her name had, after all, been placed on a list for veteran certificates.[35]

Negotiations on the issue dragged on frustratingly for months. The British insisted that in a third exchange, the disparity in numbers of the previous two exchanges must be made up by the Germans. While consenting in principle, the Germans had trouble finding people still alive whose names were on the lists supplied to them. They were often dilatory in replying to communications on the subject, which passed through the Swiss Foreign Ministry. The British government naturally tended to place the interests of its own citizens held by the Germans ahead of those of other nationalities. The Dutch government in London, for its part, had to weigh the claims of Jewish candidates for exchange against those of other Dutch citizens. Moreover, there never seemed to be enough German civilians under Allied control to meet the insatiable demand for exchange of Jews in German hands. Many of the Templers in Palestine had been removed to Australia. Others had no wish to go to Germany, and it was decided that they should not be repatriated against their will. And there were additional problems: for example, the general manager of the Palestine Railways wrote angrily about being saddled with responsibility for supplying a train to carry exchangees. He protested that he had none available that had lavatory or water provision.[36]

Even those whose names were on exchange lists turned out not to be immune from deportation to death camps. On July 20, 1943, when numbers were short for a transport from Westerbork, several hundred people who held Albersheim letters or who had actually been approved for exchange found themselves called on to make up the deficiency and were deposited on the train to the east.[37]

On November 11, Camp Commandant Gemmeker attended a meeting in The Hague with Eichmann and reported that four hundred Jews were ready for the Palestine exchange. A further one thousand, he said, were being prepared for eventual inclusion.[38]

In Westerbork, responsibility for interviewing candidates for exchange was assigned to Wilhelm Zoepf's assistant, Gertrud Slottke, who paid several visits to Westerbork for that purpose. Her task was to locate and verify the identities of persons on the British-supplied lists. To this end she questioned claimants in order to establish their bona fides. Supposed Uruguayan citizens, for example, would be quizzed on the geography of the country and asked to name its capital.[39] Where there were absences or discrepancies, perhaps because people had already been deported or were in hiding, Slottke had authority to add names to the lists by including persons who could produce a document demonstrating some claim to inclusion. Those who successfully passed examination by Slottke were given papers stating that they would be "transferred under the Palestine-exchange scheme to another camp."[40]

That camp was Bergen-Belsen in northwest Germany. In the spring of 1943, Himmler had ordered that part of the prisoner-of-war section of Bergen-Belsen be converted to a holding area for so-called *Austauschjuden* (exchange Jews). Many of those moved there were subsequently deported to death camps, but a residual number were retained for potential use in exchanges. According to guidelines issued in August 1943 by the chief of the Gestapo, Heinrich Müller, these Jews were to be regarded "not as prisoners but as camp inmates." In particular, they were to be permitted some degree of correspondence with relatives abroad.[41]

On January 11, 1944 a group of 1,037 prisoners, including 436 earmarked for a Palestine exchange, left Westerbork for Bergen-Belsen. The fact that they were transported in third-class passenger carriages aroused hopes that they might be treated like human beings rather than animals. The family of Fré Tal-Vaz Dias were among those who left. Gertrude, however, was not included in the transfer. Two further groups left for Bergen-Belsen in February, but again Gertrude remained behind.

As very few Jews, other than those who had gone "under water," remained at large in the country, departures from Westerbork now exceeded arrivals, and the camp population began to decline. By early February 1944, there were no more than sixty-five hundred prisoners left, nine hundred of whom were in the camp hospital. On February 4, Gemmeker sent an urgent cable to Zoepf in The Hague, recommending the immediate deportation, "regardless of infectious or feverish illnesses, of all sick Jews." He added: "I have the impression that if a radical deportation of the sick Jews were carried through, they would get better very quickly and no longer seek refuge in the hospital."[42] Aus der Fünten visited the camp and set aside many exemption certificates, including those protecting hospital patients. "When he comes to stay at Westerbork, something terrible always happens," commented a prisoner diarist.[43] On February 8, a transport left for the east with 1,015 prisoners, including people on exemption lists and invalids, some of whom were pushed on to the cattle trucks "alongside and on top of one another, just as one would push coffins into a hearse."[44] Again, Gertrude eluded deportation. "The mouse-trap has many doors which are left closed or are opened quite at random," wrote the diarist.[45] By February 25, just 4,230 Jews remained in the camp.

On March 2, Gertrude sent a message to Saly Mayer. It was transmitted by Rita Vuyk, daughter of Gertrude's deceased friend, Pieter Vuyk. Gertrude said that she was in good health and was still in the country (i.e., had not yet been deported).[46] The same day, Rauter reported to Himmler that "the actual Jewish problem in Holland can be regarded as having been solved." Within the next ten days, the last "full Jews" would be deported to the east from Westerbork.[47]

Gertrude was finally sent away from Westerbork by rail on March 15, together with 209 other candidates for exchange. Also in the group with his family was Heinrich Mainz, her collaborator in the Palestine exchange effort, and Eli Dasberg, whose departure for Switzerland Gertrude had tried unsuccessfully to arrange in December 1942. Gertrude was fortunate to be included, since she had not originally been on the approved list for exchange at this time.[48] Among those she left behind in Westerbork were her ex-husband's brother Alfred van Tijn and the two former co-chairmen of the Jewish Council, Cohen and Asscher, though they had all been on earlier exchange lists.[49]

There was a full moon that night, and the prisoners could see the surrounding countryside clearly. The train took a roundabout route through Hanover and other German towns that "seemed to be nothing more than a mass of ruins—a gruesome sight to us—and to such a pass has mankind come—a source of rejoicing."[50] After thirty-six hours they reached the station at Bergen, a few miles from the concentration camp. From the station they were force-marched for three hours to the camp in pouring rain.

"The camp was the most dismal place I had ever seen. It was a picture of barbed wire, SS guards, watchtowers every few yards and again barbed wire." What most shocked Gertrude were the changes that had overtaken the group of prisoners who had come from Westerbork in January. They had left Holland "in good mental and physical condition." "Already the men looked emaciated, ill-kept, cowed—a shadow of their former selves."[51] Their acquaintances in Bergen-Belsen were equally dismayed at the appearance of the new arrivals: "They all have dysentery. Very unbalanced nutrition. Obsessive requests for proper food."[52]

Conditions in Bergen-Belsen at this time were a shade less horrific than in other concentration camps. Some limited correspondence with the outside world was allowed, and Gertrude was able to send word to Saly Mayer, again via Rita Vuyk, of her removal to Germany.[53] But by comparison with Westerbork, the regime at Bergen-Belsen was much more spartan. The work norm was seventy-one hours a week. Meals consisted chiefly of dry bread and turnip broth. On days when there was no soup, the prisoners got a soupspoonful of jam, quark (curd cheese), or herring salad. Gertrude was fortunate in being able to supplement these rations with food parcels that she received from Amsterdam once a week. The wooden, double-decker box beds were filled with sacks stuffed with paper and wood shavings. An inmate recalled that taking a bath at

Bergen-Belsen was "a veritable torture": "By the hundreds we were driven to the baths in columns of five, men and women separately, though the SS was also in charge of the women. We were ordered to undress, hurriedly, in a cold room, and at the sound of a whistle we had to run to a shower bath. The whole procedure lasted six minutes. We returned to the barracks, again in columns of five, marching in the goose step."[54] With its endless roll calls, petty humiliations, and harsh physical conditions, existence in Bergen-Belsen, Helmuth Mainz later wrote, "resembled life in an animal cage."[55]

Upon arrival, Gertrude was put in the camp hospital, as she had developed a high temperature. Unlike the hospital in Westerbork, this one was miserably equipped, overcrowded, and insanitary. Medicines were in short supply, and when some arrived in parcels, they were confiscated by the Germans. In the hospital her condition deteriorated, and a doctor told her she was "in for pneumonia."[56]

On the evening of April 7, the patients held a Passover seder. The youngest child, according to custom, asked the traditional four questions: *Ma nishtano halailo haze mikol haleiloys* ("Why is this night different from all other nights?). The chief rabbi of Leeuwarden, A. S. Levisson, whose bed adjoined Gertrude's, recited the familiar liturgy in Aramaic and Hebrew, with its promise of redemption from slavery: *Ho lakhmo anyo* ("This is the bread of affliction"). "There was suppressed sobbing from many people."[57] Levisson, in Gertrude's eyes "a saintly man," survived until the liberation of the camp but died ten days later.

After several weeks, Gertrude recovered, whereupon she was put to work taking apart old shoes and salvaging reusable parts. Mirjam Bolle, a former secretary in Gertrude's office and now a fellow prisoner, worked with her in the "shoe-barrack," which, she wrote in her diary, was "indescribable. Dirty, stuffy, dark, cold . . . the filthiest work there is."[58]

"At the exit from the camp to the work barracks," Bolle noted, "stands a small shed, three by four meters, with a double-bunk bed. Two young men live there. They do nothing all day but are not allowed out, because they work in the crematorium and probably see too much. We go past them as we go to the shoes. Mrs Van Tijn, who craned her neck to see the guys, got a slap with the words: 'You inquisitive old goat.' "[59]

Whereas in Westerbork inmates had retained a measure of self-government, prisoners in Bergen-Belsen were under the direct control of the SS. Gertrude recorded, however, that two Greek Jews from Salonica had been placed in charge of labor organization: their conduct was "absolutely disgraceful."[60] Discipline was harsh. Punishments, sometimes collective, for minor infractions included being forced to stand for hours on end, imprisonment in unheated isolation cells, or worse. Gertrude reported that "beatings were the rule of the day," although she added that with a single exception, there had been no instance in her experience of ill-treatment resulting in injury.[61] One of the only sources of encouragement was the sight and sound of Allied bomber aircraft formations passing over the camp on their way to pound German cities.

Gertrude got up at 4:30 a.m. every day, attended roll call at 6:10, and then marched to work. There was another roll call at 11:30, then a hurried lunch, a third roll call at 12:30, more work until 6:30, and then the evening roll call. She later reflected that "a certain serenity of temper and temperament helped me to get through in relatively good condition." Most of the prisoners, she noticed, "quarrel violently." Although normally a gregarious person, she found the overcrowding unbearable. "Never one single moment alone or not under observation; even the latrines were 24 in 2 rows without any partition. . . . That was for me the worst; this never-to-be alone for a second and always voices and noise and smell and filth."[62] Given the lamentable sanitary conditions, it is hardly surprising that dysentery was rampant.

Camp life was an incongruous mixture of the brutal and the banal. One day Gertrude saw a rabbit on the other side of the fence. Over the next few days, it kept coming back. "It seemed to have no fear, and watching it gave us somehow a sense of freedom. Then, one Sunday, a German, who must have watched us from his tower, shot the rabbit. The shock and senseless brutality of it made me ill."[63]

Between January 1 and July 31, 1944, the number of *Austauschjuden* held at Bergen-Belsen grew from 379 to 4,100, but only 524 actually left Nazi territory before the end of the war.[64] On April 26, there was a collective, electric shock of hope when all holders of "Palestinian papers" were ordered to step out of the early afternoon assembly. They were then individually called up and examined by the commandant and a civilian official, from either the German Foreign Ministry or the International Red Cross. Out of 1,300 people assembled, only 272 were summoned; and of these, 22 did not appear, as they were in the hospital. The 250 who remained, one of whom was Gertrude, were ordered to go and collect their belongings and reappear in an hour. They were then marched off to a "quarantine" barrack, where they were held under somewhat improved conditions for four weeks, without being told what was to become of them.

On May 28, in the middle of an air-raid alarm, they were ordered out for another inspection by the commandant. Again the list of names was read out. Proceedings were interrupted when Allied planes flew overhead, occasioning inward excitement among the prisoners, who did not dare, in the presence of the commandant, to look up to the sky. When the reading of the list resumed, some of the persons present were not included, leaving just 222 who were told to prepare for departure. The remainder were ordered to return to the ordinary barracks. Among those who had been excluded was Abel Herzberg.

Gertrude had already discovered how easy it was to be knocked off an exchange list, but her friends had been working hard to save her. On May 19, Moses Leavitt, head of the Joint, had written to Lawrence Lesser, a senior figure on the staff of the War Refugee Board. This was the executive agency established by order of President Roosevelt the previous January to "rescue the victims of enemy persecution who are in imminent danger of death."[65] The letter, which followed an earlier conversation, urged that special efforts be made on behalf of six persons (and their families) who had played a role in rescue and relief activities in western Europe in collaboration with the Joint. Five of these were French; the sixth was Gertrude, who appeared at the head of the list. Leavitt stressed that she had "stuck to her post at the risk of her life even though she had many opportunities to escape."[66] The Joint was also in touch with the Dutch government in London. Whether because of the Joint's pressure or through sheer luck, Gertrude's name remained on the list.

On May 31 came news that they would leave the next day. At 7:00 a.m. on June 1, all stood ready to go. But nothing happened. They sat on their luggage and waited. And waited. Then two SS men appeared and announced that they were not leaving after all. Gertrude collapsed. "I had—although nobody noticed it, a real breakdown then—two heart attacks; and I slept for two days and two nights. The disappointment was too terrible."[67] Whether she really suffered heart attacks we cannot know. But she evidently came closer than ever before to opening her little yellow tin and taking the cyanide pill.

On June 6 they were ordered to leave the "quarantine" barrack and return to the main camp.[68] Lingering hope turned to despair. "We weren't marching off towards freedom but back to a slave existence that we had believed we had already escaped," one of the prisoners later recalled.[69] A few hours later, the roller coaster of emotions switched direction again as news filtered through of the Allied landings in Normandy. But days once more lengthened into weeks, and their spirits sank. On one occasion, Allied bombers raided a nearby SS installation. Several people, both SS personnel and non-Jewish prisoners in a neighboring camp, were killed. Gertrude had a narrow escape during this "diving attack."[70]

Suddenly, at five in the morning on June 29, guards told them to get ready to leave. Theresa Klee, the German-Jewish widow of a member of the Jewish Council's *Beirat*, remained behind voluntarily in Bergen-Belsen to look after her granddaughters. She perished; the girls survived.[71] Helmuth Mainz and his family were added to the list at the last moment as substitutes. Gertrude, too, might have declined to leave if Brahn had been in the camp with her. But without him, she had nothing to hold her there. The entire day of June 29 was devoted to a meticulous search of the prisoners' belongings and persons. All papers except official documents were destroyed. Gertrude's cyanide pill was confiscated by an SS officer.

At dawn on June 30, Gertrude left Bergen-Belsen as part of the group of 222 people. About two-thirds were females and one-third males, most of the latter either boys or men above the age of forty-five. There were 99 Dutch citizens and 77 German Jews. The rest were mainly holders of Latin American papers. Just four were Palestinian citizens.

Escorted by guards and dogs, they were marched out of the camp to the railway station. "It is still dark," wrote Helmuth Mainz. "The chimney of the crematorium (Kesselhaus) rises black to the star-glittered sky."[72] "At the station," Gertrude later recalled, "our hopes rose. Waiting for us was an ordinary train, not the sealed, windowless freight cars used to transport Jews to Poland."[73]

The journey to Vienna took two days. In Nuremberg, the passengers could see the devastation caused by RAF bombing two months earlier. They stayed overnight in Vienna in a hostel for the homeless. This was "the very home in which Hitler had spent some time when as a young man he had been without work and shelter."[74] The six-story building at 27 Meldemannstrasse in the suburb of Brigittenau, said to be the most modern such establishment in Europe when it opened in 1905, had been financed partly by donations from Jewish families, including the Rothschilds.[75] There was room for up to 544 residents. For the first time in several months, Gertrude encountered a clean washroom and proper beds with sheets. The severely undernourished prisoner-guests were served hot meals and, luxury of luxuries, sweetened tea and coffee with Viennese specialty cakes. "We felt as if we were in the Grand Hotel in St Moritz," wrote Helmuth Mainz.[76] Remarkably, they received a visit from an assistant to Josef Löwenherz, who still functioned as the nominal head of the Jewish community but "could not come personally." The man reported that of the city's prewar Jewish population, which he said had been 210,000, no more than 182 were still living there above ground.

In Vienna, the group was joined by a further sixty-one prisoners, mainly from the camp at Vittel in France. The next day they all resumed their journey from the Ostbahnhof. Their train now had sleeping accommodations and a restaurant car. The carriages, emblazoned with swastikas on the outside, boasted plush upholstered seats. The group was accompanied by three German policemen, a German Foreign Ministry representative, two German Red Cross nurses, and a Swiss diplomat. As the train rattled through Budapest at night, they saw fires burning from more Allied bombing. In the course of this stage of the journey, they were authorized to remove their yellow-star badges. Gertrude kept hers carefully with the few other relics of her ordeal. Traversing northern Yugoslavia, the train seemed to come under aerial attack. It came to a halt for several hours as the passengers listened to nearby explosions and wondered whether, on the cusp of liberation, they might become victims of their enemies' enemies. In Belgrade, oil storage tanks near the station were ablaze. Passing through the Bulgarian countryside, the train was assaulted at every halt by swarms of peasant women and children offering fruit for sale.

On July 6, they reached Istanbul. At last on neutral territory, they could begin to breathe freely. Representatives of the Jewish Agency welcomed them at the station. Gertrude sent cables to Saly Mayer and to her children.[77] The travelers were placed aboard a coastal steamer, which took them on a sightseeing trip around the Bosphorus and the Sea of Marmara. The German officials left in order to escort the 114 German exchangees, mainly Templers from Palestine, back to the homeland that most of them had never seen. The two groups never came face to face. The Germans were accorded a festive welcome when they reached Vienna. But on arrival at their final destination, Stuttgart, they were struck by a British air raid in which ten of them were killed.

Leaving behind one woman who had taken ill en route and died in a hospital in Istanbul, 282 Jews continued their journey from Haydarpaşa station on a high-class train across Anatolia. At Meydan Ekbez on the Turkish-Syrian border, Palestinian Jewish and British police officers met the train to accompany them on the last leg of their journey through Syria and Lebanon. As they crossed the frontier into the Holy Land at Ras al-Nakura (Rosh Ha-Nikra), the passengers joined hands and sang *Hatikva* ("Hope," the Zionist anthem).

Gertrude's route from Westerbork to Haifa, 1943–1944

Their ten-day journey ended on the afternoon of July 10, when they reached Haifa. They were greeted with flowers. Among those waiting on the platform was Mirjam de Leeuw, who called it "one of the happiest moments of our lives."[78] The arriving passengers could hardly believe their good fortune. A reporter noted "tears of happiness rolling down their emaciated faces."[79] But among the waiting crowd were many grief-stricken faces of people disappointed in their hope of meeting loved ones. A Palestine government report noted that the arriving Jews "were physically in very poor condition."[80]

Gertrude and the others were taken to an internment camp at Athlit, which had recently been vacated by the departing Germans.

A military commission questioned them. Gertrude, though realizing that some form of screening was necessary, could barely stomach to be once again in an internment camp. Of course, it was not a Nazi concentration camp; in fact, conditions were relatively comfortable. "But still, there was little privacy, and wherever we looked, we saw that cursed barbed wire."[81] From Athlit, Gertrude was sent to Haifa to be interrogated by British security personnel. By coincidence, the officer who questioned her had once inhabited the same house near Johannesburg where Gertrude and her family had lived in the 1920s. They happily exchanged memories of the luxuriant gardens of the Inanda estate. He released her immediately. At last she was free, in body if not in spirit.

CHAPTER ELEVEN

Aftermath

"It is really like being re-born and I am still really rather dazed," Gertrude wrote to her daughter in America a few days after her arrival in Palestine. "I am quite slender again and my hair is quite white. . . . If only life did not include sleepless nights and remembrance of all I have seen."[1] The "serenity of landscape and manner of living" in Palestine formed "too much of a contrast with the rather tumultuous thoughts" that tormented her.[2]

Gertrude's friends rejoiced in her escape from Europe. "When we saw your name on the back of an envelope from Palestine, I must confess we really got a chill up our spines," wrote Morris Troper. "It was truly miraculous."[3]

A little later, Gertrude distributed a circular letter to friends: "Don't expect a coherent letter from me just yet. The change from a German camp to freedom—the change from certainty that one would not live to life itself is so great that somehow it absorbs all my self-control to behave normally." She related what she knew about the fate of those deported to Poland, about conditions in Westerbork and Bergen-Belsen, and about the exchange. She also laid great stress on her differences with David Cohen: "I was in open and fierce opposition to the Joodsche Raad—for some time before the deportations I had already serious conflicts with Cohen, but after the deportations started I was in *open* and *declared* opposition. I had withdrawn from every responsible post and did not carry any responsibility any more politically." She emphasized the "frightful strain" under which she had worked and "the conflict that I had to fight out with myself almost everyday."[4]

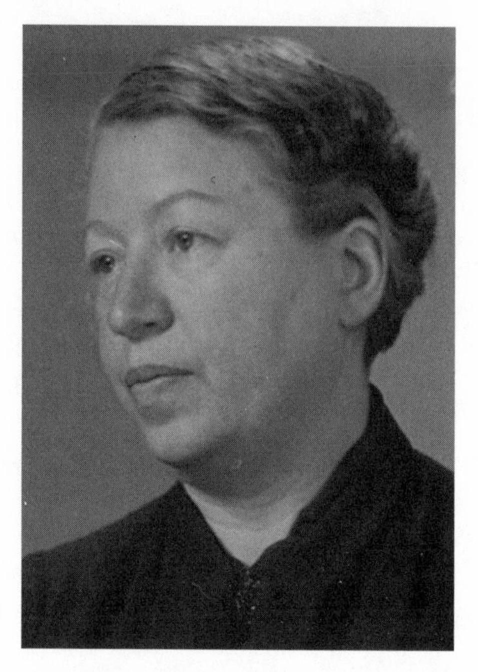

Gertrude after her release from Bergen-Belsen, 1944 *(American Jewish Joint Distribution Committee Archive)*

She wrote a heartfelt letter to Saly Mayer: "I never for one moment thought I would get out. That made me bear everything with such extreme equanimity." Her old friend Henrietta Szold, leader of the women Zionists, had invited her to join her work. But Gertrude decided her first task must be to write a much more detailed report for the Dutch government and the Joint. Then she hoped to be drafted into reconstruction activity in Europe. "What I really want is to go to Theresienstad[t] immediately after the war." That was where she knew Max Brahn had been sent, and she hoped to be reunited with him. Above all, she looked forward to seeing her children: Chedwah was studying in New York, and David was serving in the Princess Irene Brigade, the Dutch contingent in

Eisenhower's Allied army in France. She inquired whether her entry permit to Switzerland was still valid. "I have an idea that Switzerland will be one of the few countries where (from a Jewish point of view) you won't break your heart when you see it back." And she added presciently, "In Holland nothing is left and then there will be the awful questions about co-operation during the war etc etc."[5]

The "awful questions," in fact, haunted her. After staying a short time in Haifa, with a brother of Mirjam de Leeuw, she went to the northern coastal resort of Nahariya and settled down for a month to write an account of what she had witnessed in Holland over the previous four years. It was written at the urgent request of the Dutch foreign minister, Van Kleffens, who cabled the Dutch consulate-general in Jerusalem on August 5 asking for a report from Gertrude on her "experiences outside the Netherlands."[6] She decided to expand this into a full-scale history of the Jews in Holland since 1940.

She found this "heartbreaking document" very hard to write. Given that she had not been permitted by the Germans to bring a single piece of paper, other than her identity documents, out of Bergen-Belsen, and had only limited published documentation available to her in Palestine (though she had access to the annual volumes of Louis de Jong's contemporary chronicle, *Je Maintiendrai*, published in London, from which she could derive a basic chronological and legal framework),[7] her narrative was a remarkable achievement of historical reconstruction. Measured against the massive published and archival documentation now available, it is largely corroborated by the established historical record and is probably the single most significant eyewitness account of the destruction of Dutch Jewry.[8]

Gertrude insisted that her report was only a draft and merely recounted "plain facts." Proceeding in chronological order, she provided a narrative of the successive stages of German policy. She discussed the reactions of the Dutch Jews and of the general population, analyzed the history of the Westerbork camp, and provided a critical commentary on the conduct of the Jewish Council.

Although she tried to produce an objective account, she did not write *sine ira ac studio.* She warned at the outset: "Let those who have not lived under such terrible stress beware before they lightly judge those whose hands were forced to act against their own people and therefore—I am afraid when the real reckoning comes—against themselves."[9] Yet in the end the report was an indictment of the leaders of the Jewish Council of which she had been a staff member for more than two years. Gertrude acknowledged that Asscher and Cohen had "honestly believed that by carrying out German orders they avoided worse things happening to the Jews." But she showed that this constantly repeated refrain became a rationalization for pitiful abasement before the Germans' genocidal policy.

The memorandum was couched in a much more personal style than any of her earlier reports to the Joint or the Jewish Council. The first person intruded repeatedly, as Gertrude drew on her own direct knowledge and experiences. Far from diminishing its value, this personal ingredient renders the narrative all the more authentic as a historical source. Sensitive to the tragic dimensions of her subject, Gertrude wrote in a sober and measured tone, only occasionally sharpened by an uncharacteristic note of asperity.

One of the earliest, best-informed, and most clearly written accounts of the fate of a Jewish community under Nazi occupation, the report had a significant effect in shaping the contemporary view—and later accounts—of the Nazi genocide in the Netherlands, notably Louis de Jong's monumental *Het Koninkrijk der Nederlanden in de Tweede Wereldoorlog.* This standard history of the German occupation of the Netherlands, which devotes extensive consideration to the persecution of the Jews, relies, as one of its authorities, on Gertrude's testimony.[10] De Jong nevertheless noted that "like nearly everyone," Gertrude found it "easier to evaluate others critically than herself."[11]

Commending the report's mixture of objectivity and personal experience, a recent German historian writes that its "openness and directness" gives the reader the impression that it was written by "a person who thinks and feels."[12] Yet surprisingly, this major historical document has never appeared in print. At the moment of its completion, Gertrude considered turning it into a book but decided that she did not wish to make money out of such a thing. She also felt that the issues discussed were so sensitive that it was "for the few only."[13] Indeed, it could not possibly have been published as long as the war was being waged, since publicity might have endangered several of those she mentioned. She was nevertheless concerned that it be read not only by the Dutch government in London but also by influential people in Palestine and the United States. She pressed the Rescue Committee of the Jewish Agency and the top ranks of the Zionist leadership in Palestine for permission to present it in person.[14] Before distributing it, she appears to have had second thoughts about some of her harsh judgments of the leaders of the Jewish Council, softening these somewhat.[15]

A few weeks after her arrival, the Dutch consul-general in Jerusalem, Charles Marie Dozy, invited her to come see him and suggested that she take up a position in the Dutch Ministry of Social Affairs.[16] The ministry had established a Repatriation Commission to prepare for the reception and reintegration of Dutch citizens who had been deported from the country. Gertrude was invited to become a repatriation commissioner, with special responsibility for deportees returning "from Poland." She would start work in London and proceed, as soon as possible, to the continent. Although the consul-general presented the proposal as his own idea, it had been initiated by the Dutch government in London, following consultations among senior ministers.[17] Evidently Gertrude's reputation had preceded her.

In spite of her long-standing sympathy for Zionism, Gertrude had never contemplated living in Palestine. The government's offer, she hoped, would enable her to participate in the liberation of the camps. She told the consul-general she was inclined to accept, asking only that she be allowed to maintain her long-standing association with the Joint.[18]

When the appointment became known, it immediately aroused opposition. Leib de Leeuw, in his capacity as chairman of the Dutch Immigrants' Association, went to see Dozy to object. He said the appointment "would lead to resistance among Dutch Jews" on the ground that Gertrude had held a leading position in the Jewish Council.[19] Dozy refused, however, in the absence of any supporting evidence of misconduct by Gertrude, to forward this protest to his government.

Failing with the consul-general, De Leeuw and his wife held two meetings with Gertrude herself. The couple did not believe that Gertrude had not solicited the official position. "Though I was outwardly unruffled and serene, these attacks hurt. It was the first time I heard of attempts to brand me, and all other people who had worked under the occupation, as collaborators. . . . If the Dutch government thought I could help, no petty jealousies among Dutch Jews in Palestine would prevent my going to London."[20] Seeing that Gertrude was not to be moved, the De Leeuws promised the cooperation of their association.[21] They parted on a superficially amicable note, but one of Gertrude's oldest friendships had ended.

Before leaving Palestine, Gertrude called to have lunch with Chaim Weizmann and his wife at their home in Rehovot. She regarded this reunion with the Zionist leader, whom she had first met in Amsterdam more than twenty years earlier, as "one of the most moving and most memorable events" of her life.[22] She also paid a touching farewell visit to Henrietta Szold, who died a few weeks later. In a kibbutz she met a former Wieringen student, who had arrived as a young girl in 1939 on the *Dora* and whom Gertrude had allowed to travel even though others had judged her too young.

Gertrude left Jerusalem at the end of November, traveling first to Cairo and then to London. She was shocked at the devastation that had been wrought on the city by the Blitz, the V1 flying bombs, and the V2 rockets, which were still causing severe damage and loss of life. She stood in the middle of what had been Fleet Street and burst into tears.[23]

One of her first calls was on the Dutch prime minister, Pieter Gerbrandy, at Brown's Hotel, where he was living. The head waiter still remembered her from prewar visits with her husband; her meeting with Gerbrandy went less well. As minister of justice in 1939, he had shown some sympathy for the predicament of Jewish refugees on the *Dora*. Now it seemed to Gertrude that he "did not really care about the fate of the Dutch Jews." She upbraided him mercilessly. Abashed, he "repeated over and over again that they [the Dutch government] had been, and still were, powerless." Subsequently, however, she decided that she had wronged him. "He was a deeply religious man, without racial prejudice, and possibly more concerned than he cared to show."[24]

The harshness of this encounter notwithstanding, the government kept its promise to employ her. She was assigned an apartment in a fashionable building on Piccadilly, not far from the government's seat at Stratton House and the repatriation department on St. James's Street. In London she found a little Holland-in-exile, consisting of the royal family, politicians and officials, elements of the reconstituted Dutch armed forces, a Dutch club, and many civilians, including some Dutch Jews. But there was little to satisfy her desire to engage in effective war work. Only the south of the Netherlands had been liberated thus far, so she could not yet return to Amsterdam.

In March 1945 she traveled to Switzerland, ostensibly on official business "to try and do a few things which ought to have been done long ago." "But before I do anything," she wrote to Saly Mayer, "I want to see you. . . . My dear it's quite useless to try and say how much I am looking forward to this meeting.—You have no idea what your kind thoughts have meant to me through all these difficult years. . . . It means so much to me to be able to write 'au revoir soon.' "[25]

Her visit to Switzerland proved to be less idyllic than she had imagined. Upon interviewing some former prisoners from Theresienstadt whose release Mayer had obtained, she learned that Max Brahn was dead. He had insisted on accompanying his wife when she was deported to Auschwitz. Brahn's daughter, Ursula, was in Switzerland, and Gertrude had to break the news to her.

Gertrude found that some of the Jewish refugees from Holland whom she and Mayer had helped to escape to Switzerland earlier in the war were now engaged in bitter financial wrangles with Mayer. They complained that insufficient funds had been allocated to the dispatch of food parcels to Jews in concentration camps, demanded continued support from the Joint or the Swiss Jewish community, and claimed that Mayer was discriminating against them in allocation of funds. They had drawn the International Red Cross, the U.S. War Refugee Board, and other bodies into the disputes. With some difficulty, Gertrude managed to compose these quarrels. At any rate, she sent a report to the Joint claiming to have done so—but the bickering did not stop.[26]

Israel Polak, a semitropical fruit importer from The Hague, whose wartime passage to Switzerland had been facilitated by Gertrude and Mayer, later sued both of them, as well as the Joint.

He claimed reimbursement of money he had paid to Gertrude in Holland, which should have been refunded to him when he reached Switzerland. The case eventually reached the Raad voor het Rechtsherstel (Council for Redress), a special Dutch court established after the liberation to deal with such cases. It concluded that Polak was owed nothing. Commending Gertrude for her wartime actions, the court declared that by utilizing money paid in Holland by Polak and others, she had managed to give succor to those Jews who remained in Amsterdam under threat of death.[27] Gertrude took considerable satisfaction in this formal vindication and in the "very nice things [that the court had said] about me personally and all the work I did in Holland during the war."[28]

On a personal level, her visit to Mayer appears to have been a little uneasy. A stiff, rather deaf, conventional, and unforthcoming character, he seems not to have reciprocated Gertrude's predilection for intense, if platonic, relationships with older, married men. He gave her a watch, and they parted on cordial terms, but Gertrude had apparently overestimated the depth of his feeling for her.

From Switzerland, she traveled to Paris and then to Brussels. There, on April 12, she had an emotional reunion with her son, David, whose army unit was stationed nearby. She had not seen him for five years. News had just arrived of the death of Roosevelt, and people were weeping in the streets. David had just 48 hours' leave. Then he rejoined his unit, and they both went their separate ways to liberated south Holland.

Now came the moment that she had both yearned for and dreaded since her liberation. "It is all this that I think of at night when I cannot sleep," she had written in Palestine the previous October. "What and whom are we going to find when we shall come back into a liberated Holland? Into an occupied Germany? . . . How many of those who were human beings—ordinary human beings—when the Germans came, will be alive and—if alive—what will be their condition when the curtain rings down on the final act?"[29]

She entered a devastated and traumatized land. The Dutch provinces north of the Rhine and Waal Rivers remained under German occupation. After the failure of the Allied landings at Arnhem the previous autumn, the Germans had subjected the Dutch population to brutal reprisals for sabotage attacks by the resistance. The *hongerwinter* of 1944–1945 was one of bitter endurance for Dutch civilians, deprived of food and driven to eating cats, dogs, and tulip bulbs. In desperate search for fuel, they burned furniture, doors, and floorboards, including much of what remained of empty Jewish apartments in Amsterdam.

When Gertrude arrived on Dutch soil, she found chaos, a tangle of red tape, but little for her to do. From Breda she wrote to Mayer on April 20:

> My darling, . . . We are all waiting for "V" day in Breda—it may be announced any moment now, so everybody thinks Fancy celebrating "V" day in Breda. But anywhere is all right as long as this slaughter will stop at last.—We are all terribly worried about our friends and relatives in occupied Holland.—Things are much worse there than people generally realize. Your watch keeps perfect time; to say that I think of you when I wind it at night is a gross understatement. I think of you ever so often at all odd moments during the day and only hope that we may meet again soon. . . . I know you won't find time to write to me privately ever.—But it doesn't really matter. Only look after yourself and keep well and unchanged until we meet again . . . Love, Gertrude

On May 2, still in Breda, frustratingly unable to return either to Amsterdam or to London, she added a postscript: "Darling, I am still in Breda—desperate."[30] Mayer replied a month later, briefly describing a visit he had made to liberated Dachau but avoiding any personal matters and signing, "With my heartiest greetings and all my love, sincerely yours."[31]

Westerbork was liberated by Canadian troops on April 12, 1945: 876 Jews were found alive there. Amsterdam had to wait until all German forces in the Netherlands surrendered on May 5. Two days later, news came that the war was over. Gertrude, stuck in Breda, celebrated with her son amid a population "kissing, hugging, shouting, drinking, singing songs in Dutch and English, the *Wilhelmus* and *God Save the King* over and over again."[32]

A total of 107,000 Jews had been deported, mainly to death camps in Poland. About 5,500 returned. Among the deportees were over 19,000 children, of whom at least 18,000 had been murdered. Of an estimated 28,000 *onderduikers,* perhaps 17,000 had survived in hiding in the Netherlands. A few thousand more Jews had escaped across the frontier or were among the handful spared by the Nazis. The Jewish community that was painfully reconstructed after the liberation was a shattered remnant, numbering no more than 30,000 persons.

Most of those directly responsible for the mass murder of Dutch Jewry were eventually tried and punished. About fifteen thousand Dutch and German citizens were arraigned in Dutch courts for war crimes committed in the Netherlands. Death sentences were passed on 154, of whom 40 were executed. Among these was Hanns Rauter. The former Reichskommissar, Seyss-Inquart, was among the "major war criminals" tried at Nuremberg in 1945–1946. Unrepentant to the end, he was sentenced to death and hanged in October 1946.

Albert Gemmeker, the former commandant of Westerbork, faced a court in Assen, not far from the camp, in 1949. He declared that he did not feel in any way guilty: "Befehl ist Befehl" (Orders are orders).[33] Kurt Schlesinger, the German-Jewish former *Oberster*

Dienstleiter of the camp, offered testimony on his behalf. Gemmeker was sentenced to ten years in prison, of which he served six.

A death sentence passed on Ferdinand Hugo aus der Fünten in December 1949 was commuted to life imprisonment six months later by the minister of justice. In the 1970s, Aus der Fünten became known as one of the "Breda Three"—Nazi war criminals about whose continued incarceration a bitter controversy developed. He was released in 1989 and died a few months later.

Willy Lages was also sentenced to death but was subsequently spared execution. In both cases, the men owed their lives to strong pressure by Queen Juliana, who opposed the death penalty.[34] In a letter to the Dutch government in March 1950, the West German federal chancellor, Konrad Adenauer, urged the Dutch government not to execute any more German war criminals. The minister of justice declared, however, that this intervention had had no bearing on the government's decision making.[35] Lages remained in jail in Breda until 1966, when he was released on account of serious illness. He died in 1971.

Lages's former assistant, Klaus Barbie, achieved notoriety in 1942–1944 as the "Butcher of Lyons." After the war, he was engaged in anti-Communist activities for the American army's counterintelligence corps. With American aid, he eluded arrest by the French and fled to Bolivia, where he lived under an assumed name from 1951 until 1983, when he was extradited to France. In 1987, he was found guilty by a court in Lyons of crimes against humanity and sentenced to life imprisonment. He died in prison in 1991.

Wilhelm Zoepf remained at large in Germany for many years after the war, working as a sports therapist and company registrar. Following pressure from the Netherlands, he was eventually tried in Munich in 1967. He was found guilty of participation in the murder of 54,982 persons and sentenced to nine years in prison.

His former assistant, Gertrud Slottke, led a below-radar existence after the war as secretary of the South German Plant Breeders Association in Stuttgart. She was tried with Zoepf. A newspaper report at the time described her as "a small woman, bitter and stubborn; her voice is energetic, with a sharp sound."[36] She exhibited "the most imperious defiance" towards the court.[37] Slottke was sentenced to five years, of which she served less than three.

Feeling within the Jewish community against former members of the Jewish Council was intense, and many people were disinclined to make fine distinctions. Among those who returned from the camps alive was Eli Dasberg, who had been deported with Gertrude from Westerbork to Bergen-Belsen in March 1944. Unlike her, he had not been included in the Palestine exchange. In early 1945, however, he was suddenly pronounced eligible for a further exchange of seventy-two persons to be conducted via Switzerland. All the members of the group except Dasberg and his family held British, United States, or Latin American citizenship. The Dasbergs perhaps owed their inclusion to the earlier efforts of Gertrude and Mayer to place them on an exchange list. Together with the others, the Dasbergs were moved towards the Swiss border. But before they were able to cross, a new order was received, and they were sent instead to an internment camp in southern Germany. Upon arrival at the railway station at Breda on June 28, Dasberg was immediately asked to stand aside and was denounced as a collaborator. The accusation was soon withdrawn, but Dasberg's return to his native land was full of bitterness, expressed in dark verses that he wrote at the time.[38] He later emigrated to Israel.

In spite of her record of opposition to the council's leadership, Gertrude encountered hostility among surviving Jews. Even before she arrived, Abraham de Jong, a leader of the Jewish Coordination Commission for the Liberated Dutch Area, which had been established in January 1945 at Eindhoven, objected to her appointment:

"When they are repatriated, Jews do not want to see again the same person that they had seen in the service of the Jewish Council helping them leave."[39] Leib de Leeuw, in a letter from Palestine to De Jong, reported on his exchanges with the Dutch consul-general, and took the opportunity to propose himself as a suitable alternative candidate for the job of repatriation commissioner.[40]

Gertrude soon understood that her position in the shattered Dutch Jewish community was untenable. "The moment I talked to them, I felt an icy rejection. Once I saw one of my oldest friends on the street and went to meet him, both arms outstretched. He looked at me, turned on his heels without saying a word, and left me standing, rooted to the ground."[41]

Having narrowly missed each other in Breda, Gertrude and Ernst Laqueur did not meet during her visit to Holland. Their relationship had been marred by the enmity of his wife and family. Laqueur's younger daughter, Liselotte, noted in her diary on May 14 that Gertrude was in Eindhoven, but she hoped not to see her because, despite all the help she had given, Gertrude had caused many quarrels between her parents. A few days later, she recorded that Gertrude had written her father a long letter asking for his assistance in rebutting attacks on her on account of her work for the Jewish Council. "Mrs van Tijn is a bitch [*een loeder*]," she remarked.[42]

In the meantime, Gertrude had been instructed by her superiors to go back to London. She had hoped to return to Amsterdam, but there was no time. She was not sorry to leave. She had been given next to no work and found everything in the country "heartbreakingly disappointing."[43]

After a long wait for a United States visa, she was finally able to travel to New York in early June 1945. There, at last, she was reunited with her daughter. She moved into an apartment in Washington Heights, an area of Manhattan where many German-

Jewish refugees had settled. From New York she wrote to Mayer, pleading with him to visit her.[44] He replied by cable saying he could not do so, offering "heartiest greetings as of old, Saly Mayer."[45]

A less welcome communication arrived shortly afterwards from another former colleague. David Cohen, together with his wife and daughter, had been moved from Westerbork to Theresienstadt in late 1944. He survived and returned to Amsterdam, where he was restored to his university chair. His letter to Gertrude (which has not been found) appears to have queried financial transactions that she had conducted during the war. In her reply, Gertrude gave him some information, noting, "there are still several amounts to be claimed on account of dollar sales, but I think I had better settle this with the Joint." She added, "I am glad to see from your letter that you are back at the University. I do not think it is of any use to talk about the things that happened in the past. I always told you that the differences between us went deeper than you thought and would make working together in the future quite impossible. This does not mean, however, that I do not wish you privately the chance to work at your beloved studies for many years to come."[46] Cohen's response (also not found) seems to have been less cordial, apparently impugning Gertrude's financial probity. She replied on September 30:

> The contents as well as the tone of your letter rather surprised me. . . .
>
> Whether you can rightly call me a member of the "staff" seeing that I drew no salary after July 1942—the date the deportations started and the date at which I went into well known opposition against the policy of the J.R. [Jewish Council] I do not know. But it is a fact that I remained both head of the emigration department and head of the charitative department H[ulp] a[an] V[ertrekkenden] [Help for the Departing] (which had nothing to do with the politics of the J.R.). I practically

> daily hesitated between "going under" and remaining at my post, but always thought I had to do the latter—no matter what my attitude and feelings. . . .
>
> I am sorry we had to have this correspondence. It would have been better if you had not started it, as every attempt to recall past happenings is bound to raise our old controversy. Although I do not intend to live in Holland again, still I am interested for the sake of my children to have my name cleared if there should be any talk about my attitude during the years of the occupation. . . .
>
> Personally I had hoped that it would have been possible to let all these old things rest and start rebuilding. That those who would cause feelings of bitterness should not be the ones to do this reconstruction work seems to me logical. As soon as I heard that there was a certain opposition against me (to my mind unjustly) I immediately withdrew. Fortunately many of my friends who knew my political attitude have come back and I can safely leave it to them to clear up this point if this should become necessary.[47]

The correspondence appears to have ended there.

Cohen continued, however, to snipe at Gertrude from the rear. She had not sent him a copy of her report on wartime Holland (she could not in any case have done so before his liberation). When, in early 1947, he finally secured a copy, he was deeply affronted. He complained that it was "full of lies and intrigues against my collaborators and myself." He declared that he proposed "to write . . . a counter-report [that] . . . will be so sharp and convincing that it will break down the career of Mrs van Tijn. I must confess that it should be my duty to do this; I think that she has become a danger for every organization in which she works, because I have the proofs that she was full of intrigues already in the last year in which we cooperated. And Mrs van Tijn knows very well that when I am really angry (and I am) I am not to be trifled with." Cohen remained "convinced that the line along which I worked was the right one in those days; otherwise I could not live now."[48]

This blustering denunciation was reported to Gertrude. She professed to feel "no personal resentment against Professor C." Their differences were "entirely political." This was "best proven," she maintained, "by the fact that for a long time during the occupation I had been telling Professor C. on many occasions that if we both live to see the end of this I would never again at the end of the war sit down at one table with him." She insisted on the veracity of her report but declared that she wanted to "close this chapter." "I went through too much during the occupation and later in camp, and cannot afford to be constantly reminded of it."[49] From the point of view of Gertrude's mental health, this was probably a wise attitude. Cohen took a different line: for the rest of his life he obsessively defended his wartime policy, which he characterized as one of "passive resistance."[50]

Others placed greater emphasis on the adjective than the noun. In 1946–1947, a Jewish *Ereraad* (Court of Honor) examined the wartime records of Cohen and Asscher. It decided that the former co-chairmen of the Jewish Council had acted dishonorably and should be excluded from any position in the Jewish community for the rest of their lives. They were also barred from attending synagogue services. Although they were not formally excommunicated from the community (in the manner of the *cherem* that had been imposed on Baruch Spinoza in 1656), the verdict represented a severe moral censure. After efforts to set up an appeal tribunal failed, however, the verdict was set aside by a narrow vote of the standing committee of the Ashkenazi Jewish community.

In the course of his defense, Cohen prepared a lengthy rebuttal of Gertrude's report. He admitted that he had previously always admired her reports for their rigor and lucidity. By contrast, this one was the worst he had ever read. She constantly gave herself *le beau rôle* in the narrative, he observed. The report, indeed, had "such a subjective character" that it did not deserve to be called a "contribution to the history of the Jews in the Netherlands during the German Occupation" (a title that Gertrude appears to have given it at a late stage).

Cohen conceded that Gertrude had displayed outstanding organizational talents in her prewar work for the refugees committee, and he maintained that notwithstanding some frictions, they had worked well together. But "from 1941 this good understanding changed." She had shown lack of political understanding. "The hatred for her, that already existed before the war among many even of her closest colleagues, grew constantly. I myself had always defended her and continued to defend her." But she had conspired against him with people such as Bondy and Edelstein. She had always sought prominence; for example, she had ousted him from his position as the primary representative of Dutch Jewry to the League High Commission for Refugees and the Joint. He maintained that when, in May 1943, she had offered her resignation, he had refrained from accepting it only in the hope of keeping some control over her "lies and intrigues." Worse, he alleged that she had known how "in some to me mysterious way to obtain favours from the Germans." Later she had wangled her way from Palestine to London and then to Switzerland, where "her arrogant behavour aroused hatred all round."

All this was merely by way of prefatory remarks. There followed a page-by-page rebuttal of Gertrude's "famous report," in which Cohen attempted to demonstrate its utter historical unreliability, colored as it was (so he alleged) by prejudice, self-promotion, "viciousness," "subjectivity," "scandalous accusations," and, above all, systematic and unscrupulous falsehoods.[51]

This was an astonishing outpouring of invective, all the more so in that it emanated from a normally courteous and mild-mannered man. Cohen seemed almost more furious with Gertrude than with the German war criminals with whom he had dealt. His eight-thousand-word philippic, though catching her report out on some minor details, did not, however, undermine Gertrude's narrative on any substantial issue.

At times, Cohen's critique descended from apologetics (understandable, perhaps, in that his memorandum was prepared as part of his legal defense) into delusions of self-sacrifice. Referring to the visit from Prague to Amsterdam in 1941 of Jacob Edelstein, Gertrude had written: "I think it was he who told Prof. Cohen that he would probably be made the mouthpiece of such dreadful news concerning the Jews that he would become hated and despised by his own people."[52] Commenting on this passage, Cohen saw it as another example of Gertrude's bias against him. "I remember, however, such a conversation, where we talked about the martyrdom of every leader of Jewish people."[53]

On some major points, notably the critical events of July 1942 and May 1943, Cohen's memorandum tended to corroborate rather than discredit Gertrude's account. His quibbles about details only reinforce the foundations of Gertrude's narrative. His repeated complaints about her "intrigues" were, for the most part, conspiracy theorizing; if anything, the repetitive vehemence of Cohen's remonstrances on this score bears out her claim to have distanced herself definitively from the council leaders' policies. In the end, Cohen's single-minded effort to disparage Gertrude's report was, in a way, an implicit acknowledgment of its importance and of the irreparable damage it could—and did—cause to his reputation.

In November 1947, Asscher and Cohen were arrested by order of the public prosecutor in Amsterdam and held for a few weeks. Official inquiries dragged on until July 1950, when the case was dropped "in the public interest," though it was announced that this should not be seen as an exoneration of the two men.[54] Asscher had in the meantime died "isolated and embittered" and, at his express wish, was buried in a non-Jewish graveyard.[55] Cohen persisted until his death in 1967 in his battle to vindicate his conduct during the war. He attributed his prosecution in large measure to the malevolent influence of Gertrude's 1944 report.[56] When confronted with testimony by Aus der Fünten that Gertrude had protested against the registration of Dutch Jews, he dismissed this as "indeed somewhat humorous, since I always had to defend Mrs van Tijn against the charge that she favoured German Jews."[57] In an interview with the Netherlands State Institute for War Documentation in 1952, Cohen denounced Gertrude's version of wartime events as "unbelievable lies."[58]

Cohen adopted a more emollient tone in a volume of memoirs, covering the prewar years, that he published in 1955. He praised Gertrude's "great gifts in the sphere of organization and financial management." He acknowledged her as the chief initiator of the Wieringen *werkdorp*. But he could not refrain from adding a note in response to a comment by Joseph Schwartz of the Joint, who had praised Gertrude for not taking the opportunity, in Lisbon in 1941, to flee to America. Cohen pointed out that she was not alone: none of his fellow workers had sought personal escape that would have brought down vengeance on others.[59]

In November 1945, Gertrude joined the staff of the Joint Distribution Committee. Although she had been closely associated with it for more than a decade, this was the first time she formally became one of its employees. She did not, however, return to Europe. We do not know why. Perhaps she wanted to get as far away as possible from all the horrors she had witnessed. Or perhaps the Joint directors felt it would be more prudent not to send her back to a continent where feeling against the Jewish councils, and by extension against her, was so strong.

Instead, in early 1946, she went to Shanghai. Her mission was to ameliorate the plight of the twenty thousand Jewish refugees from central Europe who had survived the war there. She was employed by the United Nations Relief and Rehabilitation Administration (UNRRA), an agency founded in 1943 to tackle the immense refugee and welfare problems that confronted the Allied nations in areas liberated from Axis control. At the same time, she worked closely with the Joint's representative in the Far East, Charles Jordan.

The Jewish refugee problem at the end of the war was, if anything, even more acute than it had been in 1939. It had now morphed into what was called, in the jargon of the time, a "displaced persons" problem, as survivors of the Nazi camps and ghettos sought new homes outside Europe. The Jewish refugees in Shanghai were in a unique position, having survived the war under the Japanese occupation.[60] Although the Japanese did not share their Nazi allies' anti-Semitic outlook, they crowded most of the Jews into a quasi-ghetto, or "designated area," in Hongkew—a squalid slum area of Shanghai—for the duration of the war. Some died of malnutrition, but most survived and thought only of leaving China. They owed their survival in large measure to the Joint, which contrived, by a variety of means, to provide aid to them through much of the war. Most now wanted to go to the Americas or Australia; a few keen Zionists looked to the Promised Land; and thirty-two hundred, only half-conscious of the scale of the tragedy that had befallen Europe, registered for return to Germany or Austria.[61]

Gertrude addressed this problem with her usual energy. "I sometimes wish I was a little less dynamic," she wrote to her children, "because I am plainly a nuisance to people, but on the other hand if I were I would probably not achieve as much as I do." Personally, however, she felt "disjointed, dislocated, pretty bewildered."[62]

Solomon Trone, who now worked for the Chinese government, met her in Shanghai. He found her "in quite a nervous condition."[63] It was proving extremely difficult to move refugees out of Shanghai. The United States still maintained its long-standing quota restrictions on immigration. Other countries, beset with the manifold tasks of postwar reconstruction, had little appetite for sharing in any new burden. In Palestine, the British mandatory authorities continued to limit Jewish immigration as the country descended into civil war. Germany and Austria, each divided into occupation zones of the four great powers, were already inundated with vast numbers of refugees from east-central Europe. And even where destinations could be found, shipping space out of Shanghai was at a premium.

In March 1946, there were still 13,475 Jewish refugees registered with the Joint in Shanghai, most of them in desperate circumstances, wholly or partly dependent on the organization for survival. Most were stateless, as they had been deprived of their German, Austrian, or Polish citizenships. Gertrude was responsible for rehousing some of them in newly built, sanitary refugee camps. She also tackled her old specialty: securing emigration visas. In the course of her work, she met personalities such as Madame Sun Yat-sen, widow of the founder of the Chinese republic, and the celebrated adventurer General Morris "Two-Gun" Cohen. For most of her time in Shanghai she stayed at the Park Hotel, one of the most modern hotels in the city, but at that time fallen into shabby decrepitude. Although she found satisfaction in her work, her health suffered from the humid heat and insanitary conditions in some of the camps; she suffered from DDT poisoning and contracted dengue fever. After a few months, she had had enough, deciding to resign and return to America.

En route, she stopped in Australia to visit her brother, Ernst. While there, she negotiated with the government on behalf of the

Gertrude (front left, holding flowers) with Jewish refugees and representatives of the Joint Distribution Committee in Shanghai, 1946 *(private collection)*

Joint about the immigration of refugees from Shanghai. Relatives were anxious to bring in their families, but the broader Jewish community was not keen to push the matter in the face of considerable anti-Semitic and xenophobic feeling. Gertrude noted "very concerted attacks in Parliament and—more so—the violent reactions of the Press every time a boat with Jewish immigrants comes to Australia."[64] The problem was compounded by what Gertrude called "jealousies and incompatibilities of personalities" among Jewish leaders and by hints of corruption in the issuing of immigration permits.[65]

Government policy towards immigration of Europeans responded to a mixture of populist and pragmatic impulses. Unknown to Gertrude, at the very same time that a large section of Australian public opinion was agitating against the admission of Jewish refugees, the Australian government was secretly discussing with the British and Palestine authorities plans for the admission of several hundred German Templers who remained in Palestine (some of them still interned there nearly two years after the end of the war). Many of these wished to be reunited with members of their families who had been deported, largely on account of Nazi sympathies, to Australia. It was also proposed to allow the deportees in Australia to remain there. The British high commissioner for Australia candidly informed the British government of the reason for the surprising Australian openness to accepting this group of potential immigrants: "It is understood that the Commonwealth Government have been informed by these persons that their assets in Palestine amount to many millions of pounds and that the Commonwealth authorities are not uninfluenced by the hope that these assets may be transferred to Australia, a matter which they will at a later stage raise."[66] (The hope was not vain. A total of over £3,274,000 was eventually transferred to the government of Australia by the Custodian of Enemy Property in Palestine.)[67]

Notwithstanding this unpropitious background, Gertrude found a sympathetic ear in the minister of immigration, Arthur Calwell. He was a convinced supporter of large-scale immigration, but even Calwell bent to the xenophobic wind. He told her that "he did not wish one boat to bring, say, a thousand Jewish immigrants" all at once. "The figure of 25% [of Jews on any one boat] was repeatedly mentioned."[68] Calwell later wrote, "We had to insist that half the accommodation in these wretched vessels must be sold to non-Jewish people. It would have created a great wave of anti-Semitism and would have been electorally disastrous for the Labor Party had we not made this decision."[69] He nonetheless gave approval for an influx of around two thousand to twenty-five hundred Jews from Shanghai.[70] It was further agreed that a certain number of Jewish "Displaced Persons" would be admitted from Europe. By

January 1947, Gertrude was able to pronounce her "mission here . . . successful beyond everybody's expectations."[71] Australia admitted some Jews from Shanghai, but the Jewish refugee problem there was not resolved until the end of the decade.

The Joint was pleased with her performance in the Far East and would have extended her contract. But on returning to New York, she decided that she could no longer face the grueling demands of refugee work. Instead, she accepted a job offer from Julius Simon, a Dutch Zionist and old friend, who headed the Palestine Economic Corporation. This body, connected with the Joint, organized Jewish investment in Palestine. The work was routine and unemotional, a far cry from everything she had done over the previous fourteen years.

Since leaving Europe, she had continued to correspond with Ernst Laqueur. In 1947, he planned a visit to New York, and Gertrude looked forward eagerly to their reunion.

> Through all these years, [she wrote to him] your letters have meant much to me; but one hour together will be better than all those many pages. . . . Almost too much has happened since I saw you last at the Amstel station. I do not know in what way these years have changed me. One thing has surely not altered: my love for you. From your letters it seems the same is true for you. I still refuse to dye my hair. I still drink coffee, black and strong, all day. I still chain-smoke. . . . I am taking a week's holiday when you arrive and shall meet the boat. To think that this will really be my last letter for a long, long time."[72]

But they never met again. Shortly afterwards, while on holiday in Switzerland, Laqueur died suddenly of a heart attack. Gertrude learned of his death when she opened the *New York Times* and saw his obituary.[73] Her last letter to him was returned unopened.

Grief stricken, she gave up her job and set off on a long road trip through America with her friend Miriam Schloessinger, who had moved from Palestine to New York in 1939. Struck by the arresting beauty of Taos, New Mexico, and by the presence of an artists' and writers' community, Gertrude decided to settle there and build a new life for herself. Laqueur had left her a small bequest, and with the help of this she bought an old adobe house. Over the next few years she wrote commentaries on international affairs for the local newspaper, *El Crepusculo*, and made friends among the town's cosmopolitan residents, including Frieda Lawrence, widow of D. H. Lawrence.

She also wrote her memoirs. James G. McDonald and Curt Bondy tried to help her find a publisher but without success. The problem was not lack of literary quality, since the book was written with flair, color, and zest. And as regards her depiction of the war period, it is now possible, as in the case of her report of October 1944, to check her account against other surviving evidence; with few exceptions, it passes the test of historical veracity. But perhaps that in itself was the problem. Gertrude's record of gray wartime realities was too ambivalent for those who sought a comfortingly black-and-white version of history. She never found a publisher; the manuscript languished and was eventually consigned to an archive.

In 1958, Gertrude moved to Oregon to be close to her daughter, who had married and was working there. Family worries, financial difficulties, and health problems began to weigh on her. But she remained active in liberal politics, even participating in Martin Luther King Jr.'s march on Washington in August 1963. She returned to Europe for a year in 1964, revisiting London and Amsterdam, and meeting old friends. She also traveled to Israel, where she was treated as an honored guest. On a trip to New York in 1967, she was reunited with Gideon Rufer, her fellow conspirator in the voyage of the *Dora*, who, as Gideon Rafael, was serving as Israeli ambassador to the United Nations.

Although she was now what she called a "cookie-jar grandmother," she found new causes.[74] In 1968, she campaigned for the anti-war presidential candidacy of Eugene McCarthy. She wrote an article on the history of the Wieringen *werkdorp*.[75] Her research brought her back in touch with many of the *werkdorp*'s former students, scattered round the world, who wrote her letters full of memories and appreciation for what she had done for them.

The historian Yehuda Bauer, who visited her in May 1968 to talk about her wartime experiences, found her a "very sharp, determined lady, furious at the whole world."[76] A few months later, Gertrude gave an interview, rather reluctantly, to the local Jewish newspaper in Portland. The paper reported that she continued to live a full social and cultural life in her "pleasant, book-stacked apartment," above all valuing "the serenity of privacy."[77] But the deaths of close friends—Solomon Trone in 1969, and Miriam Schloessinger and Curt Bondy in 1972—saddened her, and she felt increasingly lonely.

Gertrude died on July 7, 1974, in Portland, three days after her eighty-third birthday. Friends were urged not to send flowers (not customary at Jewish funerals) but to make contributions to the Jewish Welfare Federation or the American Civil Liberties Union. Later that month, her cremated remains were scattered from the air about forty-five miles east of Portland, above the slopes of Mount Hood—the highest point in Oregon and a dormant volcano.

CHAPTER TWELVE

A Reckoning

The life of Gertrude van Tijn, especially the record of her activity between 1933 and 1945, touches on some of the central moral-historical issues of the twentieth century. Those were famously articulated and addressed by Gertrude's contemporary Hannah Arendt in her book *Eichmann in Jerusalem*. There, she excoriated the Jewish councils in occupied Europe, whose members she portrayed as pusillanimous instruments of the Nazi genocidal apparatus.

Gertrude shared many characteristics with Arendt. Both were products of the assimilated German-Jewish bourgeoisie; both were brought up barely conscious of their Jewish origin; both acquired in their twenties a sudden awareness of and profound interest in Jewishness and Zionism; both were well-educated, sophisticated, and independent-minded; both worked on behalf of Jewish refugees in the 1930s; both were interned in camps during the war but managed to get out. The two never met, but their paths crossed on one occasion: in Lisbon in early May 1941, just as Gertrude was arriving, Arendt embarked for America. Gertrude, too, could have fled across the Atlantic, and no one would have blamed her, just as no one thinks of blaming Arendt for choosing to escape. Gertrude, however, chose the more morally challenging path of returning to her post in Amsterdam.

Arendt's attack on the Jewish councils owed much to the influence of the pioneer historian of the *shoah*, Raul Hilberg. In his *Destruction of the European Jews*, he explained what he saw as the complicity of the councils in the annihilation of their own people by referring to what he alleged was the traditional passivity of Jewish society in eastern Europe. An obvious objection to this interpretation arose from the fact that the councils (or similar bodies, such as the Reichsvereinigung) in largely nontraditional Jewish communities—such as those of Germany, France, and the Netherlands—exhibited patterns of behavior very similar to those of their analogues in Poland and other countries of east-central Europe. Hilberg later modified his views on the subject.

An alternative explanation for the conduct of the Amsterdam Jewish Council has been proposed by some historians who stress the conformist nature of Dutch society, the efficiency of Dutch bureaucracy, and the general inclination of Dutch Jews to follow what they saw as the instructions of the Dutch government. The first interpretation saw the council as hobbled by supposedly essential Jewish characteristics; the second, by supposedly essential Dutch ones.[1]

Gertrude's critique of the Amsterdam Jewish Council, followed in large measure by the historian Jacques Presser in his book *Ashes in the Wind*, focused more on the personal attributes of the council's leaders, Asscher and Cohen: on the alleged weaknesses of their personalities, and on the fatal errors in their decision making. The effectiveness of Gertrude's attack on the Council was, however, undermined by her own participation in its work during almost the whole of its history.

Conscious of this potential opening for criticism, Gertrude was determined to distinguish her position from that of the council's heads and to rebut censure of her own actions. The report that she wrote in Palestine in October 1944 must be seen, in part, as an exercise in self-exculpation, designed to anticipate and repudiate any attempt to impugn her conduct between 1940 and 1943. In this it had only limited success. As we have seen, Gertrude encountered strong hostility from many Dutch Jews even before her return to the Netherlands in the first days of the liberation.

On June 8, 1945, two days before she left England, Gertrude decided to address the issue head-on in a letter to the Jewish Advisory Commission to the Dutch Government in London: "It has come to my knowledge that certain rumours are current in Holland regarding my conduct in Holland during the occupation in connection with Jewish work done by me. If this is the case I should appreciate it if a full official investigation were to be held and I should be grateful if you were to take the necessary steps to assure that this be done." Noting that she was about to leave for the United States, she declared herself "willing to return at any time to Holland if this should become necessary."[2] Gertrude later wrote that an official investigation had been carried out and had cleared her.[3] Although no details of any formal inquiry appear to survive, the government archives contain a letter to the ministry of justice, dated May 1, 1945, from the foreign department of the Netherlands police in London confirming that "from the political point of view nothing [was] known against" her.[4] She was in any case already clearly regarded as trustworthy, since in November 1944 the Dutch consulate-general in Jerusalem had authorized her to deliver sealed official dispatches to the Dutch legation in Cairo. For this purpose, she was granted a quasi-diplomatic laissez-passer, which was renewed for two years in 1946.[5] In 1949, as we have noted, she was accorded judicial vindication by a Dutch court in the Polak case. Gertrude also stated in her memoir that "my name was cleared by the Dutch Zionist Organization, when, some time later, they held their own private trial."[6] No record has been found of that in the archive of the Netherlands Zionist Federation—which remains, however, in a state of some disorder.

Censure of Gertrude's wartime behavior was not limited to Holland. As soon as she arrived in Palestine in 1944, she found herself the target of criticism and backbiting. In particular, she fell out with Mirjam de Leeuw. Much later, in 1978, when both Mirjam and Gertrude were dead, Mirjam's widower, Leib, wrote a savage denunciation of Gertrude, which he lodged at the Netherlands State Institute of War Documentation. He said that he considered it his duty to do so "in order that researchers in the future know that they should be very careful with her information."

Strangely, De Leeuw's attack focused not so much on Gertrude's actions in occupied Amsterdam as on her conduct in 1944. He complained that immediately upon arrival in Istanbul, en route to Palestine with the other exchangees, she had sent a telegram to Queen Wilhelmina in London, offering to go to England to report on German persecution of the Jews in the Netherlands. He noted that Gertrude had blamed Mirjam for her non-inclusion in the first list of proposed exchangees.[7] When the De Leeuws learned that Gertrude was writing a report on the destruction of Dutch Jewry, they offered to help her write it "so that it would have greater value." Leib even went to visit her in Nahariya two or three times to persuade her to agree to their proposal. She refused. "I am writing the report on my own and I know what I must write and will write," he recalled her saying.

The De Leeuws were evidently furious at what they appear to have regarded as Gertrude's usurpation of the role of custodian of the Dutch Jewish memory. Perhaps they were also fearful of what her report might contain by way of criticism of their committee. They found her "aggressive, morbidly ambitious, avid for power, and not always honest in her writings, speech, and actions. She always had to play first violin." Gertrude's failure to furnish them with a copy of the report made the couple even more angry. In his

1978 memorandum, De Leeuw alleged that Gertrude had deliberately held back lists of proposed exchangees for days or even weeks and then come forward with them, claiming that she herself had drawn them up.[8]

This memorandum was apparently designed to dissuade its recipient, Louis de Jong—head of the institute—from continuing to regard Gertrude's report as reliable evidence of events in Holland during the occupation.

The attack, however, fails to carry conviction. The accusation that Gertrude wished to be "first violin" does not conform to much of what we know about Gertrude's work in the decade after 1933, when she worked in the shadow of David Cohen and rarely thrust herself forward or sought publicity or honors. Gertrude's telegram to the queen from Istanbul (if it was sent)[9] was not publicized. Gertrude undoubtedly, and not unreasonably, regarded it as important to inform the Netherlands authorities in London as soon as possible of everything she knew about the annihilation of Dutch Jewry. She was at that moment in a better position than almost anyone else to provide such information. The monarch was known to welcome communication with recently exiled subjects, as she wished to remain in touch with events in her country.[10] In a broadcast to her people in October 1942, she had declared herself "personally affected" by "the systematic extermination" of the Dutch Jews.[11] As we have seen, when Gertrude eventually reached London, she called on Prime Minister Gerbrandy and pulled no punches in her condemnation of what she saw as the London government's inaction in relation to the Dutch Jews.

As for the attempt to undermine the veracity of Gertrude's report, De Leeuw's memorandum is long on vituperation but short on specific detail. De Leeuw does not, indeed, adduce a single piece of evidence that would serve to cast doubt on its accuracy on any substantial point. Nor, one might surmise, was he in a position to do so on a firsthand basis, since he and his wife had been resident in Palestine throughout the period covered by Gertrude's narrative, whereas she had been an eyewitness to the catastrophe in Holland. Quite why they felt they could add "more value" to the report therefore remains unclear. In the memorandum, De Leeuw asserts that he could produce five witnesses who would support his critique; but he does not supply their names, and from what he writes, their disapproval was more of Gertrude's character than of her account of events.

The precipitant of this imbroglio was evidently the difficult birthing of the exchange lists. The De Leeuws seemed to regard Gertrude as a competitor for the honor of having brought about the exchange. There is no evidence to support one of the few specific allegations of De Leeuw—that Gertrude delayed submission of lists. The holdups seem to have occurred elsewhere.[12] Given the many obstacles that bedeviled the exchange negotiations, it is understandable that all those involved felt a certain frustration. But it is hard to see what Gertrude might have thought to gain by procrastination. What is certain is that she was excluded from the list that Mirjam submitted to the Jewish Agency on March 19, 1943. Perhaps the De Leeuws felt a twinge of guilt on this account and therefore sought to turn tables by accusing the friend whom they had wronged.

These recriminations were more than just a miserable squabble among old friends. Gertrude's conduct in the decade after 1933 inevitably gives rise to several hard questions. How, then, should we assess Gertrude's conduct during the twelve years of Nazi power?

This question can be answered, in part, in quantifiable terms. From its formation in 1933 until the end of 1940, the Committee for Jewish Refugees facilitated the emigration from Holland of 18,494 people (of course, more left under their own steam), most of them refugees from Germany and Austria. Of these, at least 350 were students of the *werkdorp* at Wieringen. To these numbers must be added the 300 or so emigrants who left Amsterdam for Palestine on the *Dora* in the summer of 1939, the nearly 2,000 whose departure from the Third Reich via ports in Italy or Scandinavia in the autumn of 1939 was facilitated by the Amsterdam committee, the 66 who left Lisbon in December 1940 for the Dutch East Indies, and at least some of the passengers on the three voyages of the SS *Mouzinho* from Lisbon to New York in 1941.

Several hundred more were able to leave Holland between 1941 and 1944, thanks at least in part to Gertrude and her co-workers. These included a small number of legal emigrants, the few hundred who were able to proceed to Spain or Switzerland thanks to various bribery schemes, and the exchangees who traveled with Gertrude from Bergen-Belsen to Palestine in the summer of 1944.

Were it not for the work of Gertrude and her colleagues, the great majority of these 22,000 or so German, Austrian, and Dutch Jews would probably have perished at the hands of the Nazis. This was a significant lifesaving achievement, accomplished against enormous odds and in the face of a myriad of conflicting pressures and constraints.

Of course, Gertrude did not achieve this by herself. Much of her efficacy, indeed, arose from her capacity to work with others. David Cohen, of whose wartime conduct she was so critical, must certainly share much of the credit for what was achieved for refugees in Holland between 1933 and 1940.

The committee's work has not, however, won universal praise. Historians have found fault with its subservience to government restrictionism, its bias against Communists, and its willingness, in the early years, to send refugees back to Germany.[13] Although, as we have seen, there is substance to all three criticisms, there is little ground for concluding that a different stance by the committee on any of these fronts would have made much difference to the outcome. More persuasive is the view expressed by De Jong and others that the compliant attitude of the committee towards the Dutch authorities prefigured and to some degree paved the way for the submissive mien of Cohen and his colleagues towards the occupation regime.

Is Gertrude's conduct after May 1940 open to similar criticism? Was she, from the outset, a dupe of the Nazis in her belief that Jewish emigration might still be possible? Was the decision to send her to Lisbon simply a ploy to disguise the Nazis' true intentions? De Jong opts for this view, calling it a "form of deception" and a ruse.[14] But that was by no means certainly the case. Nazi policy makers in the Netherlands in the spring of 1941 were still jockeying for position and assessing various alternative forms of anti-Jewish action. They had not yet received clear and unequivocal orders from Berlin on the "final solution." While it is very doubtful that any mass exodus of Jews from the Netherlands was feasible at that stage, Nazi actions elsewhere in western Europe indicate that, so far as they were concerned, the exit doors were not yet sealed. Although Gertrude's Nazi interlocutor in Amsterdam professed disappointment in the response she brought back from the Joint, the most fundamental obstacles to the success of her mission were the scarcity of passenger shipping space across the Atlantic and the refusal of the United States and British governments to soften their immigration policies in relation to Jewish refugees. Gertrude's optimism after her return from Lisbon about obtaining German permission for large-scale Jewish emigration may in retrospect seem naive. But in the context of the time, it appears quite logical, especially when considered against the backdrop of Nazi encouragement and stimulation of the departure of half of all the Jews in Germany since 1933. At any rate, Gertrude cannot be criticized for exploring every possible opportunity, however farfetched, for extricating Jews from Nazi Europe.

If Gertrude is to be censured for naiveté, the Wieringen episode of June 1941 must bulk large. Of all her wartime actions, this troubled her most for the rest of her life. In her interview with Yehuda Bauer in 1968, she admitted that "she felt guilty of one mistake, and that was the fact that she handed over a list of the Wieringen group to the Nazis." Their assurance that they merely wanted to return the students to the farm had "seemed reasonable enough at the time," but Gertrude nevertheless "felt that she had committed a grave error in giving them any names at any time."[15]

For years afterwards, Gertrude was bitterly attacked for her part in this. Citing postwar testimonies by Willy Lages and Abel Herzberg, the historians of the *werkdorp* find the criticism overblown and suggest that Gertrude was guilty at most of credulity.[16] But they also consider that Gertrude and the Jewish Council may be blamed for not drawing correct conclusions soon enough from the affair. "In this respect," they write, "Mrs van Tijn was insufficiently decisive and the Jewish Council embarked on a slippery slope."[17]

No doubt Gertrude was deceived by Klaus Barbie in this instance, but no conscious sacrifice was made. Years later, Cohen attempted to shuffle off responsibility, from the Jewish Council to the directors of the foundation that administered Wieringen.[18] Later still, he was more self-critical but entered a plea in mitigation: "my only excuse, if excuse it be, can be that we had no conception at that time of the villainous nature of these people. Barbie had invoked his honour as a German officer."[19]

In the relationship between Cohen and Gertrude and its ugly denouement, we come to the heart of the dilemma that confronted Jewish leadership in occupied Europe. In a second volume of memoirs covering the wartime years, published only after his death, Cohen disputed the notion that Gertrude had been any more of a resister than he himself.[20] He attributed their falling-out not to disputes over policy but to amour-propre and pique on her part.

> The difficulty was that she wanted to extend her influence to other areas and could not bear that the advice of other staff members had more influence on me than her expert advice had had before the war. She therefore presented herself as an opponent of my policy and as an opponent of the Jewish Council even though she herself had gone along with it. She was especially irritated that I had not allowed her to attend the daily meetings of our secretariat. However, this was impossible because many of her closest associates distrusted her so much that her presence at those meetings would have given rise to the greatest complication. My staff warned me strongly against her because she was by nature a great intriguer—something of which I became aware only later as her efforts bore no fruit. I considered her work, however, of such importance that I never wanted to let her go. She then issued a report in wartime in which she attacked not only me but even more strongly some of our colleagues who were her friends. This document, that was sent to the London government, is full of easily detectable lies. I cannot describe it in any other way, because she possessed an excellent memory and her reports before the war in our Jewish organizations were famous for their accuracy. That is why I was through with her after the war. Her attempts to shake off responsibility for the actions of the Jewish Council failed utterly.[21]

Cohen's final onslaught was notable for its refusal to acknowledge any substantial political difference with Gertrude.

He rejected the notion that Gertrude's departments on Lijnbaansgracht had operated independently, insisting that the Jewish Council had been a single entity.[22] Cohen dismissed Gertrude's statement that after the Wieringen episode, she had determined never again to hand over any lists of Jews to the Germans. He denied that she was alone in this attitude. He and his colleagues, too, he maintained, never again submitted any lists, save for requests for exemption from anti-Jewish measures.[23] Cohen pointed out that Gertrude herself had been responsible for drawing up *that* kind of list—for example, the Palestine exchange lists. He denied flatly that he had ever handed over to Aus der Fünten any lists of Jews for deportation.

This claim might be considered difficult to sustain, given Cohen's authorization for the preparation by his staff of the Zentralstelle's *cartothèque* and, above all, his selection of council employees to be deported in May 1943.[24] That, after all, was the critical point at which the council leaders moved, as one historian has put it, from "negative" to "positive" selection.[25] Anticipating such an objection, Cohen contrasted Gertrude's absolute refusal to hand over lists to Aus der Fünten, which, he wrote, simply resulted in the German threatening to round up the Jews anyway, with his own effort in such cases to resort to delay. That, he declared, was "invariably effective." Even in the case of the selection of Jewish Council employees in May 1943, he averred, "this system, though dangerous, was pursued with success."[26]

The difference between the attitudes of Cohen and Gertrude may seem slight and, in each case, self-serving. Yet the distinction between their positions was of significance both in Jewish religious law and in a broader moral calculus.

In his *Collaboration with Tyranny in Rabbinic Law* (1965), the legal scholar David Daube examined the subject (without specific reference to the Nazi period). Daube showed that there was a general consensus among rabbis of the Talmudic period on the principle that "thou shall not give up a single soul from Israel." At the same time these ancient authorities (whose deliberations form the basis of *halachah*—Jewish religious law) recognized the complexity of situations that might arise from enemy occupation and consequently drew certain distinctions. In general, their view was that whereas a particular, named person might be handed over, if that were necessary to save a remnant of their persecuted nation, a demand to hand over "simply any odd person for execution" must never be met. The reason for the distinction was that where the surrender of a named person was demanded, compliance at least would not involve the guilt of selection.[27]

Cohen, by selecting persons for deportation in May 1943, crossed what Yehuda Bauer has called "the last moral barrier."[28] Gertrude, by stubbornly refusing to get involved in such selections, stopped short of it. Her position, at least by this calculus, was thus closer to Jewish traditional teaching than Cohen's. Whether she or Cohen was aware of that is very doubtful. Gertrude's moral compass—guided, no doubt, by humane instinct rather than religious precept—nevertheless led her to hold back at that point.

Our understanding of Gertrude's wartime role, as of that of the Jewish Council in general, must depend to a large extent on the degree of her (and the council's) knowledge of the fate of the Jews who were deported from Holland.

After the war, Gertrude always maintained that she had been fully aware of the Nazi program of mass murder. "Very few people in Holland knew what happened to the deportees," she wrote in 1947. "I did, and so did Professor C[ohen]."[29] Many years later she insisted that she had known as early as her visit to Lisbon in the spring of 1941 of the gassings at Auschwitz. She told Bauer in 1968 that "she knew of the gassings in Auschwitz, but had never told anyone."[30] "She feels," Bauer noted, "that to have told others would have merely created panic and would have served no useful purpose, because the people in the camp were helpless in any case and could not escape the transports." It was a strange claim, since the earliest recorded gassings of Jews by the Nazis took place only in December 1941 (at Chelmno in Poland). Moreover, the Dutch Jews were, in the main, not yet "in the camp" in 1941. And even later, when they passed through Westerbork, escape remained much less difficult than from other points of the Nazi prison-camp system.

Gertrude's claim to such early knowledge of "the wholesale extermination of Jews in gas chambers" is, however, absent from her long report of October 1944, in which she even expresses faint hope that some Jews might return from Poland after the war. It first appears in her autobiography, written in the 1950s.[31] There she states that she had told Cohen "about gas chambers in Poland when I returned from Lisbon." She added, "We had at the time agreed to keep the story secret to avoid alarming people unnecessarily."[32] No corroboration has been found for this. Possibly what she repeated were rumors of such German atrocities. She had certainly discussed Nazi policy with German-Jewish leaders in Berlin and with the Joint representatives in Lisbon. In both places, she no doubt heard gruesome accounts of what had already occurred in Poland. The most likely explanation is that, wishing to differentiate her position from that of David Cohen, she subconsciously backdated her knowledge of mass murder to May 1941.[33]

On July 25, 1942, Prime Minister Gerbrandy spoke movingly on Radio Oranje, the voice of the Dutch government-in-exile in London, condemning the deportations.[34] Another broadcast four days later mentioned gas chambers.[35] On December 17 the American, British, Soviet, and other Allied governments, including the Dutch, collectively denounced Nazi mass murder. The declaration, pronounced in a memorable scene in the House of Commons by the foreign secretary, Anthony Eden, was given wide publicity in Allied propaganda, including BBC broadcasts to occupied Europe. Louis de Jong, at the time working for Radio Oranje, participated in such a broadcast to Holland. After the war, Cohen admitted that he had known of Eden's declaration in 1942. Eden's statement referred explicitly to "all the occupied countries."[36] Cohen nevertheless insisted that both De Jong, in his broadcast, and he himself had understood it to refer only to Polish Jews.[37] There is no doubt that, in spite of the declaration, reality took time to sink in. A year later, De Jong, by then fully convinced of the veracity of recently received reports on the "Final Solution," showed them to the Dutch prime minister. Gerbrandy responded with shocked surprise and skepticism.[38]

Yet in October 1942, a thirteen-year-old girl, hiding in an attic in Amsterdam, almost completely cut off from the rest of world, wrote in her diary: "The English radio says they're being gassed." And in March 1943, "These poor people are being shipped off to filthy slaughterhouses like a herd of sick and neglected cattle."[39] Cohen, with far greater access to information and responsibility to seek and interpret it than Anne Frank, remained oblivious until the very end. The classical historian, with his penchant for ancient analogies, seems to have imagined that the Jews were being sent into a modern version of the Babylonian captivity, from which they would return, led by himself as a latter-day Ezra. As late as September 1944, in Theresienstadt, he offered a parting reassurance to a fellow prisoner who was about to leave for Auschwitz: "Take care. You are young and healthy. As you know, it's just for work."[40]

After the war, Cohen insisted that he had not known about the death camps at the time of the mass deportations: "I was told about it for the first time in the spring of 1945 at Theresienstadt."[41] Even Cohen's sympathetic biographer finds the claim implausible.[42] Could he really have persuaded himself that orphan children, the blind, the insane, and the limbless were being transported to perform "labour service" for the Reich? At the very least, Cohen must have operated between the summer of 1942 and the spring of 1945 in an extreme state of wishful thinking if not willful blindness. Gertrude at any rate made no such claim.

But if Cohen's profession of ignorance was a transparent attempt to shirk responsibility for the consequences of his actions, does Gertrude's admission of knowledge place a proportionately greater weight of responsibility on her shoulders? Under interrogation after the war, Willy Lages, the former SD chief in Amsterdam, declared that "without the Jewish Council we would not have achieved anything."[43] Should not Gertrude, especially if she had a clearer appreciation than Cohen of the likely fate of the deportees, face a no less damning indictment?

The question arises, most particularly, in relation to her work in 1942–1943. What, after all, was the role of her department Help for the Departing? Did it really help the departing, or was it another cog in the machine of destruction? Did it function as yet another ruse by means of which the Germans, through their instrument, the Jewish Council, deluded their victims into the belief that they really were heading towards some bearable future in "labour service" in Germany? On balance, did the rucksacks, baby diapers, sanitary pads, coats, boots, and the rest ease the last days of the Jews en route to the death camps, or, in the final reckoning, did the entire operation of the department accrue more to the benefit of the ultimate recipients of many of these goods: German soldiers and civilians, German women, and babies?

One answer is given by Etty Hillesum, the young woman who worked for a time in Gertrude's department and was later deported from Westerbork to Auschwitz. She recorded in a letter in December 1942 that in Westerbork, she had noticed that "it made a great difference whether people arrived prepared, with well-filled rucksacks, or had been suddenly dragged out of their houses or swept up from the streets." And she recalled the plight of "all those who went to face the winter in Eastern Europe without any clothes, if we remember the single blanket that was sometimes all we were able to dole out in the night, a few hours before departure."[44]

Most historians have been less impressed. Jacques Presser, in general a fierce critic of the Jewish Council, expresses a guarded admiration for Gertrude, recognizing the efficiency of her department in fulfilling its mandate of "rendering help and advice to all those going to Germany on labour service." "Unfortunately," he continues, "the bureau never gave the advice not to go at all." Presser, who survived the later part of the war in hiding but whose wife was captured in a *razzia* and perished at Sobibor, adds "the bitter rider" that "by advising others to go, the staff of the bureau was able to stave off their own departure for a time."[45] Louis de Jong rejected Gertrude's argument that the work of her department was purely charitable. Though acknowledging that it eased the lot of the deportees, he did not accept that it had nothing to do with politics. "It had *everything* to do with the politics of the Jewish Council. . . . Help to the departing was a consequence of help for deportation."[46] More recently, Bart van der Boom has written, "The entire philosophy of compliance was packed up in the rucksacks: the assumption that deportation was probably inevitable and could be mitigated by following instructions from above."[47]

A rather different picture, of course, emerges from Gertrude's postwar memoir. She contends that her department not only helped people prepare for deportation but also helped "a great number of people" to escape: "People who decided to send their children into hiding were without exception enabled to do so. With great personal risk to themselves, workers from the Expositur or HAV [Help for the Departing] helped children to reach organizations who in turn sent them into securer hiding places."[48] She also claims to have channeled "black money" that was at her disposal "to the underground and to people in hiding."[49] While there is no reason to doubt these statements, it is difficult to form any precise impression of the effectiveness of such aid. Still, the sums available to her between 1941 and 1943 from residual Joint funds; from the Swiss consular agent, Ernest Prodolliet; and from deposits left with her by departing Jews such as Polak were substantial. If distributed effectively to Jews who went "under water," they must have made a significant difference to their survival prospects.

Gertrude describes a few instances in which she gave direct help to people who "went under." One was the mother of her ex-sister-in-law, who lived in a home for the elderly in The Hague. Gertrude went to the place in Amsterdam where this woman and other residents of the home were detained prior to deportation: "They seemed completely oblivious of what was going to happen to them. It was a gruesome scene. The old people, none under seventy, had no luggage. They had been shoved into a dilapidated, sparsely lit building, devoid of any furniture. It was bitterly cold and damp. The old people were supposed to sleep on the floor without blankets. Most of them hardly knew what had happened; they just muttered incoherently to themselves." Gertrude arranged for non-Jewish friends to smuggle the old lady into hiding. She survived the war.[50] The story is corroborated (albeit with different details) by Jacques van Tijn's second wife in a postwar letter to him from Amsterdam.[51]

There is no doubt that Gertrude advocated a more militant posture than that adopted by the leaders of the Jewish Council. But even if she was not a member of the council itself, the fact remains that she was a department head of the very organization whose leaders she attacked so bitingly. Her distinction between the council's "political" and "charitable" activities is not wholly convincing when one recalls, for example, her department's menacing warnings to German Jews to register "for emigration;" and the scenes in which its representatives, accompanied by SS men, turned up at arrested people's homes to collect their luggage for forwarding to Westerbork.

Gertrude would no doubt have done better, from the point of view of protecting her reputation, if she had either not worked at all for the Jewish Council or resigned definitively from it at an early stage. But in spite of the "first violin" accusations against her by De Leeuw and others (which may be understood at least in part as the natural reactions of males in a patriarchal age to a woman who dared to express her own contrary opinions), she understood that the only hope even of minimal effective action to counter the Nazi threat was as an ensemble player rather than a soloist.

In her humane endeavors, Gertrude courted physical and moral dangers. She was concerned less with striking attitudes than with saving lives. Sometimes that involved acquiescing in orders from the Germans (for example, registering potential emigrants in the hope of securing exit permits). Sometimes it involved defying the policies of the British (for example, by her part in the *Dora* episode and in "trading with the enemy"). But unlike some who simply crumpled into obeisance to brute force, she drew a line beyond which she would not go—at any rate, following her experience with Barbie in 1941.

Both Cohen and Gertrude took morally hazardous decisions in order to save lives. But Cohen was ready to sacrifice some lives in order to save others, and he dared to take it upon himself to distinguish those less worth saving. Gertrude balked at that.

When a local Jewish newspaper in Portland interviewed her in 1969 and called her a "heroine," she was embarrassed. "The last thing I would call myself is "heroine," she wrote to a former colleague at the Joint.[52]

How, then, should we understand her life and, most particularly, her conduct during the supreme crisis of European Jewry? The magnitude and complexity of the horrors of her time preclude

Gertrude in retirement *(private collection)*

any simple categorization of the responses of those caught up in Nazism's tentacles. As we have seen, several of the decisions that Gertrude took are open to criticism. But at least she did not respond passively or fatalistically. Guided by the social and political ideals she had imbibed as a young woman in Berlin and London before the First World War, educated in the wiles of the world in Africa and Mexico in the 1920s, drawing on large personal reserves of courage, energy, and compassion, and impelled by a burning desire to help the persecuted and downtrodden, she battled selflessly against impossible odds to save lives.

Gertrude's story is a study in the ambiguity of virtue. She was an altruist who saw no reason to damp down her natural idiosyncrasy; a woman of principle, who understood the need to compromise—up to a point. Supremely practical and down-to-earth, she had yet a spiritual dimension, untrammeled by conventional religion. She was her own kind of feminist and her own kind of Zionist. She was a humanitarian who drew her values from the great store of the European enlightenment, to which the German-Jewish bourgeoisie, into which she was born, was heir.

Quoting Goethe's "*Lebensregel*" ("Rule of Life"), she chose her own epitaph:

> Inquire into the meaning of each day,
> What each day means, itself will say;
> In thine own actions, take thy pleasure,
> What others do, thou'lt duly treasure;
> Ne'er let thy breast with hate be supplied.
> And to God the future confide.[53]

Epilogue

In the summer of 2011, as I began to write this book in Amsterdam, my wife suggested that we take a look at the different addresses where Gertrude had lived in and around the city. We started at 585 Keizersgracht, Gertrude's home in Amsterdam during the First World War. A few weeks later, we visited the "Wooden House" in Blaricum, to all external appearance little changed since it had been the Van Tijn family's residence in the 1930s. Next we called at the former "Prins Hendrik" boardinghouse at 28 Prins Hendriklaan, where Gertrude had rented a small flat in 1941–1942. This is an elegant building, today the headquarters of Gazprom EP International.

Finally we searched for her last listed address in Amsterdam, at 32 Nieuwe Amstelstraat. This street was in the heart of the old Jewish quarter in the city center. Several of the houses have been knocked down and replaced since the war, and the numbering seemed to have changed. We were about to give up, when I decided to walk to the end of the street, just to make sure. The last house, now number 70, was the only one on the street that, almost miraculously, still bore the old number plate: 32.

This corner building, close to the Blauwbrug (Blue Bridge) over the River Amstel and down the street from the Ashkenazi Great Synagogue, today the Jewish Historical Museum, exactly matched Gertrude's description. From the upper windows Gertrude had a view of the bridge, the nearby Waterlooplein, and the whole of the surrounding area.

Plaque on wall of 32 Nieuwe Amstelstraat, Amsterdam, bearing inscription: "*DIE GODE GEHOORSAAMT GEHOORSAEMEN D'ELEMENTEN*" ("The elements obey him who obeys the Lord") *(Amsterdam City Archives)*

Above the lintel of the front door of the house was a wall plaque with a relief depicting the famous biblical scene in which Joshua made the sun stand still to enable his army to wreak revenge on the enemies of the children of Israel. This was the original "longest day." The massed soldiery of the Israelites are depicted, all wearing helmets, as a storm of hailstones descends on the heads of the fleeing hosts of the Amorite kings. The plaque carries the inscription in old Dutch, "*DIE GODE GEHOORSAAMT GEHOORSAEMEN D'ELEMENTEN*" ("The elements obey him who obeys the Lord").

The words are not a quotation but rather an interpretation of the biblical passage (Joshua 10:12–14), which, in the Authorized Version, records:

> Then spake Joshua to the LORD in the day when the LORD delivered up the Amorites before the children of Israel, and he said in the sight of Israel, Sun, stand thou still upon Gibeon; and thou, Moon, in the valley of Ajalon.
>
> And the sun stood still, and the moon stayed, until the people had avenged themselves upon their enemies. . . . So the sun stood still in the midst of heaven, and hasted not to go down about a whole day.
>
> And there was no day like that before it or after it, that the LORD hearkened unto the voice of a man: for the LORD fought for Israel.

The story, with its suggestion that God performed a miracle at the behest of a human being, is one of the most debated in biblical literature, often invoked in a variety of contexts. It was cited against Galileo by the Inquisition and by Clarence Darrow at the Scopes "monkey" trial in 1925. During the German occupation of Holland, the text was quoted by a Christian sermonizer as a veiled attack on the occupiers (or perhaps not so veiled; a week later, the newspaper in which the homily was published was subjected to a two-month ban).[1]

"It is one of our most exquisite plaques that portrays this moment . . . apparently—like so many reliefs—based on an old print," wrote H. W. Alings in his pleasant little guide to Amsterdam wall plaques, published in 1943.[2] By "this moment," Alings no doubt meant the moment that the sun stood still. But in the twilight world of occupied Europe, where so much had a double meaning, his words might also be read as alluding to *this* moment, that is, 1943. For the plaque, although created around 1650, could hardly have been more appositely designed to furnish a bitterly ironic reflection of the lurid scene that unfolded before Gertrude's eyes in that building on the night of the floodlit *razzia* on May 25–26 that year.

At the doorpost of the house were three bells, one for each floor. Suddenly I got a shock: the name, slightly faded, on the middle bell was "Van Tijen." Surely the label could not have survived there since Gertrude's arrest and departure in 1943? I was tempted to ring and inquire, but I decided not to disturb the residents.

The apartment had been plundered within hours of Gertrude's arrest on April 29, 1943. Ernst Laqueur, who had a duplicate key, went to collect some of her things but found the place quite empty except for some heavier pieces of furniture. It therefore seemed inconceivable that anything worthwhile for my biographical purposes would remain there nearly seventy years later.

I was nevertheless sufficiently intrigued to inquire further. I soon ascertained that the "Van Tijen" in question was Tjebbe van Tijen, who had nothing to do with Gertrude, save the coincidental similarity of his surname. That seemed to resolve the matter. But *nomen est omen*. Some time later I decided to send a message to Mr. Van Tijen, asking whether I might see the apartment. He said I was welcome. He added a remarkable detail: while remodeling the house in the late 1970s he had discovered, hidden behind a wall, the papers of a Jew who had lived there during the war.

When I eventually called at the apartment, I could immediately see why Gertrude had loved the place. In her day, it was a modern building, constructed in 1928 to house a branch of the Twentsche Bank. The apartment, occupying five rooms on two levels, had been the residence of the bank manager. It was bright and sunny and, as the building occupied a triangular corner site, had windows looking out in three directions. The view is very different now. Two large trees partly block what in Gertrude's day was an unimpeded vista towards the Blue Bridge over the River Amstel. On the right, the Waterlooplein has been completely redesigned and all the buildings on one side knocked down to make way for the modern Amsterdam City Hall. Across the road is visible an incongruous line of white granite paving stones, placed in 1989. It marks the site of the Megadlé Jethomiem orphanage, from which the children were deported in February 1943.[3]

My host showed me the location of the crevice where he had found the old documents. Then he produced a carton with the faded relics that constituted the *trouvaille*. The papers were those of an Amsterdam Jew, Levie (Lion) Cohen, who had run a music shop in Amsterdam before the war. There was his passport, his record of service in the Dutch army in the First World War, some photos, an envelope containing a few old banknotes, and assorted bric-a-brac.

Among the latter was a little round cardboard box. When I opened it, I was momentarily disappointed: it held nothing but coffee beans. Then an association flashed into my mind: in all those wartime letters and cards that Gertrude had sent to Saly Mayer in Switzerland, there was one recurring refrain: she constantly thanked him and Joseph Schwartz, the Joint representative in Lisbon, for regularly sending her packets of real coffee, almost unobtainable in Amsterdam during the occupation. "It's so important for me," she wrote in February 1942, "because of the heart murmurs from which I suffer more than ever as a result of the continual physical and mental strain, and for which, actually, the only remedies are strong coffee or alcohol."[4]

The discovery of those seventy-year-old beans left me with the feeling that I had discharged my assignment as a historian. This reminder of Gertrude's little indulgence was a salutary admonition that what I was dealing with was not a remote figure from the

The little box of coffee beans found with other items, *c.* 1979, in a crevice behind a wall at 32 Nieuwe Amstelstraat, Gertrude's last home in Amsterdam *(photograph by Tjebbe van Tijen)*

past but a human being, with all the natural cravings and frailties to which our kind are susceptible.

Mr. Van Tijen had one more surprise for me. The last item in his collection was a small notebook, a pocket diary for 1942, though the entries, which cross from one date to the next, were evidently not written on the printed dates. The contents appeared to be not a diary but a kind of commonplace book, with aphorisms or quotations from literary works in Dutch. The back pages contained miscellaneous notes, a list of "recipes to be asked for," a shopping list, names, addresses, and telephone numbers, including those of several employees of the Jewish Council. There was also a version of the list, issued by Gertrude's department, of items to be packed in anticipation of deportation. On one of the last pages, inscribed in block capitals, were Gertrude's name and personal details (date of birth, and so on), together with the words "Arrived 17 November 1942." On the opposite leaf, also in block letters, was a similar entry for Gertrude's housekeeper, Lucie Ascher.

Levie Cohen worked in Gertrude's department at the Jewish Council. His wife and daughter were deported and killed in October 1942. The city's housing registration records do not indicate exactly when he moved to the address. But a city police report of late October 1942, in which he complained of a theft of his belongings from the apartment, shows that he had been resident there since some time before that date.[5] Evidently, once his wife and daughter were gone, he shared this apartment with Gertrude and her housekeeper. He was one of the four employees for whose exemption from deportation Gertrude made a special appeal to David Cohen in March 1943.[6] But the immunity, if it was accorded, did not protect him for long. He was sent to Westerbork on May 20, 1943. From there he was deported on May 25 (the night of the floodlit *razzia*) and murdered on arrival in Sobibor three days later.[7]

The notebook, coffee beans, and the rest remain today in the apartment, eerie relics of those six months that Gertrude, Lucie, and Levie Cohen lived under the same roof. The handwriting in the diary is not Gertrude's. Wondering whether the entries might be in code, I submitted the notebook to an expert cryptanalyst. After careful examination, he concluded that there was no secret message embedded in the text. As the notebook was found with various belongings of Levie Cohen, the most likely explanation appeared to be that he was the writer.

On the other hand, the cryptanalyst as well as other readers noticed a few minor errors in Dutch, subsequently corrected, of a kind that suggested that the writer was not a native Dutch speaker.

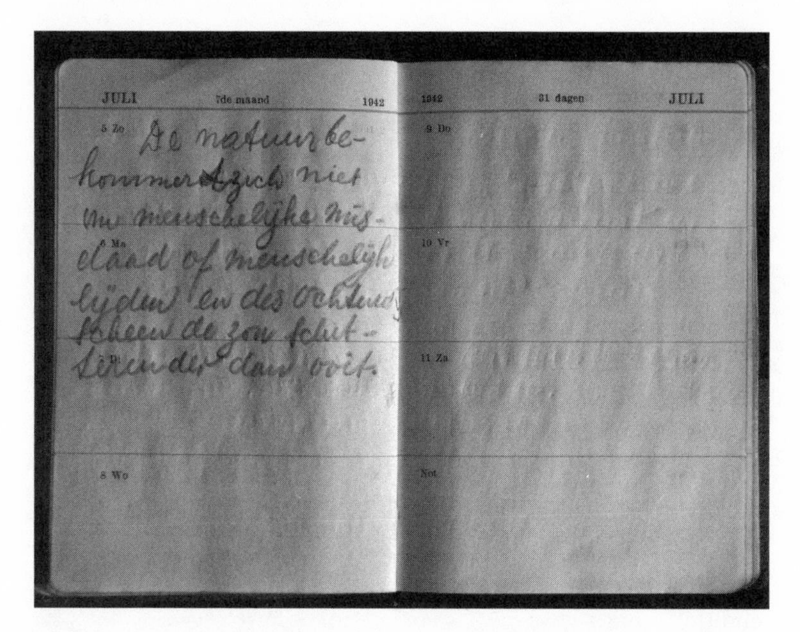

Page from 1942 pocket diary (this entry was probably written in 1943); the notebook was found, *c.* 1979, in Gertrude's last home in Amsterdam *(photograph by Tjebbe van Tijen)*

It seemed as if these fragments had been read out, as a dictation exercise, to a person who wanted to learn to write the language.

Strangely, at least three of the passages were translated sentences from a popular English-language novel, published in 1913, which, so far as can be ascertained, had never appeared in Dutch.[8] Only someone able to translate from English at sight could have dictated these passages in Dutch.

Whiling away the long nights of curfew in the winter of 1942–1943 in her sitting room with her German-born housekeeper, did Gertrude read out these *dictées* to Lucie in Dutch in order to help her learn the language properly? Like most Jews left in Amsterdam by this time, Lucie was a nominal employee of the Jewish

Council (or so, at any rate, she is recorded in the notebook). Perhaps the object was to train her as a secretary, or maybe the two women simply wanted to soothe their nerves.

On the face of things, most of the literary extracts in the notebook are of no intrinsic significance, as if from books plucked from the shelf and opened at random. Yet a few, like the wall plaque on the outside of the building, offer an uncannily pertinent commentary on the agony of wartime Amsterdam. So it is with the last such entry. If we exercise our imaginations, we can almost hear Gertrude's voice calmly dictating it to Lucie on their last evening together, as the enemies of the children of Israel massed outside: "Nature pays no attention to human crimes or human suffering and that morning the sun was shining more brilliantly than ever."[9]

Sources

Unpublished Sources

Unfortunately, Gertrude burnt many of her papers in May 1940 at the time of the German invasion. More were lost as a result of German raids during the war and when she was taken from her last home in Amsterdam in September 1943. She destroyed others in 1970 before sending some of the remainder to the Leo Baeck Institute. Much of her story must therefore be reconstructed from other sources. Fortunately, these are abundant.

An important source for her life up to the 1950s is her unpublished memoir, which exists in several forms. The first autobiographical document is the long report (over a hundred pages of single-spaced typing with some handwritten corrections) on wartime events in the Netherlands, that she wrote shortly after her arrival in Palestine in 1944. This covers only the years 1940 to 1944. Copies of the typescript are held in the Central Zionist Archives in Jerusalem, the Leo Baeck Institute Archives in New York, and the Netherlands Institute of War Documentation in Amsterdam (in a Dutch translation), as well as in other repositories. There are some minor differences among these versions. Quotations here are from the Leo Baeck Institute copy.

Gertrude's memoirs, properly so called, were written in the 1950s in New Mexico. Entitled "The World Was Mine," they relate the whole of her life story up to that point. The passages dealing with the wartime period were obviously based on her 1944 report. There is also a fifty-four-page memorandum of "Supplementary Data," supplied by Gertrude to the Leo Baeck Institute. It differs, however, only very slightly from the early chapters of her memoirs. When the memoirs were revised with a view to publication, some of the names were changed, notably those of David Cohen and Abraham Asscher. A shortened version of part of it was later redacted by Gertrude's granddaughter Roberta Stein. None of these, however, ever appeared in print. All quotations here are from the version of the autobiography held by the Leo Baeck Institute.

I have drawn on these memoirs freely but with some reserve. Wherever feasible, I have preferred to rely on contemporary evidence. This is voluminous, particularly for the critical years 1933 to 1945, with which this book is primarily concerned. Only in the case of Gertrude's early life have I been compelled by the paucity of other material to rely heavily on her autobiography. In the main, wherever it has been possible to compare her memories with other documentation, the latter has been found to corroborate her account.

Archives

Archiv für Zeitgeschichte, Zürich
Arquivo Histórico Municipal de Cascais
Bibliotheca Rosenthaliana, University of Amsterdam
British National Archives, Kew
Central Zionist Archives, Jerusalem
Columbia University Library Archival Collections
Ghetto Fighters House Archive, Kibbutz Lohamei Hagetaot
Harry Ransom Center, University of Texas at Austin
International Institute of Social History, Amsterdam
Jewish Historical Museum, Amsterdam
Leo Baeck Institute Archives, Center for Jewish History, New York
Netherlands Institute for War Documentation, Amsterdam
Netherlands National Archives, The Hague
Netherlands Red Cross Archive, The Hague
Niedersächsisches Landesarchiv—Staatsarchiv Wolfenbüttel
Papers in possession of Tjebbe van Tijen
Papers in possession of Sasha Trone
Papers of the Van Tijn (New Jersey), Bergman (Laren), and Stein (Seattle) families
Stadsarchief Amsterdam

Stadsarchief's-Hertogenbosch
Stadtarchiv Braunschweig
Streekarchief Gooi en Vechtstreek, Hilversum
Swiss Federal Department of External Affairs Archive
Tresoar, Leeuwarden
United Nations Archives, New York
United States National Archives, Washington, DC
Wiener Library and Archives, London
Yad Vashem Archives, Jerusalem
YIVO Institute for Jewish Research, New York

Dissertations

Braber, Ben. "De activiteiten van Barbie in Nederland in de jaren, 1940–1945." Kand. scriptie, Universiteit Amsterdam, 1984.

Hummel, Ben. "De Derde Duits-Palestijnse Uitwisseling of hoe 281 Joden in Juli 1944 Gered Werden." Doctoraal-scriptie, Rijksuniversiteit Groningen, 1987.

Michman, Dan. "Ha-plitim ha-yehudiyim mi-germanyah be-holand bashanim, 1933–1940." PhD diss., The Hebrew University of Jerusalem, 1978.

Newman, Joanna. "Nearly the New World: Refugees and the British West Indies, 1933–1945." PhD diss., University of Southampton, 1998.

Schütz, Raymund. "Vermoedelijk op transport." Masterscriptie archiefwetenschappen, Universiteit Leiden, 2011.

Website

Joods Monument: www.joodsmonument.nl/

Published Sources

Newspapers

Avondblad-Algemeen Handelsblad
Ha'aretz
Het Joodsche Weekblad (Amsterdam, 1941–1943)
Het Vaderland

Het Volksdagblad
Leeuwarder Nieuwsblad
Ochtenblad–Algemeen Handelsblad
Palestine Post

Books and Articles

Aalders, Gerard. *Nazi Looting: The Plunder of Dutch Jewry During the Second World War.* Oxford, 2004.

Alings, H. W. *Amsterdamsche Gevelsteenen.* Amsterdam, 1943.

Arendt, Hannah. *Eichmann in Jerusalem: A Report on the Banality of Evil.* London, 1964.

Avneri, Aryeh L. *Mi-"velos" ad "taurus:" asor rishon le-ha-apalah be-darkhei ha-yam, 1934–1944.* Tel Aviv, 1985.

Avni, Haim. *Spain, the Jews, and Franco.* Philadelphia, 1982.

Barlas, Haim. *Hatsalah bimei shoah.* Tel Aviv, 1975.

Bauer, Yehuda. *American Jewry and the Holocaust: The American Jewish Joint Distribution Committee, 1939–1945.* Detroit, 1981.

———. "The Judenräte—Some Conclusions." In *Patterns of Jewish Leadership in Nazi Europe 1933–1945: Proceedings of the Third Yad Vashem International Historical Conference, Jerusalem April 4–7, 1977.* Jerusalem, 1979.

———. *My Brother's Keeper: A History of the American Jewish Joint Distribution Committee, 1929–1939.* Philadelphia, 1974.

Berg, Meike. *Judische Schulen in Niedersachsen: Tradition—Emanzipation—Assimilation.* Cologne, 2003.

Berghuis, Corrie K., ed. *Joodse Vluchtelingen in Nederland, 1938–1940: Documenten betreffende toelating, uitleiding en kampopname.* Kampen, 1990.

Berkley, K. P. L. *Overzicht van het onstaan de werkzaamheiden en het streven van den Joodsche Raad voor Amsterdam.* Amsterdam, 1945.

Blom, J. C. H., R. G. Fuks-Mansfeld, and I. Schöffer, eds. *The History of the Jews in the Netherlands.* Oxford, 2002.

Bolle, Mirjam. *Ik zal je beschrijven hoe een dag er hier uitziet: Dagboekbrieven uit Amsterdam, Westerbork en Bergen-Belsen.* Amsterdam, 2003.

Brasz, Chaya. *Irgoen Olei Holland: De ontstaansgeschiedenis van de Nederlandse immigrantenvereniging in Israël.* Jerusalem, 1993.

———. "'Dodenschip' Dora," *Vrij Nederland,* May 1, 1993.

———. *Transport 222: Bergen-Belsen—Palestina, Yuli 1944.* Jerusalem, 1994.

———. *Removing the Yellow Badge: The Struggle for a Jewish Community in the Postwar Netherlands 1944–1945.* Jerusalem, 1995.

Breitman, Richard, and Kraut, Alan M. *American Refugee Policy and European Jewry, 1933–1945.* Bloomington, 1987.

Breitman, Richard, Barbara McDonald Stewart, and Severin Hochberg, eds. *Refugees and Rescue: The Diaries and Papers of James G. McDonald, 1935–1945.* Bloomington, 2009.

Caron, Vicki. *Uneasy Asylum: France and the Jewish Refugee Crisis, 1933–1942.* Stanford, 1999.

Castan, Joachim, ed. *Hans Calmeyer und die Judenrettung in den Niederlanden.* Göttingen, 2003.

Cohen, David. *Zwervend en Dolend: De Joodse Vluchtelingen in Nederland in de Jaren, 1933–1940.* Haarlem, 1955.

———. *Voorzitter van de Joodse Raad: De herinneringen van David Cohen (1941–1943).* Edited by Erik Somers. Zutphen, 2010.

Croes, Marnix, "The Holocaust in the Netherlands and the Rate of Jewish Survival." *Holocaust and Genocide Studies* 20, no. 3 (2006): 474–99.

Croes, Marnix, and Peter Tammes. *"Gif laten wij niet voortbestaan:" Een onderzoek naar de overlevingskansen van Joden in de Nederlandse gemeenten, 1940–1945.* Amsterdam, 2004.

Daube, David. *Collaboration with Tyranny in Rabbinic Law.* London, 1965.

de Jong, Louis. *Het Koninkrijk der Nederlanden in de Tweede Wereldoorlog.* 14 vols. The Hague, 1969–91. [All citations here refer to the "scientific edition," available, except for illustrations, at www.niod.nl/nl/koninkrijk.]

———. *The Netherlands and Nazi Germany.* Cambridge, MA, 1990.

Dwork, Debórah, and Robert Jan van Pelt. *Flight from the Reich: Refugee Jews, 1933–1946.* New York, 2009.

Favez, Jean-Claude. *The Red Cross and the Holocaust.* Cambridge, 1999.

Fijnaut, Cyrille. *De Geschiedenis van de Nederlandse Politie: Een staatsinstelling in de maalstroom van de geschiedenis.* Amsterdam, 2007.

Fishman, J. S. "On Jewish Survival during the Occupation: The Vision of Jacob van Amerongen." *Studia Rosenthaliana* 32, no. 3 (1999): 160–73.

Flim, Bert Jan. *Omdat Hun Hart Sprak: Geschiedenis van de Georganiseerde Hulp aan Joodse Kinderen in Nederland, 1942–1945.* Kampen, 1996.

———. *Saving the Children: History of the Organized Effort to Rescue Jewish Children in the Netherlands, 1942–1945.* Bethesda, MD, 2005.

Foot, M. R. D. ed. *Holland at War Against Hitler: Anglo-Dutch Relations, 1940–1945*. London, 1990.

Frank, Anne. *The Diary of a Young Girl: The Definitive Edition*. London, 1997.

Friedländer, Saul. *The Years of Extermination: Nazi Germany and the Jews, 1939–1945*. New York, 2007.

Friedman, Philip. *Roads to Extinction: Essays on the Holocaust*. Philadelphia, 1980.

Frishman, Judith, and Hetty Berg, eds. *Dutch Jewry in a Cultural Maelstrom, 1880–1940*. Amsterdam, 2007.

Gigliotti, Simone. "'Acapulco in the Atlantic': Revisiting Sosúa, a Jewish Refugee Colony in the Caribbean." *Immigrants and Minorities* 24, no. 1 (2006).

Griffioen, Pim, and Ron Zeller. *Jodenvervolging in Nederland, Frankrijk en België, 1940–1945: Overeenkomsten, verschillen, oorzaken*. Amsterdam, 2011.

Habas, Bracha. *Portsei ha-shearim*. Tel Aviv, 1960.

Hájková, Anna. "The Making of a Zentralstelle: Die Eichmann-Männer in Amsterdam." *Theresienstädter Studien und Dokumente* (2003), 353–81.

Hamann, Brigitte. *Hitler's Vienna: A Dictator's Apprenticeship*. New York, 1999.

Harari, Jacob. *Die Ausrottung der Juden im besetzten Holland: Ein Tatsachenbericht*. Tel Aviv, 1944.

Heinrich, Crista, Hans Winterberg, Merete Vargas, Jürgen Bock, and Roger Meintjes, eds. *Lissabon 1933–1945: Fluchtstation am Rande Europas*. Akademie der Künste, Berlin, 1995. Exhibition catalog.

Herrmann, Simon Heinrich. *Austauschlager Bergen-Belsen: Geschichte eines Austauschtransportes*. Tel Aviv, 1944.

Herzberg, Abel J. *Kroniek der Jodenvervolging, 1940–1945*. Amsterdam, 1985.

Hilberg, Raul. *The Destruction of the European Jews*. Rev. ed., 3 vols. New York, 1985.

Hirschfeld, Gerhard. *Nazi Rule and Dutch Collaboration: The Netherlands under German Occupation, 1940–1945*. Oxford, 1988.

Houwink ten Cate, Johannes. "Heydrich's Security Police and the Amsterdam Jewish Council (February 1941–October 1942)." In *Dutch Jewish History* 3, edited by Jozeph Michman, 381–96. Assen, 1993.

Huiskes, Gino, and Reinhilde van der Kroef, eds. *Vluchtelingenkamp Westerbork*. Westerbork Cahiers 7, Assen, 1999.
Independent Commission of Experts Switzerland—Second World War, *Switzerland, National Socialism and the Second World War: Final Report*. Zürich, 2002.
Joods Historisch Museum, Amsterdam. *Documenten van de Jodenvervolging in Nederland, 1940–1945*. Amsterdam, 1965.
Kaplan, Marion A. *The Making of the Jewish Middle Class: Women, Family, and Identity in Imperial Germany*. Oxford, 1991.
Koestler, Arthur. *Scum of the Earth*. London, 1941.
Koker, David, *At the Edge of the Abyss: A Concentration Camp Diary, 1943–1944*. Edited by Robert Jan van Pelt. Evanston, IL, 2012.
Kolb, Eberhard. *Bergen-Belsen, 1943–1945*. Göttingen, 2002.
Krausnick, Helmut, and Martin Broszat. *Anatomy of the SS State*. London, 1970.
Kuiper, Arie. *Een wijze ging voorbij: Het leven van Abel J. Herzberg*. Amsterdam, 1998.
Levine, Paul. *From Indifference to Activism: Swedish Diplomacy and the Holocaust, 1938–1944*. Uppsala, 1998.
Lindwer, Willy, ed. *Het fatale dilemma: De Joodsche Raad voor Amsterdam, 1941–1943*. The Hague, 1995.
Litvinoff, Barnet, ed. *The Letters and Papers of Chaim Weizmann*. Series B, vol. 2, Dec. 1931–April 1952. New Brunswick, NJ, 1984.
Lochery, Neill. *Lisbon: War in the Shadows of the City of Light, 1939–1945*. New York, 2011.
Lozowick, Yaacov. *Hitler's Bureaucrats: The Nazi Security Police and the Banality of Evil*. London, 2002.
Lubell, Samuel. "War by Refugee." *Saturday Evening Post*, March 29, 1941.
Luijters, Guus. *In Memoriam: De gedeporteerde en vermoorde Joodse, Roma en Sinti kinderen, 1942–1945*. Amsterdam, 2012.
Maass, Walter B. *The Netherlands at War, 1940–1945*. New York, 1970.
Mason, Henry L. "Testing Human Bonds within Nations: Jews in the Occupied Netherlands." *Political Science Quarterly* 99, no. 2 (1984): 315–43
Mechanicus, Philip. *Waiting for Death: A Diary*. London, 1968.
Meershoek, Guus. "De Amsterdamse hoofdcommissaris en de deportatie van de joden." *Oorlogsdocumentatie 40/45, Jaarboek van het Rijksinstituut voor Oorlogsdocumentatie* 3 (1992): 9–43.

———. *Dienaren van het gezag: De Amsterdamse politie tijdens de bezetting.* Amsterdam, 1999.

Melkman [Michman], J. "David Cohen." *Studia Rosenthaliana* 4 (1970): 219–27.

Micheels, Pauline. *De vatenman: Bernard van Leer (1883–1958).* Amsterdam, 2002.

Michman, Dan. "The Committee for Jewish Refugees in Holland (1933–1940)." *Yad Vashem Studies* xiv (1981): 205–32.

———. "The Uniqueness of the Joodse Raad in the Western European Context." In *Dutch Jewish History* 3, edited by Jozeph Michman, 371–80. Assen, 1993.

Michman, J. "The Controversy Surrounding the Jewish Council of Amsterdam." In *Patterns of Jewish Leadership in Nazi Europe, 1933–1945: Proceedings of the Third Yad Vashem International Historical Conference, Jerusalem April 4–7, 1977* (Jerusalem, 1979), 235–57.

Middelberg, Mathias. *Judenrecht, Judenpolitik und der Jurist Hans Calmeyer in den besetzten Niederlanden, 1940–1945.* Göttingen, 2005.

Moore, Bob. *Refugees from Nazi Germany in the Netherlands, 1933–1940.* Dordrecht, 1986.

———. *Survivors: Jewish Self-Help and Rescue in Nazi-Occupied Western Europe.* Oxford, 2010.

———. *Victims and Survivors: The Nazi Persecution of the Jews in the Netherlands, 1940–1945.* London, 1997.

Mulder, Dirk, and Ben Prinsen, eds. *Vluchtelingenkamp Westerbork.* Westerbork Cahiers 7, Hooghalen, 1999.

Oppenheim, A. N. *The Chosen People: The Story of the "222 Transport" from Bergen-Belsen to Palestine.* London, 1996.

Pinkhof, Menachem. "Reshit ha-mahteret ha-halutsit be-holand." *Yediot beit lohamei ha-getaot* 13 (Jan. 1956): 16–21.

Posthumus, N. W., ed. "The Netherlands during German Occupation." *Annals of the American Academy of Political and Social Science* 245 (May 1946).

Presser, Jacob. *Ashes in the Wind: The Destruction of Dutch Jewry.* London, 2010.

Ramati, Alexander. *Barbed Wire on the Isle of Man: The Wartime British Internment of Jews.* New York, 1980.

Ravid, Benjamin. "Alfred Klee and Hans Goslar: From Amsterdam to Westerbork to Bergen-Belsen." In *The Dutch Intersection: The Jews and the Netherlands in Modern History*, edited by Yosef Kaplan, 348–68. Leiden, 2008.

Rose, Norman, ed. *The Letters and Papers of Chaim Weizmann*. Series A, vol. 19, Jan. 1939–June 1940. New Brunswick, NJ, 1977.

Rothkirchen, Livia. *The Jews of Bohemia and Moravia: Facing the Holocaust*. Lincoln, NE, 2005.

Rüter, C. F., and D. W. de Mildt, eds. *Justiz und NS-Verbrechen: Sammlung Deutscher Strafurteile wegen Nationalsozialistischer Tötungsverbrechen, 1945–1999*. Vol. 25. Amsterdam, 2001.

Schellekens, Mark. *Walter Süskind*. Amsterdam, 2012.

Schorr, Daniel. *Staying Tuned*. New York, 2001.

Schrijvers, Piet. *Rome, Athene, Jeruzalem: Leven en werk van prof. dr. David Cohen*. Groningen, 2000.

Schulze, Rainer. "'Keeping Very Clear of Any "Kuh-Handel': The British Foreign Office and the Rescue of Jews from Bergen-Belsen." *Holocaust and Genocide Studies* 19, no. 2 (2005): 226–51.

Schwarz, Fred. *Züge auf falschem Gleis*. Vienna, 1996.

Sereni, Enzo Chaim. *Ha-aviv ha-kadosh: yomanim, mikhtavim, maamarim: kovets*. Edited by Kalev Ḳasṭelbolonzi. Tel Aviv, 1946.

Sijes, B. A. *De Februari-Staking, 25–26 Februari 1941*. The Hague, 1954.

Smelik, Klaas A. D., ed. *Etty: The Letters and Diaries of Etty Hillesum, 1941–1943*. Grand Rapids, MI, 2002.

Sneader, Walter. *Drug Discovery: A History*. Chichester, 2005.

Stegeman, H. B. J., and Vorsteveld, J. P. *Het Joodse Werkdorp in de Wieringermeer, 1934–1941*. Zutphen, 1983.

Steiner, Zara, *The Triumph of the Dark: European International History, 1933–1939*. Oxford, 2011.

Stiftung Topographie des Terrors. *Topography of Terror: Gestapo, SS, and Reich Security Main Office on Wilhelm- and Prinz-Albrecht-Straße*: A Documentation. Berlin, 2010.

Tartakower, Arieh, and Kurt R. Grossman. *The Jewish Refugee*. New York, 1944.

ten Have, Wichert. *De Nederlandse Unie: Aanpassing, vernieuwing en confrontatie in bezettingstijd, 1940–1941*. Amsterdam, 1999.

Tsameret, Shmarya. *Boker tamid: igrot u-reshumot*. Tel Aviv, 1966.

Tweede Kamer der Staten-Generaal Enquêtecommissie Regeringsbeleid 1940–1945. *Verslag Houdende de Uitkomsten van het Onderzoek*. Vols. 6A&B and 7A&B. The Hague, 1952, 1955.

Unabhängige Expertenkommission Schweiz—Zweiter Weltkrieg, *Die Schweiz und die Flüchtlinge zur Zeit des Nationalsozialismus*. Zürich, 2001.

———. *Die Schweiz und die deutschen Lösegelderpressungen in den besetzten Niederlanden: Vermögensentziehung, Freikauf, Austausch 1940–1945 Beiheft zum Bericht Die Schweiz und die Flüchtlinge zur Zeit des Nationalsozialismus*. Bern, 1999.

Urquhart, Clara, and Peter Ludwig Brent. *Enzo Sereni: A Hero of Our Times*. London, 1967.

van den Bergh, S. *Deportaties*. Bussum, 1945.

van der Boom, Bart. *"Wij weten niets van hun lot:" Gewone Nederlanders en de Holocaust*. Amsterdam, 2012.

van der Leeuw, A. J., ed. *Le-Ezrath Ha-am: Het Volk ter Hulpe*. Assen, 1985.

van der Ros, B., ed. *Geschiedenis van de christelijke dagbladpers in Nederland*. Kampen, 1993.

van Ditzhuijzen, Jeannette. *A Shtetl under the Sun: The Ashkenazic Community of Curaçao*. Amsterdam, 2011.

van Galen-Herrmann, Ruth. *Calmeyer, dader of mensenredder? Visies op Calmeyers rol in de jodenvervolging*. Soesterberg, 2009.

van Tijen, Tjebbe, and Akiko Tobu. *Memoraphilia*. Tokyo, 2004. [Also at http://socialhistory.org/sites/default/files/docs/arts-of-oneself.pdf.]

van Tijn, Gertrude. "Werkdorp Nieuwesluis." *Leo Baeck Institute Year Book* 14 (1969): 182–99.

Veld, N. K. C. A. in't, ed. *De Joodse Ereraad*. The Hague, 1989.

———. *De SS in Nederland: Documenten uit SS-Archieven, 1935–1945*. 2 vols. The Hague, 1976.

Warmbrunn, Werner. *The Dutch under German Occupation, 1940–1945*. Stanford, 1963.

Wasserstein, Bernard. "Ambiguities of Occupation: Foreign Resisters and Collaborators in Wartime Shanghai." In *Wartime Shanghai*, edited by Wen-hsin Yeh. London, 1998.

———. *Britain and the Jews of Europe, 1939–1945*. Rev. ed. London, 1988.

———. *Secret War in Shanghai*. London, 1998.

Weber, Ronald, *The Lisbon Route: Entry and Escape in Nazi Europe*. Lanham, MD, 2011.

Wijsmuller-Meijer, Truus. *Geen Tijd voor Tranen*. Amsterdam, 1961.

Wischnitzer, Mark. *To Dwell in Safety: The Story of Jewish Migration since 1800*. Philadelphia, 1948.

Wolff, Anni. *Schliesslich waren wir alle jung und lebenslustig: Erinnerungen: Von Berlin nach Israel.* Berlin, 1993.

Wyman, David S.. *Paper Walls: America and the Refugee Crisis, 1938–1941.* New York, 1985.

Ziegler, Sandra. *Gedächtnis und Identität der KZ-Erfahrung: Niederländische und deutsche Augenzeugenberichte des Holocaust.* Würzburg, 2006.

Zweig-Strauss, Hanna. *Saly Mayer (1882–1950): Ein Retter jüdischen Lebens während des Holocaust.* Cologne, 2007.

Abbreviations

AJDCNY	Archives of the American Jewish Joint Distribution Committee, New York
Bibl. Ros.	Bibliotheca Rosenthaliana, University of Amsterdam
BNA	British National Archives, Kew
CZA	Central Zionist Archives, Jerusalem
GFH	Ghetto Fighters House archive, Kibbutz Lohamei Hagetaot
GvT	Gertrude van Tijn
GvT, TWWM	Gertrude van Tijn, "The World Was Mine" (memoir), Leo Baeck Institute Archives, New York
IISH	Archive of the International Institute of Social History, Amsterdam
LBINY	Leo Baeck Institute Archives, Center for Jewish History, New York
NIOD	Archive of the Netherlands Institute for War Documentation, Amsterdam
NL-HaNA	Netherlands National Archives, The Hague
NL-HaNRK	Netherlands Red Cross Archive, The Hague
SM AfZ	Saly Mayer papers, Archiv für Zeitgeschichte, Swiss Federal Institute of Technology Zürich MF 11 & 12
YIVO	YIVO Archives, Center for Jewish History, New York

Notes

Prologue

1. Ronald Weber, *The Lisbon Route: Entry and Escape in Nazi Europe* (Lanham, MD, 2011), 15.

1. "Ruined Woman"

1. GvT, TWWM, I, 1.
2. Information from Stadtarchiv Braunschweig.
3. GvT, TWWM, I, 3.
4. Records of the school, Niedersächsisches Landesarchiv—Staatsarchiv Wolfenbüttel 167N/81 & 83. See also Meike Berg, *Jüdische Schulen in Niedersachsen: Tradition—Emanzipation—Assimilation* (Cologne, 2003).
5. GvT, TWWM, I, 3.
6. Ibid., 4.
7. Ibid., 6.
8. Ibid., 6–7.
9. Marion A. Kaplan, *The Making of the Jewish Middle Class: Women, Family, and Identity in Imperial Germany* (Oxford, 1991), 214.
10. GvT, TWWM, I, 7.
11. Ibid., 9–10.
12. Ibid., 11.
13. Ibid., 15.
14. Ibid., 16.
15. Ibid.
16. GvT to Chedwah van Tijn, 20 Aug. 1944, Chedwah Stein papers.
17. GvT, TWWM, I, 17.
18. Ibid., 20.
19. Ibid., 24.
20. Ibid.
21. Ibid., 28.
22. Ibid.
23. Gertrude Cohn to JNF, 3 Aug., 1916, CZA KKL1/224/2/217.
24. See Kaplansky to Gertrude Cohn, 14 Feb. 1917, CZA KKL1/57/30 and Cohn to Kaplansky, 15 Feb. 1917, CZA KKL1/57/29.

25. See cables between Vuyk and Felix Warburg, Jan.–Dec. 1915, AJDCNY 1914–18 1/2/1/18.1 & 19.1.
26. GvT, TWWM, I, 32.
27. Ibid., 193.

2. Rebuilding Lives

1. GvT, supplementary memoir, LBINY ME 1335, 26.
2. GvT diary entry, Baarn, 18 Aug. 1924, Van Tijn family papers.
3. GvT, TWWM, II, 3.
4. Central British Fund to GvT, 16 Jan. 1934, NIOD 181b/354.
5. Yehuda Bauer, *My Brother's Keeper: A History of the American Jewish Joint Distribution Committee, 1929–1939* (Philadelphia, 1974), 22.
6. Kahn to Jewish Refugees Committee, Amsterdam, 23 Jan. 1934, NIOD 181b/354.
7. GvT to Kahn, 2 Feb. 1934, ibid.
8. See H. B. J. Stegeman and J. P. Vorsteveld, *Het Joodse Werkdorp in de Wieringermeer, 1934–1941* (Zutphen, 1983), 34–5.
9. Report by GvT, 6 Nov. 1936, LBINY AR 3477/33.3/53.
10. Gertrude van Tijn, "Werkdorp Nieuwesluis," *Leo Baeck Institute Year Book* 14 (1969), 185, 189.
11. McDonald's resignation letter, 27 Dec. 1935, in Richard Breitman et al., eds., *Refugees and Rescue: The Diaries and Papers of James G. McDonald, 1935–1945* (Bloomington, 2009), 102.
12. See fund-raising pamphlet, 1935, LBINY AR 3477/33.3/51.
13. Van Tijn, "Werkdorp Nieuwesluis," 194.
14. Anni Wolff, *Schliesslich waren wir alle jung und lebenslustig: Erinnerungen: Von Berlin nach Israel* (Berlin, 1993), 24.
15. GvT to Joseph Rosen (Joint Distribution Committee, Paris), "streng vertraulich," 8 Sept. 1935, NIOD 181b/355.
16. Gertrude van Tijn, "Werkdorp Nieuwesluis," 194.
17. M. Rosenblueth (Jewish Agency, London) to C. Barlas (Jewish Agency Immigration Dept., Jerusalem), 8 Nov. 1935, CZA S7/288/35–36.
18. Report by GvT on Stichting Joodsche Arbeid, 6 Nov. 1936, LBINY AR 3477/33.3/53.
19. Arie Kuiper, *Een wijze ging voorbij: Het leven van Abel J. Herzberg* (Amsterdam, 1998), 183.

20. Stegeman and Vorsteveld, *Het Joodse Werkdorp in de Wieringermeer*, 92.
21. Gertrude's words were quoted in a letter from Eitje to Gertrude, 22 November 1934, cited in Dan Michman, "Ha-plitim ha-yehudiyim mi-germanyah be-holand ba-shanim 1933–1940" (PhD diss., The Hebrew University of Jerusalem, 1978), 198.
22. Robert T. Cohen to GvT, 1 June 1968, LBINY AR 3477/33.3/53.
23. Stegeman and Vorsteveld, *Het Joodse Werkdorp in de Wieringermeer*, 186.
24. Szold to GvT, 13 Oct. 1935 (copy), CZA A125/66.
25. GvT to D. J. Schweitzer, 27 July 1934, NIOD 181b/354.
26. GvT to B. Kahn, 31 July 1934, ibid.
27. J. B. Davidson, Jewish Refugees Committee, London, to GvT, 29 Jan. 1935, NIOD 181b/127.
28. GvT to Davidson, 31 Jan. 1935, ibid.
29. Wilfred S. Samuel, Jewish Refugees Committee, London, to Jewish Refugees Committee, Amsterdam, 11 December 1935, ibid.
30. GvT to Wilfred S. Samuel, 18 Dec. 1935, ibid.
31. GvT to Davidson, 31 Jan. 1935, ibid.
32. Memorandum by GvT, 7 Nov. 1935, IISH Judaica NL 14.
33. Amsterdam Jewish Refugees Committee report for 1935, 2 Feb. 1936, IISH BRO 1380.22 fol.
34. Bentwich to GvT, 23 March 1936, NIOD 181b/132.
35. Bentwich to GvT, 23 April & 1 May 1936, ibid.
36. GvT to Bentwich, 26 May 1936, ibid.
37. GvT to Bernard Kahn, 1 April 1936, NIOD 181b/356.
38. Baerwald to Felix Warburg et al., 6 May 1936, NIOD 217a/1h.
39. "Monthly Report Refugees Committee" (by GvT), 11 May 1936, IISH NL Judaica 19.
40. Amsterdam Jewish Refugees Committee report for 1935, 2 Feb. 1936, IISH BRO 1380.22 fol.
41. GvT to Stephen Jacobi (London), 25 Feb. 1937, NIOD 181b/129.
42. "Bericht" (by GvT), 18 Oct. 1937, NIOD 181b/143.
43. HICEM to Jewish Refugees Committee, Amsterdam, 9 Nov. 1937, NIOD 181b/341.
44. Jewish Refugees Committee, Amsterdam, to HICEM, 11 & 21 Nov. 1937, ibid.
45. David Cohen, *Zwervend en Dolend: De Joodse Vluchtelingen in Nederland in de Jaren, 1933–1940* (Haarlem, 1955), 95.

46. Amsterdam Jewish Refugees Committee report for Dec. 1937, 18 Jan. 1938, IISH Judaïca NL 20.
47. Stegeman and Vorsteveld, *Het Joodse Werkdorp in de Wieringermeer*, 107.
48. Speech by Rabbi Jonah B. Wise to executive of the Joint, 26 March 1935, AJDCNY 1933–44/14, 16. The girl's name is not given, and her ultimate fate is unknown.
49. GvT, Tweede rapport betreffende de werkzaamheden van het Comité voor Bijzondere Joodsche Belangen, Jan. 1934, IISH Judaica NL 7.
50. GvT to Kahn, 2 Feb. 1934, NIOD 181b/354.
51. Statement issued by Cohen on behalf of the Comité voor Bijzondere Joodsche Belangen, 1 April 1935, Bibl. Ros. Vereenigingen Comité—G.
52. "The Fate of German Returning Emigrants" (report by Jewish Central Information Office, Amsterdam), 31 March 1936, YIVO 448 (Israel Cohen Papers), series 1, file 9.
53. Jonathan I. Israel, "The Republic of the United Netherlands until about 1750," in J. C. H. Blom et al., eds., *The History of the Jews in the Netherlands* (Oxford, 2002), 89.
54. Vicki Caron, *Uneasy Asylum: France and the Jewish Refugee Crisis, 1933–1942* (Stanford, 1999), 103.
55. Ibid., 108.
56. Ibid., 111.
57. Eitje to G. van den Bergh, 23 March 1938, quoted in Dan Michman, "The Committee for Jewish Refugees in Holland (1933–1940)," *Yad Vashem Studies*, xiv (1981), 219.
58. GvT memo to AJDC, 22 July 1934, quoted in Bauer, *My Brother's Keeper*, 170–71.

3. "Death Ships"

1. GvT to Norman Bentwich, 12 Feb. 1936, NIOD 181b/175.
2. GvT, TWWM, II, 13.
3. GvT, TWWM, I, 54.
4. GvT to Jacques van Tijn, 2[7?] April 1937, [copy] Chedwah Stein papers.
5. Population register for Blaricum in Streekarchief Gooi en Vechtstreek, Hilversum.

6. Mentioned in partial reworking of GvT memoirs by Roberta Stein (GvT's granddaughter).
7. GvT, TWWM, II, 13a.
8. GvT, TWWM, II, 14.
9. HICEM to Ezra, 6 Dec. 1937, NIOD 181b/341.
10. Major Holema, Rijksveldwacht 6e District Brigade, Schagen, to District Commandant, Amsterdam, 14 Feb. 1938, NL-HaNA 2.09.45/881.
11. *Schager Courant*, 11 Feb. 1938.
12. Text of circular in Michman, "Ha-plitim ha-yehudiyim mi-germanyah be-holand ba-shanim, 1933–1940" (PhD diss., The Hebrew University of Jerusalem, 1978), 372–74. See also Bob Moore, *Refugees from Nazi Germany in the Netherlands, 1933–1940* (Dordrecht, 1986), 79–80.
13. Zara Steiner, *The Triumph of the Dark: European International History 1933–1939* (Oxford, 2011), 977.
14. Arieh Tartakower and Kurt R. Grossman, *The Jewish Refugee* (New York, 1944), 426.
15. David Cohen, *Zwervend en Dolend: De Joodse Vluchtelingen in Nederland in de Jaren, 1933–1940* (Haarlem, 1955), 103. Cohen's narrative dates this episode at November 9 (which is possible, as some isolated incidents of violence had already occurred on November 7 and 8), but it is more likely that it took place the next day.
16. Ibid., 105.
17. Ibid., 266.
18. Richard Breitman and Alan M. Kraut, *American Refugee Policy and European Jewry, 1933–1945* (Bloomington, 1987), 65.
19. Dan Michman, "The Committee for Jewish Refugees in Holland (1933–1940)," *Yad Vashem Studies*, xiv (1981), 212; also Michman, "Ha-plitim," 199, 498 (citing an interview with Wijsmuller-Meijer in 1975).
20. GvT to Baerwald , 14 Nov. 1938, AJDCNY 1933–44/695.
21. Joint (New York) to B. Kahn (London), 17 Nov. 1938, ibid.
22. German Jewish Children's Aid Committee, New York, to GvT, 17 Nov. 1938, ibid.
23. "Memorandum of telephone talk with Erich Warburg" concerning "urgent telephone message from Dr Meyer in Amsterdam," 17 Nov. 1938, AJDCNY 1933–44/703.
24. Cohen and GvT to Baerwald, 19 Nov. 1938, ibid.
25. Cecilia Razovsky (German Jewish Children's Aid Committee, New York) to JDC office, Paris, 28 Nov. 1938, ibid.

26. GvT TWWM, II, 16.
27. GvT to Joint Distribution Committee, Paris, 26 Dec. 1938, AJDCNY 1933–44/695.
28. Justice Ministry memorandum, [14] Dec. 1938, transcript in Corrie K. Berghuis ed., *Joodse Vluchtelingen in Nederland, 1938–1940: Documenten betreffende toelating, uitleiding en kampopname* (Kampen, 1990), 44.
29. Transcript ibid., 54–55.
30. "Note by Sir Herbert Emerson on Refugee Conditions in Holland," March 1939, AJDCNY 1933–44/189.
31. Form letter from D. Cohen to would-be hosts, 17 March 1939, Bibl. Ros., Vereeinigingen (Comité—G).
32. "Report on Refugee Work in Holland in February 1939," 17 March 1939 (unsigned but almost certainly by GvT), AJDCNY 1933–44/189.
33. Troper (Paris) to JDC, New York, 17 March 1938, AJDCNY 1933–44/189.
34. Gino Huiskes and Reinhilde van der Kroef eds., *Vluchtelingenkamp Westerbork* (Westerbork Cahiers 7, Assen, 1999), 25.
35. GvT report, Oct. 1944, LBINY AR 3477/33.3/51, 75.
36. See Salomon Jakob Flörsheim to David Cohen, 8 Sept. 1954, and reply by Cohen, 23 Sept. 1954 NIOD Doc I/294.
37. J. Reitsema et al. to Minister of Interior, 23 May 1939, Tresoar, Leeuwarden, 250/270.
38. "Camps," June 1939, AJDCNY 1933–44/700.
39. Cohen, *Zwervend en Dolend*, 319.
40. "Camps," report by GvT, 14 July 1939, AJDCNY 1933–44/700.
41. "General Review of Events in June," 31 July 1939, AJDCNY 1933–44/191.
42. The ship's tonnage is variously given in different sources. This information is from *Lloyd's Shipping Register* for 1940.
43. Aryeh L. Avneri, *Mi-"Velos" ad "Taurus:" asor rishon le-ha-apalah be-darkhei ha-yam, 1934–1944* (Tel Aviv, 1985), 127.
44. Shmarya Tsameret, *Boker tamid: igrot u-reshumot* (Tel Aviv, 1966), 103–4.
45. *Het Volksdagblad*, 15 July 1939; Chaja [Chaya] Brasz, "'Dodenschip' Dora," *Vrij Nederland*, 1 May 1993.
46. See Salomon Jakob Flörsheim to David Cohen, 8 Sept. 1954, and reply by Cohen, 23 Sept. 1954 NIOD Doc I/294.
47. *Het Volksdagblad*, 14 July 1939.

48. Diary of Paul Cohen, a passenger on the *Dora*, July–Aug. 1939, GFH 651.
49. Bracha Habas, *Portsei ha-shearim* (Tel Aviv, 1960), 198.
50. One of the passengers recorded that 370 boarded at Amsterdam: Paul Cohen Diary, July–Aug. 1939, GFH 651. The Minister of Justice stated that 307 embarked there: Minister of Justice to Minister of Foreign Affairs, 28 July 1939, GFH Holland 1113.
51. See, e.g., *Avondblad-Algemeen Handelsblad* and *Het Volksdagblad*, 17 July 1939.
52. Minister of Justice to Minister of Foreign Affairs, 28 July 1939, GFH Holland 1113.
53. Minister of Justice to Minister of the Interior, 22 August 1939, NIOD 181j/15; *Avondblad-Algemeen Handelsblad* and *Het Vaderland*, 26 Aug. 1939.
54. Paul Cohen Diary, July–Aug. 1939, GFH 651.
55. Tsameret, *Boker tamid*, 108.
56. *Avondblad-Algemeen Handelsblad*, 18 July 1939.
57. Handwritten note by GvT, c. 1964, LBINY AR 3477/33.3/53.
58. See correspondence and minutes in BNA CO 733/429/4. According to Haim Barlas, an official of the Jewish Agency's immigration department, the number of arriving passengers was 480. Haim Barlas, *Hatsalah bimei shoah* (Tel Aviv, 1975), 196.
59. Jewish Refugees Committee Report (by GvT) for Aug.–Oct. 1939, 25 Nov. 1939, AJDCNY 1933–44/700.
60. "Status of Jewish Refugees from Germany, Various European Countries, by H. Katzki," 5 July 1939, AJDCNY 1933–44/695.
61. Gambetta's precise words, in a speech at Saint-Quentin in 1872, varied slightly from the terser version generally attributed to him—and Oungre's quotation from memory was different again. The words were quoted by Churchill in his BBC broadcast (in French) to the French people on October 21, 1940.
62. Minutes of conference, 22–23 Aug. 1939, AJDCNY 1933–44/367.

4. Gertrude's War

1. GvT to Chedwah van Tijn, 5 Dec. 1945, Chedwah Stein papers.
2. GvT, TWWM, II, 19.
3. Werner Warmbrunn, memoir, LBINY ME 1418, 44. Warmbrunn states that on one occasion Bondy "came on" to him (ibid., 45).

4. "Camps," by GvT, 14 July 1939, AJDCNY 1933–44/700.
5. Jewish Refugees Committee, Report of Camp Department for Jan. 1940, NIOD 206/722–3.
6. Jewish Refugees Committee report submitted to the Joint, Aug.–Oct. 1939, NIOD 206/722.
7. GvT to JDC, New York, 12 Sept. 1939 (two letters and one telegram), AJDCNY 1933–44/69; Troper (Paris) to JDC, New York (cable), 12 Sept. 1939, ibid.
8. JDC, New York, to GvT, 18 Sept. 1939 (cable); JDC, New York, to Troper (Paris), 18 Sept. 1939 (cable), AJDCNY 1933–44/695.
9. Truus Wijsmuller-Meijer, *Geen Tijd voor Tranen* (Amsterdam, 1961), 119.
10. GvT to F. Borchardt, 20 Sept. 1939, AJDCNY 1933–44/658.
11. Malcolm MacDonald to Chaim Weizmann, 3 Oct. 1939, BNA FO 371/24095/54.
12. GvT to F. Borchardt, "Personal and Strictly Confidential," 20 Sept. 1939, AJDCNY 1933–44/658 and extracts in memorandum dated 3 Oct. 1939, AJDCNY 1933–44/631.
13. *Palestine Post*, 24 Sept. and 3 Oct. 1939.
14. Weizmann to Chamberlain, 29 August 1939, in Norman Rose ed., *The Letters and Papers of Chaim Weizmann*, series A, vol. 19, Jan. 1939–June 1940 (New Brunswick, NJ, 1977), 145; Ernst Nolte, "Die Vergangenheit die nicht vergehen will," *Frankfurter Allgemeine Zeitung*, 6 June 1986.
15. GvT to F. Borchardt, 20 Sept. 1939, AJDCNY 1933–44/658.
16. JDC, New York, to Troper (Amsterdam), 22 Sept. 1939 (cable), AJDCNY 1933–44/695; GvT record of conversation with Troper in Amsterdam, 10 Oct. 1939, AJDCNY 1933–44/703; Joseph Hyman (New York) to GvT, 18 Oct. 1939, AJDCNY 1933–44/631.
17. J. C. Hyman report to Executive Committee of JDC, 10 Oct. 1939, AJDCNY 1921–32/4/30/5/511.
18. Troper to Jewish Refugees Committee, Amsterdam, 16 Oct. 1939, AJDCNY 1933–44/703.
19. Yehuda Bauer, *American Jewry and the Holocaust: The American Jewish Joint Distribution Committee, 1939–1945* (Detroit, 1981), 137.
20. Ibid., 139.
21. Weizmann memorandum to British government, 18 Oct. 1939, in Barnet Litvinoff ed., *The Letters and Papers of Chaim Weizmann*, series B, vol. 2, Dec. 1931–April 1952 (New Brunswick, NJ, 1984), 375.

22. GvT for Stichting Joodsche Arbeid to Ministry of Justice, 4 Oct. 1939, and reply from J. Grevelink for Ministry of Justice, 9 Oct. 1939, NL-HaNA Ministerie van Justitie, 2.09.45/882.
23. Isabella Philip, Abraham Schüssel and Heinz Roberg were killed (Yad Vashem database of *shoah* victims); Dorothee Fliess survived (www.dorothee-fliess-fond.de/dorotheefliess).
24. Jewish Refugees Committee report, 25 Nov. 1939, AJDCNY 1933–44/700.
25. See, e.g., *Ochtenblad–Algemeen Handelsblad*, 29 Oct. 1939; *Het Vaderland* and *Leeuwarder Nieuwsblad*, 30 Oct. 1939; and *Het Volksdagblad*, 31 Oct. 1939.
26. GvT to HICEM, Paris, 24 Nov. 1939, YIVO RG 245.5 HIAS-HICEM MKM 16.8/119.
27. HICEM aide-mémoire, 26 Feb. 1940, YIVO RG 245.5 HIAS-HICEM MKM 16.8/121; HICEM to Jewish Refugees Committee, Amsterdam, 15 April 1940, ibid.
28. GvT to A. de Leeuw, 4 Dec. 1939, CZA J24/402–6.
29. "Comite voor Joodsche Vluchtelingen: Statistische Jahresuebersicht 1939 und 1940 für das American Joint Distribution Committee," Amsterdam, 15 April 1941, NIOD 217a/1g.
30. "J.D.C. Work for Refugees in Holland—1933–1942," 13 May 1942, NIOD 217a/1h.
31. Confidential report for Joint by GvT, 29 Feb. 1940, NIOD 217a/1g.
32. "Comite voor Joodsche Vluchtelingen: Statistische Jahresuebersicht 1939 und 1940 für das American Joint Distribution Committee," Amsterdam, 15 April 1941, NIOD 217a/1g.
33. See telegrams between Bondy, in Amsterdam, and JDC, New York, March–April 1940, in AJDCNY DORSA 2/2/49.
34. Debórah Dwork and Robert Jan van Pelt, *Flight from the Reich: Refugee Jews, 1933–1946* (New York, 2009), 114.
35. Enzo Hayim Sereni, *Ha-aviv ha-kadosh: yomanim, mikhtavim, maamarim: kovets*, ed. Kalev Ḳasṭelbolonzi (Tel Aviv, 194[6]), 300–301. Sereni refers to Gertrude as "V.T.," and he (or his Hebrew editor) renders the *werkdorp* as "Vorkdorf." His English biographers compound the error by locating it at "Veereenigen-Zee" (Clara Urquhart and Peter Ludwig Brent, *Enzo Sereni: A Hero of Our Times*, London, 1967, 137–39). In her personal copy of the latter work (now in the possession of her daughter), Gertrude corrected these errors.

36. Sereni, *Ha-aviv ha-kadosh*, 303.
37. Ibid., 302–4.
38. Yaacov Lozowick, *Hitler's Bureaucrats: The Nazi Security Police and the Banality of Evil* (London, 2002), 67; see also interview with Rafael in *Ha'aretz*, 2 Dec. 1994.
39. NL-HaNA, 2.09.45, Ministerie van Justitie, Rijksvreemdelingendienst (RVD), inv. 800. RVD report, 20 March 1940; and letter dated 4 April 1940 from Inspecteur der Koninklijke Marechaussee to RVD, ibid.
40. David Cohen to Minister for Home Affairs, 3 May 1940, transcript in Corrie K. Berghuis ed., *Joodse Vluchtelingen in Nederland, 1938–1940: Documenten betreffende toelating, uitleiding en kampopname* (Kampen, 1990), 162–65.
41. GvT, TWWM, II, 23.
42. Bentwich to GvT, 14 May 1940, NIOD 206/722–3.
43. Joanna Newman, "Nearly the New World: Refugees and the British West Indies, 1933–1945" (PhD diss., University of Southampton, 1998), 50.
44. Report by GvT, Oct. 1944, LBINY AR 3477/33.3/51, 3.
45. Ibid., 3.
46. Ibid., 4.
47. Ibid., 5.
48. Ibid., 4.
49. Ibid.; see also "The Persecution of Jews in Holland, 1940–1944," report by Israel Taubes, June 1945 (henceforth "Taubes report"), NIOD Ned Tau 9.1, 1.
50. Report by GvT, Oct. 1944, LBINY AR 3477/33.3/51, 4.

5. Mission to Lisbon

1. N. K. C. A. in't Veld, ed., *De SS in Nederland: Documenten uit SS-Archieven, 1935–1945* (The Hague, 1976), 2:1506; Werner Warmbrunn, *The Dutch under German Occupation, 1940–1945* (Stanford, 1963), 31.
2. Gerhard Hirschfeld, *Nazi Rule and Dutch Collaboration: The Netherlands under German Occupation, 1940–1945* (Oxford, 1988), 327.
3. Manifesto of the De Nederlandse Unie, 24 July 1941, reproduced in Wichert ten Have, *De Nederlandse Unie: Aanpassing, vernieuwing en confrontatie in bezettingstijd, 1940–1941* (Amsterdam, 1999), 16.

4. Ibid., 462–70.
5. Taubes report, NIOD Ned Tau 9.1, 1.
6. Memorandum by Joseph Schwartz (Lisbon) of conversation with Erwin Eliel, recently arrived from Amsterdam, 23 Sept. 1940, AJDCNY 1933–44/695.
7. Report by GvT, Oct. 1944, LBINY 3477/33.3/51, 6.
8. Ibid., 7.
9. GvT to JDC, New York, 4 July 1940, AJDCNY 1933–44/695.
10. GvT to JDC, Lisbon, 17 July 1940 (see also cable of same date and letter of 18 July), ibid.
11. These are presumably the twelve persons who, according to the last report of the Committee for Jewish Refugees, were "repatriated" to Germany in 1940. "Comité voor Joodsche Vluchtelingen Amsterdam: Statistische Jahresuebersicht 1939 und 1940 für das American Joint Distribution Committee," 15 April 1941, NIOD 217a/1g, 19. In her report of October 1944 (LBINY AR 3477/33.3/51, 75), Gertrude writes that sixty such refugees were handed over together with German army deserters by a Dutch military officer, who did not differentiate between the two groups.
12. GvT to Reichsvereinigung der Juden in Deutschland, 29 July 1940 (copy), NL-HaNA 2.09.45/827.
13. Report by GvT, Oct. 1944, LBINY AR 3477/33.3/51, 75.
14. Information on Emanuel Hirschhorn at Joods Monument: www.joodsmonument.nl.
15. Hirsch to Joint, 31 July 1940, AJDCNY 1933–44/695.
16. Henrietta K. Buchman (Joint) to Lawrence J. Gould (United Jewish Appeal), 6 April 1943, AJDCNY 1933–44/704.
17. Yehuda Bauer, *American Jewry and the Holocaust: The American Jewish Joint Distribution Committee, 1939–1945* (Detroit, 1981), 40.
18. GvT to German-Jewish Children's Aid, New York, 4 Nov. 1940, AJDCNY 1933–44/703.
19. GvT to Joint, New York, 28 Nov. 1940, NIOD 217a/1b.
20. GvT to Troper (Lisbon), 20 Nov. 1940, ibid.
21. GvT to Joint, Lisbon, 10 Dec. 1940, ibid.
22. Minute by Sir Nevile Bland, 4 Nov. 1940, BNA PRO FO 371/24462/462–3.
23. JDC, New York to JDC, Lisbon (cable), 16 Nov. 1940, NIOD 217a/1d; sim., 19 and 26 Nov. 1940, ibid; M. Troper for JDC to High

Commissioner for Dutch Refugees, Lisbon, 28 Nov. 1940, ibid; Joseph Schwartz for JDC, Lisbon, to M. Leavitt, JDC, New York, 29 Nov. 1940, ibid.

24. "The American Who Electrified Russia," a documentary film directed by Michael Chanan (2009).
25. GvT to Hebrew Sheltering and Immigrant Aid Society of America, 17 Feb. 1941, AJDCNY 1933–44/696.
26. GvT to Troper, 17 Feb. 1941, ibid.
27. GvT to Chedwah van Tijn, 29 May 1941, Chedwah Stein papers.
28. Louis de Jong, *Het Koninkrijk der Nederlanden in de Tweede Wereldoorlog*, vol. 4, pt. 2 (14 vols., The Hague, 1969–91), 874–5. (All citations here refer to the "scientific edition," available at www.niod.nl/koninkrijk/default.asp.)
29. Jacob Presser, *Ashes in the Wind: The Destruction of Dutch Jewry* (London, 2010), 48.
30. B. A. Sijes, *De Februari-Staking, 25–26 Februari 1941* (The Hague, 1954), 42, quoting the Communist *Het Volksdagblad* of 26 June 1940.
31. Reproduction of leaflet in Sijes, *De Februari-Staking*, opp. 110.
32. A. Asscher and D. Cohen to Rijksvreemdelingendienst, 2 April 1941, NL-HaNA 2.09.45/827.
33. *Het Joodsche Weekblad*, 27 June 1941.
34. GvT to Chedwah and David van Tijn, 8 March 1941, Chedwah Stein papers.
35. Ibid.
36. Cohen and GvT to Sicherheitspolizei, Amsterdam, 10 March 1941, NIOD 182/22.
37. "Comité voor Joodsche Vluchtelingen: Statistische Jahresuebersicht 1939 und 1940 für das American Joint Distribution Committee," Amsterdam, 15 April 1941, NIOD 217a/1g, 23.
38. Bob Moore, *Survivors: Jewish Self-Help and Rescue in Nazi-Occupied Western Europe* (Oxford, 2010), 28–31.
39. British Embassy, Lisbon, to Central Dept., Foreign Office, 15 Oct. 1940, BNA PRO FO 371/24462/464.
40. Minute by Sir Nevile Bland, 4 Nov. 1940, BNA PRO FO 371/24462/462–3.
41. GvT to Joint, Lisbon, 22 and 26 Aug. 1940, SM AfZ.
42. GvT to Troper (Lisbon), 29 Dec. 1940, NIOD 217a/1b.

43. Rijksvreemdelingendienst memorandum on meeting with Krim. Kom. Wolff, 30 Dec. 1940, NL-HaNA 2.09.45/827.
44. See my *Britain and the Jews of Europe, 1939–1945*, rev. ed. (London, 1988), 40.
45. Bauer, *American Jewry and the Holocaust*, 61–2.
46. Ronald Weber, *The Lisbon Route: Entry and Escape in Nazi Europe* (Lanham, MD, 2011), 184.
47. GvT to Troper (Lisbon), 19 Nov. 1940, NIOD 217a/1b.
48. According to Louis de Jong, *Het Koninkrijk*, vol. 5, pt. 2, 1014, Zoepf arrived in the Netherlands in March 1941. This seems to be an error. Zoepf was nominated as head of the proposed Zentralstelle für jüdische Auswanderung on April 1, 1941. But he did not immediately take up office. From 1938 to 1940 he had been stationed at the Hohenlychen Sanatorium north of Berlin, where Nazi doctors performed so-called medical experimentation on prisoners. According to his personnel file, he was not formally transferred to Holland until August 1941. He then became head of the Jewish Affairs department (known from February 1942 as IVB4) of the German Security Police in the Netherlands, with an office in The Hague. In an interrogation on August 8, 1960, he declared that he had first visited Holland in July 1941. In a later statement to the court at his trial in Munich on January 31, 1966, he stated that in early 1941 he had spent four months being trained for an "African project," the last six weeks of this period in Rome. The "loss of Abyssinia to the English," he said, led to his being ordered back to Berlin. He immediately applied for transfer to Holland. His application was approved, and "after a few weeks' holiday," he presented himself in The Hague. Since Addis Ababa fell on April 6, he is unlikely, according to this chronology, to have been present in Amsterdam in April and May 1941, when Gertrude says she met him. Of course, he may have been lying. Unfortunately, no German documentation concerning these interviews or Gertrude's visit to Lisbon has been found. Perhaps the man she met was another "Willy," Willy Lages, head of the SD office in Amsterdam. See documentation on Zoepf's prosecution and trial in NIOD 270g and Doc I/1955; also Anna Hájková, "The Making of a Zentralstelle: Die Eichmann-Männer in Amsterdam," *Theresienstädter Studien und Dokumente*, 2003, 361.

49. Documentation on Zoepf's prosecution and trial in NIOD 270g and Doc I/1955; Abel J. Herzberg, *Kroniek der Jodenvervolging, 1940–1945* (Amsterdam, 1985), 185; Stiftung Topographie des Terrors, *Topography of Terror: Gestapo, SS, and Reich Security Main Office on Wilhelm- and Prinz-Albrecht-Straße*: A Documentation (Berlin, 2010), 145; De Jong, *Het Koninkrijk*, vol. 5, pt. 2, 1035.
50. Report by GvT, Oct. 1944, LBINY AR 3477/33.3/51, 35.
51. Yaacov Lozowick, *Hitler's Bureaucrats: The Nazi Security Police and the Banality of Evil* (London, 2002), 35.
52. Rauter to Seyss-Inquart, 18 April 1941, in C. F. Rüter and D. W. de Mildt, eds., *Justiz und NS-Verbrechen: Sammlung Deutscher Strafurteile wegen Nationalsozialistischer Tötungsverbrechen, 1945–1999* (Amsterdam, 2001), 25:405–6.
53. Interview with Mirjam Bolle-Levie (one of the secretaries) in Willy Lindwer ed., *Het fatale dilemma: De Joodsche Raad voor Amsterdam, 1941–1943* (The Hague, 1995), 55.
54. See Salomon Jakob Flörsheim to David Cohen, 8 Sept. 1954, and reply by Cohen, 23 Sept. 1954, NIOD Doc I/294.
55. Livia Rothkirchen, *The Jews of Bohemia and Moravia: Facing the Holocaust* (Lincoln, NE, 2005), 122. See also Menahem Pinkhof, "Reshit ha-mahteret ha-halutsit be-holand," *Yediot bet lohamei ha-getaot* 13 (Jan. 1956): 16–21.
56. Arthur Koestler, *Scum of the Earth* (London, 1941), 244, 247.
57. Samuel Lubell, "War by Refugee," *Saturday Evening Post*, 29 March 1941.
58. Quoted in Arieh Tartakower and Kurt R. Grossman, *The Jewish Refugee* (New York, 1944), 93.
59. Report by GvT, Oct. 1944, LBINY AR 3477/33.3/51, 36.
60. GvT, TWWM, II, 36.
61. Bauer, *American Jewry and the Holocaust*, 63.
62. Richard Breitman et al. eds., *Refugees and Rescue: The Diaries and Papers of James G. McDonald, 1935–1945* (Bloomington, 2009), 250.

6. Crisis of Conscience

1. GvT to Troper, 14 May 1941, AJDCNY 1933–44/696.
2. GvT to Mayer, 28 May 1941, SM AfZ.
3. Helmut Krausnick and Martin Broszat (London, 1970), *Anatomy of the SS State*, 84.

4. Göring to Heydrich, 31 July 1941, Rüter and De Mildt, eds., *Justiz und NS-Verbrechen*, vol. 25, 407.
5. Ben Braber, "De activiteiten van Barbie in Nederland in de jaren, 1940–1945" (kand. scriptie, Universiteit Amsterdam, 1984), 12–13.
6. A. L. Scholtens for Ministerie van Sociale Zaken to Secretary-General, Department of Justice, 7 Aug. 1940, NL-HaNA 2.09.45/882.
7. James N. Rosenberg (for DORSA) to GvT, 29 Oct. 1940 (cable), AJDCNY 1933–44/696.
8. Copies of cables from GvT to DORSA, New York, 2 and 9 Dec. 1940; GvT to James Rosenberg, DORSA, 10 Dec. 1940; GvT to Troper (Lisbon), 22 Dec. 1940; and GvT to Troper, 23 Dec. 1940, AJDCNY 1933–44/696.
9. GvT and Cohen to Sicherheitspolizei, 24 March 1941, NIOD 182/22.
10. Cohen to Sicherheitspolizei, 28 March 1941, ibid.
11. Report by GvT, Lisbon, 6 May 1941, AJDCNY 1933–44/703.
12. According to Gertrude, the meeting took place at Barbie's office. According to Cohen, Barbie came to the office of the Jewish Council. Report by GvT, Oct. 1944, LBINY AR 3477/33.3/51, 16; David Cohen, *Voorzitter van de Joodse Raad: De herinneringen van David Cohen (1941–1943)*, ed. Erik Somers (Zutphen, 2010), 104.
13. Report by GvT, Oct. 1944, LBINY AR 3477/33.3/51, 16.
14. GvT to Sicherheitspolizei, 9 June 1941 (copy sent to Prof. Cohen), NIOD 182/22.
15. Report by GvT, Oct. 1944, LBINY AR 3477/33.3/51, 16.
16. Kan to Calmeyer, 18 June 1941, GFH Holland 667. Kan later resigned from the council in protest against its policies.
17. See Joachim Castan, ed., *Hans Calmeyer und die Judenrettung in den Niederlanden* (Göttingen, 2003); Mathias Middelberg, *Judenrecht, Judenpolitik und der Jurist Hans Calmeyer in den besetzten Niederlanden, 1940–1945* (Göttingen, 2005); and Ruth van Galen-Herrmann, *Calmeyer, dader of mensenredder? Visies op Calmeyers rol in de jodenvervolging* (Soesterberg, 2009).
18. Marti note, 28 Jan. 1942, quoted in Jean-Claude Favez, *The Red Cross and the Holocaust* (Cambridge, 1999), 164.
19. "Übersicht über die z. Zt. einsitzenden Häftlinge (Stichtag: 28.12.1941)," in Jacob Presser, *Ashes in the Wind: The Destruction of Dutch Jewry* (London, 2010), 71.

20. List of arrested Wieringen students with dates of death notifications, GFH Holland 667. See "Zum Geleit" (preface), diary of an unidentified Wieringen student, entry for 11 June 1941, ibid. Other sources give the number of Wieringers arrested as 60 or 61.
21. Presser, *Ashes in the Wind*, 70; Bob Moore, *Victims and Survivors: The Nazi Persecution of the Jews in the Netherlands 1940–1945* (London, 1997), 82.
22. Report by GvT, Oct. 1944, LBINY AR 3477/33.3/51, 16.
23. This is the view of Moore, *Victims and Survivors*, 82.
24. Report by GvT, Oct. 1944, LBINY AR 3477/33.3/51, 16.
25. Memorandum from J. F. Cahen to H. Viteles, 25 Aug. 1948, AJDCNY 1945–54/426.
26. GvT to Trone, 2 July 1941, Sasha Trone papers.
27. Louis de Jong, *Het Koninkrijk der Nederlanden in de Tweede Wereldoorlog*, vol. 5, pt. 2, 1006–8.
28. GvT to Troper, 23 June 1941, AJDCNY 1933–44/696.
29. De Jong, *Het Koninkrijk*, vol. 5, pt. 2, 1039.
30. Cohen, *Voorzitter*, 110.
31. Simon Heinrich Herrmann, *Austauschlager Bergen-Belsen: Geschichte eines Austauschtransportes* (Tel Aviv, 1944), 6.
32. Report by GvT, Oct. 1944, LBINY AR 3477/33.3/51, 36.
33. *Het Joodsche Weekblad*, 11 July 1941.
34. Order dated 25 Nov. 1941, Rüter and De Mildt eds., *Justiz und NS-Verbrechen*, 25:410.
35. Report by GvT, Oct. 1944, LBINY AR 3477/33.3/51, 14.
36. *Het Joodsche Weekblad*, 17 April 1941.
37. Transcript of telegram, dated 19 May, in GvT to Trone, 22 May 1941, Sasha Trone papers.
38. Ibid.
39. GvT to "my dear friends," probably Trone and his wife, 22 May 1941 (second letter of that day, a private letter, handwritten), Sasha Trone papers.
40. GvT to Trone (cable and letter), 3 June 1941, Sasha Trone papers.
41. GvT to Trone, 18 June 1941, Sasha Trone papers.
42. Compare list of names in GvT cable to Trone, 18 June 1941, Sasha Trone papers, with list of Wieringers sent to Mauthausen, GFH Holland 667.
43. See GvT to Trone, 2 July 1941; and entries in *Joods Monument* for Kanin and Mietje Kanin van der Ster.

44. GvT to H. Schnapek, 25 Aug. 1941, Sasha Trone papers.
45. Memorandum by Morris Troper, 25 Sept. 1941, AJDCNY DORSA 2/2/50.
46. Report by Rebecca Hourwich Rayher, Executive Secretary of DORSA, 18 June 1943, AJDCNY DORSA 2/2/51.
47. Ibid.
48. Simone Gigliotti, "'Acapulco in the Atlantic': Revisiting Sosúa, a Jewish Refugee Colony in the Caribbean," *Immigrants and Minorities* 24, no. 1 (2006): 34.
49. GvT to Troper (New York), 25 Aug. 1941, AJDCNY 33–44/696.
50. *Het Joodsche Weekblad*, 12 and 19 Sept. 1941.
51. Minutes of meeting of Jewish Council, 17 Sept. 1941, NIOD 182/3.
52. GvT to JDC, Lisbon, 9 Oct. 1941, AJDCNY 1933–44/696.
53. GvT to Troper (New York), 7 Nov. 1941, ibid.; GvT to Joseph Schwartz (Lisbon), 7 Nov. 1941, ibid.
54. GvT to Chedwah and David van Tijn, 27 Oct. 1941, Chedwah Stein papers. Unlike most of her family letters, this one was written in Dutch, not English.
55. Minutes of meeting of Jewish Council, 27 Nov. 1941, NIOD 182/3.
56. GvT to Chedwah Stein, 22 Nov. 1941, Chedwah Stein papers.
57. *Het Joodsche Weekblad*, 5 Dec. 1941.
58. NIOD 182/77.
59. Taubes report, NIOD Ned Tau 9.1, 12.
60. *Het Joodsche Weekblad*, 12 Jan. 1942.
61. Report by GvT, Oct. 1944, LBINY AR 3477/33.3/51, 39.
62. Record of meeting in *Documents on German Foreign Policy, 1918–1945*, series D, vol. 13 (London, 1964), 598–602.
63. Johannes Houwink ten Cate, "Heydrich's Security Police and the Amsterdam Jewish Council (February 1941–October 1942)," in Jozeph Michman ed., *Dutch Jewish History* III (Assen, 1993), 388 and 393.
64. Form letter dated 27 Jan. 1942, NIOD 182/2.
65. Presser, *Ashes in the Wind*, 100.
66. Houwink ten Cate "Heydrich's Security Police," 383, quoting Eichmann's interrogation by Israeli police prior to his trial in 1961.
67. Minutes of central committee meeting, 13 Feb. 1942, NIOD 182/38.
68. Minutes of central committee meeting, 6 Feb. 1942, NIOD 182/38.
69. GvT to Rabbi J. H. Dünner, 16 Feb. 1942, NIOD 182/11.
70. GvT to Mrs Curica Morpurgo, 17 Feb. 1942, NIOD 182/77.

71. GvT to Käthe Robinson, 2 March 1942, NIOD 182/10; GvT to C. Friedländer, ibid; GvT and B. Imbach to Frau B. Marx-Fraenkel, 2 March 1942, IISH Judaica NL 55.
72. Report by GvT, Oct. 1944, LBINY AR 3477/33.3/51, 40.
73. GvT to Mayer, 1 Feb. 1942, SM AfZ.
74. GvT to Chedwah and David van Tijn, 8 March 1942. An English translation of this German letter was forwarded from Switzerland by Saly Mayer on April 1, Chedwah Stein papers and SM AfZ.
75. GvT to Mayer, 1 April 1942, SM AfZ.
76. GvT to Chedwah van Tijn, 19 April 1942, Chedwah Stein papers.
77. *Het Joodsche Weekblad*, 24 April 1942.
78. Report by GvT, Oct. 1944, LBINY AR 3477/33.3/51, 19.
79. Harster to Wimmer, 29 April 1942, reporting on meeting of Aus der Fünten with Asscher and Cohen, in Rüter and de Mildt, eds., *Justiz und NS-Verbrechen: Sammlung Deutscher Strafurteile wegen Nationalsozialistischer Tötungsverbrechen, 1945–1999* (Amsterdam, 2001) 25:457.
80. Report by GvT, Oct. 1944, LBINY AR 3477/33.3/51, 21.
81. Ibid.
82. Presser, *Ashes in the Wind*, 123.
83. GvT to Chedwah and David van Tijn (via Saly Mayer), 5 May 1942, SM AfZ.
84. GvT to Mayer, 23 June 1940, AJDC Oral Hist. Box 9, Gertrude van Tijn.
85. Pierre Béguin, *Le Balcon sur l'Europe: Petite Histoire de la Suisse pendant la guerre 1939–1945* (Neuchâtel, 1950).
86. Hanna Zweig-Strauss, *Saly Mayer (1882–1950): Ein Retter jüdischen Lebens während des Holocaust* (Cologne, 2007), 201–2.
87. GvT to Mayer, 27 May 1942, SM AfZ.
88. GvT to Mayer, 5 Aug. 1942, ibid.
89. Minutes of meeting of Jewish Council, 4 June 1942, NIOD 182/3.
90. Cohen to James G. McDonald, 27 Dec. 1953, AJDCNY 1933–44/703.
91. Minutes of meeting of central committee, 5 June 1942, NIOD 182/38.
92. Original minutes of meeting of central committee on 12 June 1942, ibid.
93. Minutes of meeting of central committee, 19 June 1942, ibid.
94. De Jong, *Het Koninkrijk*, vol. 6, pt. 1, 261.
95. Cohen, *Voorzitter*, 133.

96. GvT to Chedwah and David van Tijn (via Saly Mayer), 15 June 1942, SM AfZ.

7. Help for the Departing

1. Interrogation of Wilhelm Zoepf, Munich, 8 Aug. 1960, NIOD Doc. I, 1955.
2. Saul Friedländer, *The Years of Extermination: Nazi Germany and the Jews, 1939–1945* (New York, 2007), 374; Pim Griffioen and Ron Zeller, *Jodenvervolging in Nederland, Frankrijk en België, 1940–1945: Overeenkomsten, verschillen, oorzaken* (Amsterdam, 2011), 395, 398.
3. Griffioen and Zeller, *Jodenvervolging*, 429; Jacob Presser, *Ashes in the Wind: The Destruction of Dutch Jewry* (London, 2010), 136.
4. Minutes of meeting of Jewish Council, 1 July 1942, in which Cohen reported on meeting with Aus der Fünten, NIOD 182/3.
5. Report by GvT, Oct. 1944, LBINY AR 3477/33.3/51, 44.
6. Information from Herinneringscentrum Kamp Westerbork, 27 Nov. 2012.
7. Friedländer, *The Years of Extermination*, 404.
8. Guido Abuys, *Het Eerste Transport—15 juli 1942 vanuit kamp Westerbork* (Westerbork, 2012), 19; information from Guus Luijters; C. F. Rüter and D. W. de Mildt, eds., *Justiz und NS-Verbrechen: Sammlung Deutscher Strafurteile wegen Nationalsozialistischer Tötungsverbrechen, 1945–1999* (Amsterdam, 2001), 25:499–501.
9. David Cohen, *Voorzitter van de Joodse Raad: De herinneringen van David Cohen (1941–1943)*, ed. Erik Somers (Zutphen, 2010), 142.
10. *Het Joodsche Weekblad*, 7 Aug. 1942.
11. L. Rein and F. Silten to co-chairmen of Jewish Council, 13 Aug. 1942, NIOD 182/13.
12. Unsigned memorandum "for the attention of Dr D. Cohen," received 11 Oct. 1942, ibid.
13. L. Rein and F. Silten to co-chairmen of Jewish Council, 4 Dec. 1942, NIOD 182/16.
14. Report by GvT, Oct. 1944, LBINY AR 3477/33.3/51, 47.
15. Ibid.
16. GvT to Mayer, 29 July 1942, SM AfZ.
17. Report by GvT, Oct. 1944, LBINY AR 3477/33.3/51, 48.

18. Minutes of meeting of central committee, 11 Sept. 1942, NIOD 182/38.
19. Minutes of meeting of central committee, 18 Sept. 1942, ibid.
20. Raymund Schütz, "Vermoedelijk op transport," Masterscriptie Archiefwetenschappen, Leiden Instituut Geschiedenis, 2010/11, 74–75. Communication from Mr Schütz to the author, 3 Jan. 2013.
21. Two versions of minutes of meeting of central committee on 18 Sept. 1942, NIOD 182/38.
22. Central committee meeting, 20 Oct. 1942, NIOD 182/38.
23. See A. Krouwer and P. H. Hendrix to co-chairmen of Jewish Council, 12 Oct. 1942, NIOD 182/13.
24. See correspondence between GvT and S. van Adelsberg, 2–30 Sept. 1942, NL-HaNRK 2050/23.
25. Cohen to GvT, 17 Aug. and 20 Aug. 1942 (and other letters of these dates), NIOD 182/12.
26. Presser, *Ashes in the Wind*, 176. See also report to Jewish Council chairmen by S. Roet, financial director of the department, 25 Nov. 1942, NIOD 182/79.
27. "Richtlijnen (tweede uitgifte)," n.d. [1942], NIOD 182/78; see also Presser, *Ashes in the Wind*, 252.
28. Copy of summons issued to Levy Hartog, 23 Sept. 1942, NL-HaNA, Ministerie van Justitie, Centraal Archief Bijzondere Rechtspleging, 1945–1949 (1952), inv. nr. 66I, verzameldossier BR.v.C.: 55/50. Hartog, aged seventy-five, was deported to Westerbork on Sept. 23, 1942, and from there to Auschwitz on Sept. 25. He was killed on Sept. 28.
29. *Het Joodsche Weekblad*, 11 Dec. 1942.
30. Taubes report, 15, NIOD Ned Tau 9.1.
31. GvT form letter to appointees to her department, 1942, NIOD 182/78.
32. Jewish Council, Lijnbaansgracht 366, form letter to Doncker family, 9 Oct. 1942, NIOD 182/88.
33. GvT to Cohen, 18 Jan. 1943, NIOD 182/17.
34. Cohen to GvT, 19 Jan. 1943, ibid.
35. GvT to chairmen of Jewish Council, 12 May 1943, NIOD 182/20.
36. GvT, TWWM, II, 57.
37. Ibid.
38. GvT, TWWM, II, 58.
39. Mark Schellekens, *Walter Süskind* (Amsterdam, 2012); Bob Moore, *Survivors: Jewish Self-Help and Rescue in Nazi-Occupied Western Europe*

(Oxford, 2010), 311; Bert Jan Flim, *Omdat Hun Hart Sprak: Geschiedenis van de Georganiseerde Hulp aan Joodse Kinderen in Nederland, 1942–1945* (Kampen, 1996), 121–64; Flim, *Saving the Children: History of the Organized Effort to Rescue Jewish Children in the Netherlands, 1942–1945* (Bethesda, MD, 2005), 46–72.

40. Cohen, *Voorzitter*, 150.
41. Presser, *Ashes in the Wind*, 276.
42. Rauter to Himmler, 10 Sept. 1942, NL-HaNA, Ministerie van Justitie, Centraal Archief Bijzondere Rechtspleging, 1945–1949 (1952), inv. nr. 66I, verzameldossier BR.v.C.: 55/50.
43. Rauter to Himmler, 24 Sept. 1942, text in N. K. C. A. in't Veld, ed., *De SS in Nederland Documenten uit SS-Archieven, 1935–1945* (The Hague, 1976), 2:1565.
44. "Entwicklung der Judenfrage in den Niederlanden (bis zum Jahresende 1942)," copy of memorandum handwritten by Gertrud Slottke (assistant to Zoepf), NL-HaNA, Ministerie van Justitie, Centraal Archief Bijzondere Rechtspleging, 1945–1949 (1952), inv. nr. 66I, verzameldossier BR.v.C.: 55/50.
45. Presser, *Ashes in the Wind*, 190–91.

8. Trading with the Enemy

1. "Tätigkeitsbericht der Auswanderungsabteilung, Lijnbaansgracht," Amsterdam, 13 Nov. 1942, ibid.
2. GvT to David Cohen, 25 Nov. 1942, NIOD 182/15.
3. GvT to Mayer, 21 Dec. 1942, SM AfZ.
4. GvT to Mayer, 14 Sept. 1942, ibid.
5. Lichtheim to Mayer, 24 Sept. 1942, ibid.
6. Ben Hummel, "De Derde Duits-Palestijnse Uitwisseling of hoe 281 Joden in Juli 1944 Gered Werden" (doctoraal-scriptie, Rijksuniversiteit Groningen, 1987), 12.
7. GvT letter to friends, Haifa, 10 Aug. 1944, NIOD Doc I/1720B.
8. Helmuth Mainz, "Erlebnisse 1940–1944" (duplicated typescript, Bibl. Ros.), 29.
9. GvT circular letter to friends, Haifa, 10 Aug. 1944, Chedwah Stein papers.
10. Hummel, "De Derde Duits-Palestijnse Uitwisseling," 12–14; *The Times*, 14 Nov. 1942.

11. A. N. Oppenheim, *The Chosen People: The Story of the "222 Transport" from Bergen-Belsen to Palestine* (London, 1996), 63, 87.
12. Mainz, "Erlebnisse," 30–31.
13. "Strictly confidential" memorandum by GvT, 21 June 1943, NIOD 182/69.
14. GvT to Jewish Council dept. in Westerbork, 30 Dec. 1942, ibid.
15. See my *Britain and the Jews of Europe, 1939–1945*, rev. ed. (London, 1988), 155.
16. GvT to Mayer, 29 June 1943, SM AfZ.
17. Report by GvT, Oct. 1944, LBINY AR 3477/33.3/51, 43.
18. GvT to Edith S. Landwirth, 24 May 1943, JHM 00001444.
19. Memoirs of her foster-father, Louis Ph. Polak, JHM 00001678/63–4.
20. Saly Mayer to Jewish Council, Amsterdam, 9 Sept. 1943, SM AfZ.
21. See, e.g., Albersheim to S. de Jong, 16 Feb. 1943, NIOD 250i/957.
22. See, e.g., GvT to J. de Jong (a minor), 24 May 1943, ibid.; also GvT to A. D. Nathans, 1 July 1943, NIOD 250i/954.
23. Memorandum by Dorothy L. Speiser, 25 Feb. 1943, NIOD 217a/1h.
24. Joanna Newman, "Nearly the New World: Refugees and the British West Indies, 1933–1945" (PhD diss., University of Southampton, 1998), 265.
25. Jeannette van Ditzhuijzen, *A Shtetl under the Sun: The Ashkenazic Community of Curaçao* (Amsterdam, 2011), 89.
26. Ibid., 90–92.
27. Independent Commission of Experts Switzerland—Second World War, *Switzerland, National Socialism and the Second World War: Final Report* (Zürich, 2002), 114.
28. According to a note by Mayer, 13 Feb. 1943, of a conversation with Roger Brunschvig, recently returned from Amsterdam, SM AfZ. A figure of SF 57,500, made available by Mayer "for work in Holland during 1943 (via G.v.T.)," is given in a memorandum by GvT, 27 April 1945, NIOD Doc I/1720B; this may include money paid by Mayer to GvT through other channels.
29. Yehuda Bauer, *American Jewry and the Holocaust: The American Jewish Joint Distribution Committee, 1939–1945* (Detroit, 1981), 276. See also GvT to Mayer, 20 Nov. 1942, SM AfZ.
30. Independent Commission of Experts Switzerland—Second World War, *Switzerland*, 117.

31. Raul Hilberg, *The Destruction of the European Jews*, rev. ed. (New York, 1985), 2:576–77.
32. Memorandum by Himmler, 10 Dec. 1942; text in Veld, N. K. C. A. in't, ed., *De SS in Nederland: Documenten uit SS-Archieven, 1935–1945* (The Hague, 1976), 1:824–26.
33. Pauline Micheels, *De vatenman: Bernard van Leer (1883–1958)* (Amsterdam, 2002).
34. Independent Commission of Experts Switzerland—Second World War, *Switzerland*, 161; Tweede Kamer der Staten-Generaal Enquêtecommissie Regieringsbeleid 1940–1945, *Verslag Houdende de Uitkomsten van het Onderzoek*, vol. 6A (The Hague, 1952), 348.
35. Hilberg, *The Destruction of the European Jews*, 2:577.
36. Leland Harrison (Berne) to State Department, 28 Oct. 1942, www.ushmm.org/assets/documents/usa/i-11.pdf.
37. Douglas Cooper to Commercial Counsellor, British Legation, Berne, 2 March 1945, www.fold3.com/image/#270079354.
38. Independent Commission of Experts Switzerland—Second World War, *Switzerland*, 9.
39. Memorandum by Dorothy L. Speiser, 25 Feb. 1943, NIOD 217a/1h.
40. Unabhängige Expertenkommission Schweiz—Zweiter Weltkrieg, *Die Schweiz und die deutschen Lösegelderpressungen in den besetzten Niederlanden Vermögensentziehung, Freikauf, Austausch 1940–1945 Beiheft zum Bericht Die Schweiz und die Flüchtlinge zur Zeit des Nationalsozialismus* (Bern, 1999), 10, 63, 137, 176.
41. GvT to Mayer, 17 Aug. 1942, SM AfZ.
42. Transcript of conversation, 25 Aug. 1942, SM AfZ.
43. GvT to Mayer, undated [probably autumn 1942] letter numbered 3487, ibid; GvT to Mayer, 23 Dec. 1942 and 4 Feb. 1943, ibid; Mayer correspondence with Eidgenössische Fremdenpolizei Emigrantenbureau, Dec. 1942–Jan. 1943, ibid.
44. Note by Mayer of conversation with Brunschvig, 13 Feb. 1943, ibid.
45. Presser, *Ashes in the Wind*, 285–86.
46. HL Deb, 24 November 1942, vol. 125, cols. 195–96.

9. To the Bitter End

1. Report by GvT, Oct. 1944, LBINY AR 3477/33.3/51, 61.
2. Monthly departmental report for March 1943, signed by GvT on 14 April 1943, NIOD 182/80.
3. According to Roet, in a memorandum dated 16 May 1952, appended to the minute book of the board of directors, Amsterdam Stadsarchief, Nederlands Israëlitisch Jongensweeshuis Megoddle Jethomim, 1205, the removal of the children took place on "5 or 6 March." However, Guus Luijters and Raymund Schütz have established, on the basis of materials in the Amsterdam City Archives and the Dutch Red Cross Archives, that the children were removed on 10 February 1943. I am grateful to them for this information. According to Roet's account, parents who tried to approach the building to see their children for the last time were held back. When they nevertheless surged forward, the Amsterdam fire brigade sprayed water to drive them away. No corroboration of these details has been found in any contemporary source.
4. Minutes of meeting of central committee, 26 February 1943, at which report was presented on meeting of co-chairmen with Lages and other German officials the previous day, NIOD 182/38.
5. Unsigned typewritten note, 3 March 1943, NIOD 182/17.
6. Minutes of meeting of central committee of Jewish Council, 5 March 1943, NIOD 182/38.
7. Monthly departmental report for March 1943, signed by GvT, 14 April 1943, NIOD 182/80.
8. E. Sluzker (Expositur) to GvT, 31 March 1943, conveying inquiry from Zentralstelle. Information on the subsequent fates of the persons sought is from *Joods Monument* (www.joodsmonument.nl/).
9. Jacob Presser, *Ashes in the Wind: The Destruction of Dutch Jewry* (London, 2010), 202.
10. GvT to David Cohen, 22 March 1943, NIOD 182/17. The four were Abraham Cohen (d. Auschwitz, 8 Jan. 1944), Lion (Levie) Cohen (d. Sobibor, 28 May 1943), Abraham Ensel (d. Auschwitz, 8 April 1944), and Ernst Maier (d. Amsterdam, 29 April 1987).
11. Minutes of meeting of central committee, 16 March 1943, NIOD 182/38; GvT to Cohen, 25 March 1943, NIOD 182/17.
12. GvT to Cohen, 12 May 1943, NIOD 182/20; Cohen to GvT, 13 May 1943, ibid.

13. GvT to chairmen, Jewish Council, 20 May 1943, NIOD 182/20.
14. Zoepf to "Judenlager Westerbork," 10 May 1943, C. F. Rüter and D. W. De Mildt eds., *Justiz und NS-Verbrechen: Sammlung Deutscher Strafurteile wegen Nationalsozialistischer Tötungsverbrechen, 1945–1999* (Amsterdam, 2001), 25:485–86.
15. Minutes of meeting of Jewish Council, 21 May 1943, NIOD 182/3.
16. David Cohen, *Voorzitter van de Joodse Raad: De herinneringen van David Cohen (1941–1943)*, ed. Erik Somers (Zutphen, 2010), 166; Minutes of meeting of central committee, 21 May 1943, NIOD 182/38. The minutes do not record the objections of Gertrude and the three others.
17. GvT to Mayer, 21 May 1943, SM AfZ.
18. Memoirs of Louis Ph. Polak, JHM 1678, 43–7.
19. GvT to Cohen, 24 May 1943 (two letters), NIOD 182/20.
20. Memoirs of Louis Ph. Polak, JHM 1678, 44.
21. Cohen, *Voorzitter*, 169.
22. Report by GvT, Oct. 1944, LBINY AR 3477/33.3/51, 64.
23. Presser, *Ashes in the Wind*, 207.
24. Report by GvT, Oct. 1944, LBINY AR 3477/33.3/51, 64–66. The account of Gertrude's release by Aus der Fünten is corroborated by Mirjam Bolle in a diary letter written in Westerbork approximately two months later. Mirjam Bolle, *Ik zal je beschrijven hoe een dag er hier uitziet: Dagboekbrieven uit Amsterdam, Westerbork en Bergen-Belsen* (Amsterdam, 2003), 130.
25. Copy of report prepared for SS Sturmbannführer Wilhelm Zoepf, "Betrifft: Aktion am 26.5.1943 im Judenviertel in Amsterdam," The Hague, 27 May 1943, NL-HaNA, Ministerie van Justitie, Centraal Archief Bijzondere Rechtspleging, 1945–1949 (1952), inv. nr. 66I, verzameldossier BR.v.C.: 55/50.
26. O. Bene (The Hague) to German Foreign Ministry, 6 June 1943 (quoting secret SD report), in Rüter and De Mildt eds., *Justiz und NS-Verbrechen*, 25:604.
27. Report by Slottke, 26 May 1943, ibid., 603.
28. Guus Luijters, *In Memoriam: De gedeporteerde en vermoorde Joodse, Roma en Sinti kinderen 1942–1945* (Amsterdam, 2012), 34; Pim Griffioen and Ron Zeller, *Jodenvervolging in Nederland, Frankrijk en België, 1940–1945: Overeenkomsten, verschillen, oorzaken* (Amsterdam, 2011), 894–95.

29. GvT to Asscher and Cohen, 4 June 1943, NL-HaNRK 2050/29.
30. Document dated 26 June 1943, LBINY AR 3477/33.3/52.
31. Memorandum dated 5 Aug. 1943, NIOD 182/1.
32. Ursula Zürcher-Brahn, "Max Brahn: Lebenslauf, nach den spärlichen übriggebliebenen Quellen zusammengestellt von seiner Tochter," LBINY ME 68.
33. Cohen, *Voorzitter*, 191.
34. Report by GvT, Oct. 1944, LBINY AR 3477/33.3/51, 21.
35. Annet Mooij, "Ernst Laqueur" in *Biographisch Woordenboek van Nederland*.
36. Hillesum diary entry, 28 Sept. 1942, Klaas A. D. Smelik, ed., *Etty: The Letters and Diaries of Etty Hillesum, 1941–1943* (Grand Rapids, MI, 2002), 534; see also 750n.
37. Walter Sneader, *Drug Discovery: A History* (Chichester, 2005), 174–76, 197.
38. *New York Times*, 16 Sept. 1935.
39. Memorandum by Wilhelm Zoepf, The Hague, 24 Feb. 1942, NIOD 77/1307.
40. Lages (SD office Amsterdam) to Befehlshaber der Sicherheitspolizei, The Hague (cable), 12 March 1942, ibid.
41. Eichmann (Berlin) to Zoepf (The Hague), 23 May 1942 (cable), NIOD 77/1307.
42. Information from P. J. Knegtmans, who is writing a biography of Ernst Laqueur.
43. P. J. Knegtmans in conversation with the author, 7 Aug. 2011.
44. Hillesum diary entry, 28 Sept. 1942, Smelik, *Etty*, 534.
45. GvT to Chedwah van Tijn, 14 Nov. 1944, Chedwah Stein papers.
46. GvT, TWWM, II, 47. NB There is some confusion in page numbering of the typescript at this point.
47. GvT to Chedwah van Tijn, 14 Nov. 1944, Chedwah Stein papers.
48. "Lijst van medewerker(sters) van den Joodschen Raad per 10 September 1943," NIOD Doc II/366A/T.
49. Copy of unsigned, undated memorandum, NIOD 182/20; minutes of meeting of central committee of Jewish Council, 13 Sept. 1943, NIOD 182/38.
50. Szold to GvT, 21 Sept. 1943, NL-HaNRK 2050/356.
51. GvT to Chedwah and David van Tijn, 6 Sept. 1943, Chedwah Stein papers.

10. Last Exit from Amsterdam

1. Hundreds of notices of such parcels are in NIOD 182/90.
2. Lichtheim to L. Lauterbach (Jerusalem), 29 Sept. 1943, CZA S26/1259–4.
3. Jewish Telegraphic Agency Daily Bulletin, 22 Oct. 1943.
4. Report by GvT, Oct. 1944, LBINY AR 3477/33.3/51, 68.
5. Ibid., 69.
6. Etty Hillesum to "two sisters in The Hague," Amsterdam, Dec. 1942, in Klass A. D. Smelik, ed., *Etty: The Letters and Diaries of Etty Hillesum, 1941–1943* (Grand Rapids, MI, 2002), 579.
7. Jacob Presser, *Ashes in the Wind: The Destruction of Dutch Jewry* (London, 2010), 430. See also Taubes report, NIOD Ned Tau 9.1, 26.
8. Etty Hillesum to Han Wegerif et al., 24 Aug. 1943, in Smelik, *Etty*, 652–53.
9. GvT, TWWM, II, 73–74.
10. Report by GvT, Oct. 1944, LBINY AR 3477/33.3/51, 86.
11. Report by GvT, Oct. 1944, LBINY AR 3477/33.3/51, 75. See also Fred Schwarz, *Züge auf falschem Gleis* (Vienna, 1996), 173.
12. Report by GvT, Oct. 1944, LBINY AR 3477/33.3/51, 84.
13. Ibid.
14. Philip Mechanicus, *Waiting for Death: A Diary* (London, 1968), 203.
15. Louis de Jong, *Het Koninkrijk der Nederlanden in de Tweede Wereldoorlog*, vol. 8, pt. 2, 738.
16. Camp registration card, International Tracing Service, Arolsen (copy in Yad Vashem Archive, Jerusalem).
17. GvT, TWWM, II, 71.
18. Taubes report, NIOD Ned Tau 9.1, 23.
19. Etty Hillesum to "two sisters in The Hague," Amsterdam, Dec. 1942, in Smelik, *Etty*, 586.
20. GvT, TWWM, II, 75.
21. GvT to Mayer, 2 Oct. 1943, SM AfZ.
22. Mayer to GvT, 5 Nov. 1943, ibid.
23. Eichmann to Befehlshaber der Sicherheitspolizei und des SD für die besetzten niederländischen Gebiete, Berlin, 5 Nov. 1943, NIOD 77/1321.
24. GvT, TWWM, II, 79–80.
25. Ibid., 80–81.

26. Ibid., 81.
27. Simon Heinrich Herrmann, *Austauschlager Bergen-Belsen: Geschichte eines Austauschtransportes* (Tel Aviv, 1944), 25.
28. Mechanicus, *Waiting for Death*, 193.
29. See British official documentation, 1943–4, in BNA FO 916/599.
30. Mirjam de Leeuw-Gerzon for Advisory Committee for Immigrants from the Netherlands to Immigration Department, Jewish Agency, Jerusalem, 3 Feb. 1943, with enclosed list, CZA S6/2832/1; revised list dated 8 March 1943, ibid.
31. GvT to Mayer, 21 May 1943, SM AfZ.
32. Julius (Jules) Gerzon to Mirjam de Leeuw, typed copy of cable, n.d. [May 1943], NL-HaNRK 2050/356.
33. Typewritten notes by Mayer of telephone conversation with Schwartz, 31 May 1943, SM AfZ.
34. L. Kohn (Jewish Agency) to Commissioner for Migration and Statistics, Jerusalem, 11 May 1943, CZA S6/2832.
35. Office Palestinien de Suisse, Genève, to GvT, 13 Aug. 1943, Chedwah Stein papers.
36. A. N. Oppenheim, *The Chosen People: The Story of the "222 Transport" from Bergen-Belsen to Palestine* (London, 1996), 64–65.
37. Taubes report, NIOD Ned Tau 9.1, 22.
38. Minutes of meeting in C. F. Rüter and D. W. de Mildt, eds., *Justiz und NS-Verbrechen: Sammlung Deutscher Strafurteile wegen Nationalsozialistischer Tötungsverbrechen, 1945–1999* (Amsterdam, 2001), 25:489.
39. Taubes report, NIOD Ned Tau 9.1, 22.
40. Ibid., 30.
41. "Richtlinien zur technischen Durchführung der Verlegung von Juden in das Aufenthaltslager Bergen-Belsen," Berlin, 31 Aug. 1943, NIOD 77/1298.
42. Gemmeker to Zoepf, 4 Feb. 1944, NIOD 270g/2/2.
43. Mechanicus, *Waiting for Death*, 243.
44. Ibid., 248.
45. Ibid., 244.
46. Rita Vuyk to Mayer, 2 March 1944, SM AfZ.
47. Rauter to Himmler, 2 March 1944, NL-HaNA, Ministerie van Justitie, Centraal Archief Bijzondere Rechtspleging, 1945–1949 (1952), inv. nr. 66I, verzameldossier BR.v.C.: 55/50.
48. Oppenheim, *The Chosen People*, 135.

49. See "5th list" in NIOD 150i/955.
50. Report by GvT, Oct. 1944, LBINY AR 3477/33.3/51, 92.
51. Ibid.
52. Bolle, *Ik zal je beschrijven*, 224 (diary entry for 18 March 1944).
53. R. Vuyk to Mayer, 22 March 1944, SM AfZ.
54. Taubes report, NIOD Ned Tau 9.1, 33.
55. Report by GvT, Oct. 1944, LBINY AR 3477/33.3/51, 99 (appendix by Mainz on Bergen-Belsen).
56. Ibid., 93.
57. Ibid., 84–85.
58. Bolle, *Ik zal je beschrijven*, 242–43 (diary entries dated 14 & 15 June 1944).
59. Ibid., 245 (diary entry dated 23 June 1944).
60. Report by GvT, Oct. 1944, LBINY AR 3477/33.3/51, 94.
61. "Information regarding Bergen-Belsen on June 28th 1944" by GvT, Haifa, 12 Aug. 1944, AJDCNY 1933–44/696.
62. GvT circular letter to friends, Haifa, 10 Aug. 1944, Chedwah Stein papers.
63. GvT, TWWM, II, 93.
64. This figure has been compiled on the basis of the latest research conducted by the Gedenkstätte Bergen-Belsen and differs from figures given in older literature; information from Bernd Horstmann via Rainer Schulze.
65. Executive Order 9417, 22 Jan. 1944, http://www.presidency.ucsb.edu/ws/?pid=16540.
66. Leavitt to Lesser, 19 May 1944, AJDCNY 1933–44/696.
67. GvT to friends, Haifa, 10 Aug. 1944, Chedwah Stein papers.
68. Testimony to author of Mirjam Bolle, June 2013.
69. Herrmann, *Austauschlager Bergen-Belsen*, 73.
70. GvT note added to narrative by Helmuth Mainz, appended to GvT's report of Oct. 1944, LBINY AR 3477/33.3/51, 112.
71. Alfred Klee (1875–1943) was a German-Jewish lawyer and communal and Zionist leader. The girls' mother was dead and Theresa Klee's son-in-law, Hans Goslar, was too ill to travel. Both Theresa and Goslar died before the end of the war. The elder of the two girls, Hanna, had been a classmate and close friend of Anne Frank. After the liberation, Hanna and her sister were sent to Holland, where they were given shelter by Otto Frank. Later they moved to Palestine. Benjamin

Ravid, "Alfred Klee and Hans Goslar: From Amsterdam to Westerbork to Bergen-Belsen," in *The Dutch Intersection: The Jews and the Netherlands in Modern History*, ed. Yosef Kaplan (Leiden, 2008), 348–68. Also information from Professor Benjamin Ravid.

72. Narrative by Mainz attached to GvT's report of Oct. 1944, LBINY AR 3477/33.3/51, 115. According to Gertrude's account (GvT, TWWM, II, 97), they did *not* march past the crematorium but in the opposite direction. There are other minor discrepancies in the several accounts given by participants in these events: Taubes report, NIOD Ned Tau 9.1, 35; memorandum by Taubes, 8 July 1944, appended to GvT's report of Oct. 1944, LBINY AR 3477/33.3/51, 117; Oppenheim, *The Chosen People*; Chaya Brasz, *Transport 222: Bergen-Belsen—Palestina, Yuli 1944* (Jerusalem, 1994); and testimony to author by Mirjam Bolle, June 2013.
73. GvT, TWMM, II, 98.
74. GvT, TWWM, II, 98.
75. Brigitte Hamann, *Hitler's Vienna: A Dictator's Apprenticeship* (New York, 1999) 158.
76. Helmuth Mainz, "Erlebnisse 1940–1944," duplicated typescript, Bibl. Ros., 82.
77. GvT to Mayer, 8 July 1944, SM AfZ.
78. Brasz, *Transport 222*, 25.
79. JTA News Bulletin, 13 July 1944. See also *Davar*, 11 July 1944.
80. J. V. W. Shaw (Chief Secretary of Government of Palestine) to Oliver Stanley (Colonial Secretary), 4 [?] Aug. 1944, BNA FO 916/925.
81. GvT, TWWM, II, 102.

11. Aftermath

1. GvT to Chedwah van Tijn, 17 July 1944, Chedwah Stein papers.
2. GvT to Chedwah van Tijn, 15 Aug. 1944, ibid.
3. Troper to GvT, 11 Sept. 1944, ibid.
4. GvT circular letter to friends, Haifa, 10 Aug. 1944, ibid.
5. GvT to Mayer, Haifa, 28 Aug. 1944, SM AfZ.
6. Van Kleffens to Dutch consul-general, Jerusalem, 5 Aug. 1944, NL-HaNA 02.05.64/3730.
7. GvT to Chedwah van Tijn, 15 Oct. 1944, Chedwah Stein papers.

8. Report by GvT, Oct. 1944, LBINY AR 3477/33.3/51.
9. Ibid., 1.
10. Louis de Jong, *Het Koninkrijk der Nederlanden in de Tweede Wereldoorlog* (The Hague, 1969–91), esp. vol. 5, pt. 2, and vol. 8 pts. 1 and 2; see also De Jong to GvT, 6 Jan. 1958, LBINY AR 3477/33.3/53.
11. De Jong, *Het Koninkrijk*, vol. 6, pt. 1, 261.
12. Sandra Ziegler, *Gedächtnis und Identität der KZ-Erfahrung: Niederländische und deutsche Augenzeugenberichte des Holocaust* (Würzburg, 2006), 341.
13. Report by GvT, Oct. 1944, LBINY AR 3477/33.3/51, 2.
14. Y. Bechar to Y. Gruenbaum, with copies to David Ben Gurion and others, 12 July 1944, CZA S6/4652.
15. J. L. Magnes to Paul Baerwald, 23 Nov. 1944, LBINY AR 3477/33.3/53.
16. C. M. Dozy to GvT, 2 Sept. 1944, Chedwah Stein papers.
17. Van Kleffens to Dozy, 5 Aug. 1944 (cable) and subsequent cables, NL-HaNA 02.05.64/3730.
18. Dozy to Van Kleffens, 25 Aug. 1944 (cable), ibid.
19. A. de Leeuw to A. de Jong, 4 June 1945, CZA J24/182–163.
20. GvT, TWWM, II, 115–16.
21. A. de Leeuw to A. de Jong, 4 June 1945, CZA J24/182–163.
22. GvT to Chedwah, 24 Nov. 1944, Chedwah Stein papers.
23. GvT, TWWM, II, 118.
24. Ibid., 120.
25. GvT to Mayer, 24 Jan. 1945, SM AfZ.
26. See GvT two reports to Joint, 27 April 1945 and other documentation, March–April 1945, in NIOD Doc I/1720B; also GvT to Joint (New York), 25 March and 3 April 1945 (cables), AJDCNY 1945–54/413; and GvT (Geneva) to Joint (New York), 29 March 1945 (cable), SM AfZ.
27. Israel Polak case file, NL-HaNA, Raad voor het Rechtsherstel, 1948–9 (2.09.48.02), Inv. 393, file R9237.
28. GvT (Portland, Oregon) to R. Pilpel (JDC, New York), 26 June 1949, SM AfZ.
29. Report by GvT, Oct. 1944, LBINY AR 3477/33.3/51, 71.
30. GvT to Mayer, 20 April 1945, SM AfZ.
31. Mayer to GvT, 8 June 1945, ibid.
32. GvT, TWWM, II, 129.
33. *Nieuwsblad van het Noorden*, 20 Jan. 1949.

34. Information from NIOD.
35. Daniel Schorr, *Staying Tuned* (New York, 2001), 39; and information from NIOD.
36. *Die Zeit*, 17 Feb. 1967.
37. Ibid.
38. See Dasberg's 1945 diary, GFH Holland 40/I.
39. Abraham de Jong in a meeting of the Commission, Eindhoven, 4 Feb. 1945, quoted in Ineke Brasz, "Bevrijdingsjaren—Jaren van Bevrijding?" in A. J. van der Leeuw, ed., *Le-Ezrath Ha-am: Het Volk ter Hulpe* (Assen, 1985), xxii.
40. A. de Leeuw to A. de Jong, 4 June 1945, CZA J24/182–163.
41. GvT, TWWM, II, 125.
42. Liselotte Laqueur diary entries, 14 and 19 May 1945, communicated by P. J. Knegtmans.
43. GvT to Chedwah van Tijn, 13 May 1945, Chedwah Stein papers.
44. GvT to SM, 21 Oct. 1945, SM AfZ.
45. Mayer to GvT (cable), 12 Nov. 1945, ibid.
46. GvT to Cohen, 30 Aug. 1945, Chedwah Stein papers.
47. GvT (New York) to Cohen, 30 Sept. 1945, Chedwah Stein papers.
48. David Cohen to Hans Mayer, 26 Aug. 1947, NIOD Doc I/294.
49. GvT to Hans Meyer, 24 Oct. 1947, Chedwah Stein papers.
50. Cohen to James G. McDonald, 27 Dec. 1953, AJDCNY 1933–44/703.
51. "Aantekeningen naar aanleiding van een rapport door Mevrouw G. v. Tijn . . . ," undated memorandum by David Cohen. NIOD Doc I/294.
52. Report by GvT, Oct. 1944, LBINY AR 3477/33.3/51, 35.
53. Cohen, "Aantekeningen," 87.
54. Moore, *Victims and Survivors*, 248.
55. Rena Fuks-Mansfeld et al eds., *Joden in Nederland in de Twintigste Eeuw: Een biografisch woordenboek* (Amsterdam, 2007), 8.
56. See D. Cohen letter to his defence counsel, 19 Aug. 1948, NIOD 181j/11.
57. Cohen to his defence counsel, 11 Nov. 1948, NIOD Doc I/294.
58. Memorandum on interview, 9 Jan. 1952, ibid.
59. Cohen, *Zwervend en Dolend*, 27, 67, 323.
60. See my *Secret War in Shanghai* (London, 1998), 140–50; and my "Ambiguities of Occupation: Foreign Resisters and Collaborators in Wartime Shanghai," in Wen-hsin Yeh ed., *Wartime Shanghai*, (London, 1998), 24–41.

61. GvT to Jennings Wong, Deputy Director, Shanghai Regional Office, CNRRA [*c.* 15 Aug. 1946], United Nations Archives, New York, S-1132-0000-0189 Repatriation and Resettlement Corr. 1944–9 UNRRA Shanghai.
62. GvT to Chedwah and David van Tijn, 12 May 1946, Chedwah Stein papers.
63. Erich Rosenberg to David Cohen, 14 March 1946, NIOD Doc I/294 David Cohen.
64. GvT to Moses A. Leavitt, 22 March 1947, LBINY AR 3477/33.3/51.
65. Ibid. Also Charles H. Jordan (Shanghai) to Moses A. Leavitt (New York), 6 Jan. 1947, AJDCNY 1945–54/97; and GvT (Sydney) to Leavitt, 1 Feb. 1947, ibid.
66. High Commissioner for Australia to Dominions Office, 19 Feb. 1947, copied to High Commissioner for Palestine, 20 Feb. 1947, BNA FCO 141/14288.
67. See documentation in BNA FCO 141/14270.
68. GvT to Moses A. Leavitt, 22 March 1947, LBINY AR 3477/33.3/51.
69. Graham Freudenberg, "Arthur Calwell," in Australian Dictionary of Biography: http://adb.anu.edu.au/biography/calwell-arthur-augustus-9667.
70. GvT (Sydney) to to Charles H. Jordan (Shanghai), 20 Dec. 1946, LBINY AR 3477/33.3/52.
71. GvT (Sydney) to Moses A. Leavitt (New York), 3 Jan. 1947, AJDCNY 1945–54/97.
72. GvT, TWWM, II, 190 (where Gertrude misdates the letter July 1948).
73. GvT, TWWM, II, 191; *New York Times*, 24 Aug. 1947.
74. GvT to Harvey P. Newton, 16 Sept. 1968, LBINY AR 3477/33.3/5.
75. Gertrude van Tijn, "Werkdorp Nieuwesluis," *Leo Baeck Institute Year Book*, 14 (1969), 182–99.
76. Bauer communication to the author, 6 Dec. 2011.
77. *Portland Jewish News*, Dec. 1968.

12. A Reckoning

1. A recent study of the destruction of Dutch Jewry subjects these, among other, interpretations to painstaking archival and statistical analysis and finds them wanting. Marnix Croes and Peter Tammes, *"Gif laten wij niet voortbestaan:" Een onderzoek naar de overlevingskansen*

van Joden in de Nederlandse gemeenten, 1940–1945 (Amsterdam 2004); an English summary of the main findings is Marnix Croes, "The Holocaust in the Netherlands and the Rate of Jewish Survival," *Holocaust and Genocide Studies* 20, no. 3 (2006), 474–99.

2. GvT to Jewish Advisory Commission to Dutch Government, London, 6 June 1945, Chedwah Stein papers (copy).
3. GvT, TWWM, II, 130.
4. Minister of Social Affairs to Minister of Justice, 5 March 1945, NL-HaNA 2.09.06/10985; and Chef den Politie-Buitendienst to Minister of Justice, 1 May 1945, ibid.
5. Laissez-passer issued by H. D. Bornstein, Dutch consulate, Jerusalem, 28 Nov. 1944, Chedwah Stein papers; and see GvT to Chedwah and David van Tijn, 14 Aug. 1946, ibid.
6. GvT, TWWM, II, 131.
7. See above, chapter 10.
8. Memorandum from Abraham (Leib) de Leeuw to Louis de Jong, 5 March 1978, NIOD Doc II/1292.
9. I am informed by the Koninklijk Huisarchief (Dutch Royal Archives) that no such telegram is in that collection, which is very sparse for the period of the queen's exile in London.
10. Louis de Jong, *The Netherlands and Nazi Germany* (Cambridge, MA, 1990), 68.
11. Tweede Kamer der Staten-Generaal Enquêtecommissie Regeringsbeleid 1940–1945, *Verslag Houdende de Uitkomsten van het Onderzoek* (The Hague, 1955), 7A: 414–15.
12. See Ben Hummel, "De Derde Duits-Palestijnse Uitwisseling of hoe 281 Joden in Juli 1944 Gered Werden" (doctoraal-scriptie, Rijksuniversiteit Groningen, 1987); and Rainer Schulze, "'Keeping Very Clear of Any "Kuh-Handel": The British Foreign Office and the Rescue of Jews from Bergen-Belsen," *Holocaust and Genocide Studies* 19, no. 2 (2005): 226–51.
13. See Dan Michman, "Ha-plitim ha-yehudiyim mi-germanyah be-holand ba-shanim, 1933–1940" (PhD diss., The Hebrew University of Jerusalem, 1978).
14. Louis de Jong, *Het Koninkrijk der Nederlanden in de Tweede Wereldoorlog* (The Hague, 1969–91), vol. 5, pt. 2, 1014–15.
15. Bauer notes on interview with GvT, 21 and 21 May 1968, AJDCNY Oral History Box 9.

16. H. B. J. Stegeman and J. P. Vorsteveld, *Het Joodse Werkdorp in de Wieringermeer, 1934–1941* (Zutphen, 1983), 125–26.
17. Ibid., 150.
18. Cohen letter to "Amice," 28 Jan. 1949 (responding to a statement by Jules Gerzon), NIOD 181j/11.
19. David Cohen, *Voorzitter van de Joodse Raad: De herinneringen van David Cohen (1941–1943)*, ed. Erik Somers (Zutphen, 2010), 106.
20. The second volume first appeared in 1982, minus one page of the text, in a special number of the *Nieuw Israëlietisch Weekblad.* A complete version was published in book form only in 2010: Cohen, *Voorzitter.*
21. Cohen, *Voorzitter,* 197.
22. Ibid., 200.
23. Ibid., 108
24. See above, chapters 7 and 9.
25. N. K. C. A. in't Veld, ed., *De Joodse Ereraad* (The Hague, 1989), 29.
26. Cohen, *Voorzitter,* 108.
27. David Daube, *Collaboration with Tyranny in Rabbinic Law* (London, 1965), 18–22.
28. Yehuda Bauer, "The Judenräte—Some Conclusions," in *Patterns of Jewish Leadership in Nazi Europe 1933–1945: Proceedings of the Third Yad Vashem International Historical Conference, Jerusalem April 4–7, 1977* (Jerusalem, 1979), 400.
29. GvT to Hans Mayer, 24 Oct. 1947, Chedwah Stein papers.
30. Bauer interview with GvT, 21 and 22 May 1968, AJDCNY Oral History, Box 9.
31. GvT, TWWM, II, 35.
32. Ibid., 48. NB There is some confusion in page numbering at this point in the typescript.
33. Cf. Bart van der Boom, *"Wij weten niets van hun lot:" Gewone Nederlanders en de Holocaust* (Amsterdam, 2012), 107, which discusses with considerable insight this discrepancy in Gertrude's narratives.
34. Tweede Kamer der Staten-Generaal Enquêtecommissie Regeringsbeleid 1940–1945, *Verslag Houdende,* 7A: 412–13.
35. Jacob Presser, *Ashes in the Wind: The Destruction of Dutch Jewry* (London, 2010), 147.
36. Hansard, House of Commons, 17 Dec. 1942.
37. "Stukken van overtuiging" by D. Cohen, 10 Jan. 1949, NIOD 181j/11, 34.

38. De Jong, *Het Koninkrijk*, vol. 7, pt. 1, 328. For further discussion of this issue, see Van der Boom, *"Wij weten niets,"* chap. 8.
39. Anne Frank, *The Diary of a Young Girl: The Definitive Edition* (London, 1997), 54, 97 (entries dated 9 Oct. 1942 and 27 March 1943).
40. S. van den Bergh, *Deportaties* (Bussum, 1945), 10.
41. Cohen to James G. McDonald, 27 Dec. 1953, AJDCNY 1933–45/703.
42. See Piet Schrijvers, *Rome, Athene, Jeruzalem: Leven en werk van prof. dr. David Cohen* (Groningen, 2000), 272–73.
43. Bob Moore, *Victims and Survivors: The Nazi Persecution of the Jews in the Netherlands, 1940–1945* (London, 1997), 246.
44. Etty Hillesum to "two sisters in The Hague," Dec. 1942, in Klaas A. D. Smelik, ed., *Etty: The Letters and Diaries of Etty Hillesum, 1941–1943* (Grand Rapids, MI, 2002), 584.
45. Presser, *Ashes in the Wind*, 251.
46. De Jong, *Het Koninkrijk*, vol. 7, pt. 1, 389.
47. Van der Boom, *"Wij weten niet,"* 397.
48. GvT, TWWM, II, 54.
49. Ibid., 65.
50. Ibid., 59.
51. Beatrix van Tijn to Jacques van Tijn, 14 April 1946, Van Tijn family papers.
52. *Jewish Review* (Portland), 9: 10 (Dec. 1968); GvT to Dorothy Speiser, 2 Jan. 1969, AJDCNY Oral History, Box 9, Gertrude van Tijn.
53. Gertrude quoted these words (in a different translation) at the end of her memoir, GvT TWWM II, 193. This translation appears in Johann Wolfgang Goethe, *The Poems of Goethe*, trans. E. A. Bowring (New York, 1881), 240.

Epilogue

1. "De verschijning van Christus op den berg van Galilea II," *De Banier* (Rotterdam), 20 May 1941. According to B. van der Ros, however, the ban was imposed on other grounds. B. van der Ros ed., *Geschiedenis van de christelijke dagbladpers in Nederland* (Kampen, 1993), 231.
2. H. W. Alings, *Amsterdamsche Gevelsteenen* (Amsterdam, 1943), 34–35. In 1943, the plaque was fixed on the other side of the house, at the corner of Waterlooplein, facing the Blue Bridge. Later it was moved to its present position.

3. See above p. 171.
4. GvT to Saly Mayer, 1 Feb. 1942, SM AfZ.
5. Stadsarchief Amsterdam, Archief van de Politie, Politierapporten 40–45: NL-SAA 20006044.
6. See above p. 173.
7. NL-HaNRK-2017 (Joodsche Raad cartotheek), personal record card of Levie Cohen.
8. The passages are: "Exit John Bennett" (appearing in the diary at 24 June); "Bob returned home next morning, shame-faced and crest-fallen, and went quietly off to his work. It was as though ten years had been added to his age" (25 June); and "To preserve the continuity of the story, we must put back the clock of time for a few days" (26–27 June). The first appears in the diary in English; the other two are in Dutch. All are quotations from John David Hennessey, *The Outlaw* (London, 1913). This story of an Australian bushranger won second prize in the Hodder & Stoughton novel competition in 1912.
9. Translated from the Dutch. The original literary source (if there is one) has not been identified.

Acknowledgments

I am particularly grateful to members of Gertrude van Tijn's family for their reminiscences of her, for answering my questions, and for making materials available.

I wish to thank my research assistants Jenna Henderson, Sylvia Rusnak, and Ori Yehudai for their indefatigable work. Many archives and libraries around the world have opened their collections to me. They are listed in the Sources, and I express my gratitude to them all. I also acknowledge with warm appreciation the help that I received from Guido Abuys, Kevin Auer, David Barnouw, Yehuda Bauer, Hubert Berkhout, Hans Blom, Mirjam Bolle, Ben Braber, Chaya Brasz, Anat Bratman-Elhalel, Calum Carmichael, Michael Chanan, Victoria Culkin, Rebecca Erbelding, Dorit Erenberg, Steven Fassberg, Joel Fishman, Peter Gohle, Adi Greenfield, Jana Haase, Eric Heijselaar, Deborah Jacobs, Alexander Joskowicz, Ana Clara Justino, Maartje van de Kamp, Patrick Kerwin, P. J. Knegtmans, Jolande van Koert, Virginia Lewick, Megan Lewis, John Löwenhardt, Guus Luijters, José Martin, Pauline Micheels, Bob Moore, Dalia Ofer, Noam Rachmilevitch, Benjamin Ravid, Gert Roelofsen, Rochelle Rubinstein, Ewoud Sanders, Christa Schepen, Simone Schliachter, Raymund Schütz, Armin Stock, Elhanan Tal, Mark Tedeschi, Anja Thieme, Tjebbe van Tijen, Sasha Trone, Wout Visser, Veronika Vogel, Silke Wagener-Fimpel, Annegret Wilke, and François Wisard.

I wrote this book largely in Uppsala, as a fellow of the Swedish Collegium for Advanced Studies, and I thank its principal, Björn Wittrock, and my colleagues there for their support.

This is the second book that I have published with Joyce Seltzer of Harvard University Press and, as on the previous occasion, it has been a privilege to work with her. Special thanks go to Edward

Wade for managing the production process of this book and to Jamie Thaman for her thoughtful copyediting of the text. My literary agents, Andrew Gordon in London and Emma Sweeney in New York, have been endlessly supportive. The maps have been drawn, with his customary clarity and precision, by Mike Shand of the University of Glasgow's Cartographic Unit.

Finally, I come to the contribution of my wife, Shirley Haasnoot, who has not only been wonderfully patient and supportive, but also saved me from many errors and gave me invaluable guidance based on her close knowledge of modern Dutch history.

Index